REAGAN'S MYTHICAL AMERICA

REAGAN'S MYTHICAL AMERICA
STORYTELLING AS POLITICAL LEADERSHIP

Jan Hanska

REAGAN'S MYTHICAL AMERICA
Copyright © Jan Hanska, 2012.

First published in 2012 by
PALGRAVE MACMILLAN®
in the United States—a division of St. Martin's Press LLC,
175 Fifth Avenue, New York, NY 10010.

Where this book is distributed in the UK, Europe and the rest of the world,
this is by Palgrave Macmillan, a division of Macmillan Publishers Limited,
registered in England, company number 785998, of Houndmills,
Basingstoke, Hampshire RG21 6XS.

Palgrave Macmillan is the global academic imprint of the above companies
and has companies and representatives throughout the world.

Palgrave® and Macmillan® are registered trademarks in the United States,
the United Kingdom, Europe and other countries.

ISBN: 978–1–137–27299–7

Library of Congress Cataloging-in-Publication Data

Hanska, Jan.
    Reagan's mythical America : storytelling as political leadership /
    by Jan Hanska.
       p. cm.
    ISBN 978–1–137–27299–7 (alk. paper)
    1. Reagan, Ronald—Oratory. 2. Political oratory—United States—
History—20th century. 3. Discourse analysis, Narrative—Political
aspects—United States. 4. Communication in politics—
United States—History—20th century. 5. United States—Politics
and government—1981–1989. I. Title.

E877.2.H356 2012
973.927092—dc23   2012013075

A catalogue record of the book is available from the British Library.

Design by Newgen Imaging Systems (P) Ltd., Chennai, India.

First edition: October 2012

10 9 8 7 6 5 4 3 2 1

Printed and bound in Great Britain by
CPI Antony Rowe, Chippenham and Eastbourne

This book is dedicated to professors
Vilho Harle
Ira Chernus
Mika Luoma-aho
. . . and the merry participants of EUK64.

I sometimes think that an awful lot of us in this country today, if not the world, are sort of like a writer who has come to a great plot problem and is really stuck and doesn't know how to make it work and finally goes back and does a little studying of the pages previously written and discovers that maybe the plot was based on a false premise.

Ronald Wilson Reagan[1]

Contents

PREFACE

I tell this story just to remind you of the magical, intoxicating power of America. We may sometimes forget it, but others do not.

Ronald Wilson Reagan[2]

Ronald Reagan has not been analyzed thoroughly with the tools of narratology as he should be. William F. Lewis wrote an excellent article about the use of narrative form in the Reagan presidency,[3] but a full-length book has been sadly missing. One of my goals is to show how the narrative approach can be used in Reagan studies, and I have taken narratology as my key empirical orientation to Reagan's texts and to explore his politics. I argue that politics creates such a work of fiction that the narrative approach dealing with stories as works of fiction can be used in the study of political narratives as well. Reagan's own life and his experiences were a crucial part of all the stories he told, but this book does not contain even a summarized biography of Reagan. Facts about his life show up on the following pages only to illustrate the points I make. As I will show, perhaps these "facts" need to be questioned because Reagan had a tendency to romanticize his own life to a degree that almost nothing unpleasant can be found in those stories.

There have been many excellent studies on Reagan from the viewpoint of rhetoric. The renowned scholar of narratology, James Phelan, sees narrative as rhetoric and writes that the narrator is "telling a particular story to a particular audience in a particular situation for presumably, a particular purpose."[4] It is not only that narrative uses rhetoric or has a rhetorical dimension, but also the fact that narrative is not just a story but action as well. This works as a good definition of the political uses of narratives, albeit I consider rhetoric and narrative to be somewhat different methods of persuasion. Rhetoric seeks to rationalize and persuade the story recipient using the power of words themselves, while narrative can penetrate deeper into the psyche of the story recipient, and not so much to give reasons and arguments, but to incite emotions. To exaggerate, rhetoric aims to convince the brain, while narrative can be at best used to set the heart blazing. There is always a rhetorical dimension within any narrative, but there exists a power somewhere beyond the words of the stories told. Regardless of the words used in the telling, the story itself can touch something primeval within us. Rhetoric creates a new way to view the world but narrative opens up new vistas and creates new worlds as mental models in form of storyworlds, a concept I shall discuss later on in more detail. Here and now it suffices to say that rhetoric is a part of the narrative framework, but the power of narrative persuasion encompasses the world of rhetoric. As Lewis wrote, the predominance of narrative form in Reagan's rhetoric has established the climate of interpretation used in understanding him. We need to be aware of the distinction between the perspectives of rationality and that of narrative. For Reagan stories were not just a rhetorical device; his entire message was a story.[5]

In order to make my methodological points and issues explicit, I wish to start with the fact that I write my study as an outsider. I cannot claim to be a part of the American culture so that I could see Reagan through the eyes of that culture and particular period of time Reagan occupied. Following the thoughts of Mikhail Bakhtin I can, nevertheless, use creative understanding in relation to Reagan's America.[6] For Bakhtin it is necessary for a person who understands to be located in time, space, and culture outside the object of creative understanding. One is not able to see one's own exterior and comprehend it. Other people are needed for that. The exterior and interior of a given culture can only be fully and profoundly comprehended by outsideness and through the eyes of another culture and time. There will exist in this book a dialogue between two separate meanings and cultures, and this hopefully will result in asking questions that may not have been common in the American culture, and meanwhile Reagan's mythical America will reveal new aspects of itself.[7] I cannot choose to inhabit a position as a complete outsider, but must immerse myself in Reagan's world to some degree, because there can exist no position for an observer outside the world he observes and indeed, the observation itself enters the world as a constituent part of what is being observed.[8] There is no totally isolated vantage point distanced by time and space such as the Archimedean immovable point, from where this book could be the metaphorical lever with which to move the world or, rather in this case, the storyworld. Storyworlds cannot be better understood from the outside than mere utterances that compose the stories, which in turn guide the construction of storyworlds. The one who tries to understand enters into the dialogue as the third party.[9]

Every text is "plurivocal, open to several readings and to several constructions."[10] Narratives are interpretive in their nature, but at the same time require interpretation as well.[11] This is because we have to interpret texts at every moment of our interaction with them and allow symbols and tools of semiotic systems to replace the actual primary experience, which we are denied forever. The act of imitating events and actions in a narrative needs the ability to ignore. Some aspects have to be left without consideration since human perception involves simplification.[12] Not all words, sentences, or even narratives are important within a given text.[13] So is the case of this book on Reagan. Because I am writing a narrative on the narrative of another narrator's narratives, the end result is my own literary creation. All I have to work on are the texts that represent only a selected and simplified reality and it is this narrated reality that I need to turn into another narrative and the meanings of both narratives are ambiguous to begin with.[14]

In 1967 William Labov and Joshua Waletzky wrote a groundbreaking paper on the mechanisms of oral narratives as a way to transmit personal experience. Their emphasis, however, is not in the "products of expert storytellers that have been retold many times, but the original production of a representative sample of the population."[15] All Reagan's narratives certainly belong to the former group of constant, practically professional retellings, but even then, some of the fundamentals of orally transmitted experience are involved. When it comes to those Reagan's public papers that were originally presented as speeches, one must consider the Bakhtinian concept of utterances, which are the real compositional units of speech communication and need speech subjects of individual speaking people to exist. The length of a single utterance is determined by a change of the speaking subject. Therefore each of Reagan's speeches consists of a single utterance and when discussing question-and-answer sessions, each response to a question forms an utterance. The length of an utterance is indeterminate, it can be only one word or, for example, an entire book. For an utterance there is an absolute beginning preceded by the utterances of others, and an absolute end followed by the responsive utterances of others. An utterance is a whole, and the change of the speaking subjects is only possible because the utterance has reached its finalization, that is, the speaker has said or written everything he wants to say at a particular moment.[16]

Bakhtin nevertheless argues that a sentence as an utterance, or a part of it, can never be repeated and even used as a quotation; it is always a new utterance. Individual sentences can be repeated identically, but the utterance as a whole is shaped by extra linguistic aspects and exists only in relation to other utterances.[17] This naturally poses a challenge for use of Reagan's quotations. New utterances have to be created, since some of the speeches are relatively long and not suitable for being reproduced here in their entirety. Therefore I must make the conscious choice of recreating utterances by shortening and cutting the original ones. Paul Ricoeur sees that the minimal meaningful unit for study in narrative discourse is a sentence, because discourse is organized in sentences. However, "Understanding a text is always more than the summation of its partial meanings."[18] Therefore words and sentences have to be combined to understand Reagan's entire metastory as a unified text, a collage of smaller stories, while short quotations have been chosen for the purpose of illustration. Reagan himself gave a word of support for my choice of how to quote him while trying to remain true to his original purpose. Reagan said,

> Anyone who expresses himself publicly from a platform of this kind must expect that his words can be used and repeated and reprinted by anyone. Once they are uttered, there can be no restriction on those who can reproduce them. Nor would we have it any other way. I retract no statements of mine that I have made in the past. My principles remain what they always have been. I will stand behind all of the quotes, if they are honestly and completely quoted.[19]

I have tried to remain honest to Reagan's narration in making choices what to include and exclude from this book. There is no doubt that some of the "major" speeches such as the speech after the destruction of space shuttle Challenger are central to the narrative construction of the American self-image and also for anyone who wants to gain a comprehensive understanding of Reagan's entire political metanarrative, but it is my argument that even speeches to smaller audiences and less publicity along with private discussions are important. To understand the goals of politics, one must recognize, following Lyotard, that "it is impossible to trust the analysis of public addresses."[20]

The desires and true intentions of the narrative political leader cannot, and indeed should not, be deciphered solely from the wording of his public addresses, the expressions he uses, or even his rhetorical flourish. If the analyst takes this approach, he must beware the fallibility of his analysis. But indeed the intentions and purposes behind any political narration are objects worthy of study since the narratives told by politicians are always told for a political purpose; either to inflict change or preserve the status quo. Public addresses are traditionally in the American context the means of "spelling the policy out loud," but there is no guarantee that there would not be a hidden agenda behind this barricade of words. The texts of important public addresses should be approached with extreme caution, since they are the most refined and thought-out expressions of the policy and less likely to offer any crack, which might be used to penetrate into the level of the intentions that lie behind the mere expression of those intentions. As Edelman writes, all public speeches and announcements are "heavily imbued with stylized and ritualistic components that justify policy to mass audiences."[21]

The most commonly found example is the inaugural speech of any president. According to John Kares Smith, the inaugural speeches fully consciously "recreates and reanimates the cosmogynic myth of the founding of the country: a litany of the great words and the great deeds of heroes past . . . a reaffirming of America as a special place chose by God for the enactment of divine purpose."[22] But from the viewpoint of narrative-based leadership of politics and the creation of myths, the inaugural speeches do carry a meaning. They are often the most illustrious verbal celebrations of the national unity and highly integrative in their nature. But the actual policy content within them is very limited. They define and strengthen identity but do not define actual political actions. One needs to peek behind the façade of ritualized and stylized aspect to deduct the purpose why a certain narrative was told instead of innumerable others that could have been put to use. There is an intention behind every story to uncover and in most cases it is this intention that actually adds the political element into the story.

Gerald Ford wrote in his memoirs that Reagan was "one of the few political leaders I have ever met whose public speeches revealed more than his private conversations."[23] To overcome the dilemma of how to use Reagan's public and private texts I have made the choice of immersing myself as thoroughly into them as possible. For this work I have read everything Reagan said publicly during his two-term presidency: all his prepresidential radio speeches; all the campaign speeches that are available at the vast archives of Ronald Reagan Presidential Library;[24] and in addition his two autobiographies,[25] the edited collections of his letters to individual people, and his diaries. In the case of the diary the narrator and the narratee are the same person, even if the diary is ultimately intended for someone else's eyes. The narrator of the diary may narrate events for his own edification and memory as well as work out his problems on paper, but essentially he is talking to himself.[26] When one uses autobiographical material as data, it is necessary to understand that is not important to determine whether biographical coherence is reality or merely an illusion. What really matters is how a person creates coherence to his life in an autobiography. "The sources of this coherence, the narratives that lie behind them, and the larger ideologies that structure them must be uncovered."[27] An autobiography is just another story, and the metanarratives that create its coherence are the most interesting factors.

Unfortunately it is impossible to arrive at a pure and unmediated story. The story I read from Reagan's papers is subtly different from any other reader's story and ultimately even the story I try to compose and recreate will result in another discourse than that of the original. While I create a new story within a new discourse, it is my claim that these nevertheless operate on the level of the storyworlds that Reagan created. To better get the true voice of Reagan included in the storytelling I follow Mikhail Bakhtin's idea of including "extraliterary utterances and their rejoinders" such as diaries and letters and things Reagan has told to biographers. In other words I create a unified utterance from heterogeneous utterances, where not only my voice and Reagan's can be heard or read, but a multitude of others as well. Thus, getting the voice of Reagan foregrounded as much as possible is essential to avoid this becoming simply my narrative. In trying to understand Reagan's utterances, I become myself a participant in the dialogue their interrelations form.[28] Barbara Czarniawska claims that "after all, reading is writing anew."[29] I cannot help writing a new story even if I try to keep as close to Reagan's as possible. But, "storytelling, to put the argument simply is what we do with our research materials."[30]

It is hard to hazard a guess as to whether the politics created Ronald Reagan, the person, or whether the person created the policies. The two processes happened simultaneously so that the life story of Reagan (which is necessarily not the one told in autobiographies) worked to create his political stories and policies, and on the other hand, the necessity for political coherence shaped the persona of the citizen-politician Reagan as well. But as Niebuhr wrote, "every 'shepherd king' in history is more king and less shepherd than he pretends."[31] There are roles a politician has to play. He can stick to the role of a stereotypical politician or attempt to break free from the bounds provided by that role. Changing the image of the role is hard after it has been established. Reagan compared politics to acting,

> In the movie business, actors often get what we call typecast; that is, the studios come to think of you as playing certain kinds of roles, so

those are the kinds of roles they give you. And no matter how hard you try, you just can't get them to think of you in any other way. Well, politics is a little like that, too. So, I've had a lot of time and reason to think about my role not just as a citizen turned politician but as an actor turned politician. In looking back, I believe that acting did help prepare me for the work I do now.[32]

Perhaps one of the reasons why the public relations move by Spencer and Roberts's company to label Reagan as a "citizen-politician" had such an appeal for Reagan was that it is, after all, "politics as Hollywood plot line."[33] Stephen Weatherford and Lorraine M. McDonnell have claimed that seeing Reagan as more actor than politician underestimates his impact by failing to take seriously the role political ideology plays.[34] One should in research evaluate and compare the ideas behind policies, their implementation, and the effects. They claim that the American political culture is so pragmatic that ideology is "scarce enough in electoral campaigns, the ideologue in power is an unprecedented occurrence."[35]

While Reagan's presidency undoubtedly can be characterized as performed or enacted at least to some degree, one cannot assert that Reagan was or even could have been solely a product of his aides or the citizenry. Reagan was an ideologue and he had his own values and policies. Despite the fact that the great rags-to-riches myth of an all-American success is personified in his life story, he was the actual person who created and crafted the policies he wanted to pursue. Because so much of Reagan's policies centered on stories and telling them, it is natural that he was himself drawn into the storyworld creation of his citizenry and was partially recreated there anew into a picture of what the story recipients wanted to see in their president. Essentially Reagan was the narrator and reasonably successful controller of the stories he told, and thus more than a speaking figurehead created to respond to the call of the citizenry.

When it comes to the narrative theories used in this text a short explanation is in order. I have not found a single theorist who would write at least in length of the narratives of the political leadership and the stories used to lead people.[36] It will be a part of the novelty and contribution of this book to show how culturally dominant narratives and myths offer tools for political leadership. I go from theorist to another, discarding some thoughts and bringing some to this text. This is due to reason of necessity since in each theoretic approach to narratology there is something valuable to increase understanding of the power of stories. And the theorists themselves do not remain set in stone either. One example of this can be found within the writings of Roland Barthes, who began as a structuralist, slowly discarding it and moving to find jouissance and even eroticism in the free textual play.[37] While I do not go so far as to suggest that there would be erotic pleasure in political texts for the reader, I claim that the story escapes from the restrictive structuralist boundaries of the text.

Northrop Frye defined literature as an area of verbal imitation between events and ideas. Poetry faces simultaneously "the world of *praxis* or action, a world of events occurring in time. In the opposite direction, it faces the world of *theoria,* of images and ideas, the conceptual or visualizable world spread out in space, or mental space."[38] Poetics is then something, which exists between the immanent and material world, partly action, partly ideas, and with the function to imitate actions in words in the world of ideas. It exists between rational thoughts and the dreams and visions of the unconscious. It creates something and this creation, the actual poem or literary product, reflects the higher world of pure ideas. Politics ideally aims at making the world better and its ultimate goal is to "create a heaven on earth." Storytelling can be a powerful political force because of its position between the often sad reality and the vision of what is conceptually possible, and it can reflect a better state of being for mankind. Poetics is, or can be, the stuff of political visions of a better future. It does not need to limit itself to depicting what is, but what *could* be.

It is a sad fact, that narratology and the study of narrative discourse are too often centered on invented stories or fictional narratives. Gerard Genette was among the first theorists to focus his attention to whether the applicability of results or even methods of narratology fit into examining factual narratives, or rather fact-based narratives.[39] But it is one of the main functions of good stories to appear as if they were not fabrications of anyone's imagination but instead true and fact-based. Stories often aim at blurring the distinction of fact and fiction, and as becomes apparent, even the "truth" of the narrative is not a clear-cut thing. The methods of studying purely fictional narratives can be used effectively to study political narratives without distortions to the stories told. One can even argue for the idea of fictionality in politics. It is not just that Reagan, as he appeared to us, was a narrated or fictional personality but that the world of politics becomes fictional when it is narrated to us. Since we most often cannot see or tangibly feel what is going on in politics, we rely on the stories told about the political process. This is most evident in the realm of international politics, since the actions in that realm are often far removed from the sphere of our daily life. We read the stories in the newspaper and see the visual narrations on the news, and can never be sure that we have been given the "true" story. The story that creates the news may have been modified and altered, but in any case, it is a story, description of states, actions and events, which has been put together or emplotted by someone, so that it would be easier for us to again emplot for the benefit of our own understanding and ultimately digestion.

Since the story of events in the realm of politics does not arrive to us in unmediated form, it is better to take it with a pinch of salt. If we start to doubt the "truth" of the news, it is only one more step to take to view them as fictional, at least to the degree that the things described are embellished to make them more reportable, and the whole array of theories concerning fictional narratives are at our disposal. The political narrative does not indeed need to be true to follow the "reality" as we know it, since it can abide by another set of rules. Since it is a story, it only needs to be plausible enough to appear life-like. Things do not need to be true as long as they appear to be true and this is a great asset for all political narratives. By treating political matters as fictional and only plausible, the politician is able to some degree supplant the "real" world of politics with a storyworld.

I will discuss many matters that are so tightly bound with each other that separations are artificial. Religious beliefs blend into myths about being American, which have influenced the culture that is in turn a shaper of the ideologies policies rest upon. This creates a web of meanings and one aspect cannot be picked out for closer study and leave the meaning in itself intact. In the realm of politics the web of beliefs, customs, and common sensical worldview join together to create a metatext, where each is partially justified by the others through intertextual means and the entire metatext will act as the legitimizer of political action. It is this entire metatext one needs to comprehend to make sense of how Reagan used parts of it in his creation of the mythical America.

The actual person of Ronald Wilson Reagan, born a poor son of a midwest shoe seller remains hidden from our eyes. This is an attempt to study Ronald Reagan, president, political narrator, storyteller, and, yes, mythmaker. The actual person, stripped of his politics and the stories he spun around himself, remains a mystery. This is because of the power of narratives in creating the public Reagan as contrasted to the private person. Reagan was an actor and his public persona was a role, drafted by himself as well as the expectations of the citizenry and the demands of how to succeed in carrying out the presidency. The stories that whirled around recreating and shaping him anew again and again are part of his mythical America and the person stripped of these stories is of no consequence in this book. To summarize what is to come in the course of the next two hundred pages or so; I can do no better than to quote Bruce Lincoln, who described his own work by saying,

> *In the following pages, my chief goal is to tell a story about the stories others have told about the stories of others still, and my point is that one should treat all these narratives with considerable care and caution.*[40]

1

The Narrative Approach to Reagan's Policymaking

There are countless forms of narrative in the world. First of all, there is a prodigious variety of genres, each of which branches out into a variety of media, as if all substances could be relied upon to accommodate man's stories. Among the vehicles of narrative are articulated language, whether oral or written, picture, still or moving, gestures, and an ordered mixture of all these substances; narrative is present in myth, legend, fables, tales, short stories, epics, history, tragedy, drama, comedy, pantomime, paintings (in Santa Ursula by Carpaccio, for instance), stained-glass windows, movies, local news, conversation. Moreover, in this infinite variety of forms, it is present at all times, in all places, in all societies; indeed narrative starts with the very history of mankind; there is not, there has never been anywhere, any people without narrative; all classes, all human groups have their stories and very often those stories are enjoyed by men of different and even opposite cultural backgrounds; narrative remains largely unconcerned with good or bad literature. Like life itself, it is there, international, transhistorical, transcultural.

Roland Barthes[1]

Barbara Czarniawska notes that there is a growing fascination among young scholars to proceed to do studies that merely show the presence of stories in their data. Czarniawska labels the resulting type of studies as "Look, Ma, there is a narrative!" Just pointing out that stories exist is not enough to produce an interesting study. The point should be what the consequences of storytelling are for those who tell them and for those who study them.[2] When one chooses to study political narratives, one of the main points of emphasis should be the consequences for the citizens or other people whose lives are affected by the narrativized politics. In the case of Reagan's political leadership one cannot help "finding narratives," since it would actually be harder to point out parts where stories are not used.

This will not be merely an isolated chapter that focuses on the narrative theory or how it can be used as a method of political analysis. It will initiate the analysis of the stories Reagan told. With the use of numerous quotations from Reagan, I will not only justify the narrative approach but also analyze specific aspects of Reagan's political storytelling and draw conclusions while presenting the reader with some essential elements of narratology. Alasdair MacIntyre claims that "man is in his actions and practices, as well as in his fictions, essentially a story-telling animal."[3] In Reagan actions and fictions blend together to create the policy.

The proper name for the study of narratives is narratology, and as David Herman notes, the mere idea of narratology is a battlefield of two competing stories. One story claims that narratology is a dead science with its "forbidding terminology and mania for taxonomies."[4] The days of high structuralism have undoubtedly passed, and the research conducted in the structuralist tradition is bound for trouble, since that particular story has been developed to its ultimate and stories have been analyzed and classified to their most minuscule detail. The other competing story argues that narratology has merely entered a state of crisis, and recent research has focused on those areas that classical narratology chose to ignore or was not able to explore. These include, for example, types of narratives that were not earlier recognized as stories at all or the extratextual effects of narrative on its reader.

One must recognize the problems involved in using narratology as a paradigm for further research and broaden and diversify the conception of stories, and provide new ways to analyze both their structures and effects. Narratology has only moved with the times into another phase. This one may not be as enthusiastic and even as utopian as that of the semiological revolution of the 1960s but compensates by not even trying to aim for any kind of unified grand theory that would once and for all explain everything within every kind of narrative. Narratology has become a more open-ended project and focuses on the areas that have been overlooked by using a more multidisciplinary approach.[5] When applied to politics more vigorously, narratology might broaden our scope of the entire concept. We tend to see politics as an altruistic system that functions rationally to make life better for each citizen. If we would gain more insight into the system by which stories operate in us and change our lives as political subjects, hitherto unforeseen vistas could open for us as the rationality of political decision making is questioned by the study of those narratives that are used to excite political passions and power plays. Stories play a larger role in our lives as citizens and political subjects than we even comprehend. They largely create who we are through establishing themselves as "common sense."

Structuring a Political Narrative

Success in politics is about issues, ideas, and the vision we have for our country and the world

Ronald Wilson Reagan[6]

Walter Fisher wrote that the relationship between politics and poetics is a tight one. Both the vision behind a political philosophy and the language used to illustrate it are aesthetic. Reagan's rhetoric invites participation from the audience but in a manner as one would participate in a drama.[7] Thus there is a need to advance beyond rhetoric and to transgress its boundaries to understand Reagan and highlight the dramatic and poetic aspects of his politics. That is, to focus on the story itself and not just on the rhetorical devices used in the telling. Now it is time to look at how to use poetics in politics and how to create a suitable story for a president to tell.

The mere concept of what constitutes a narrative varies greatly throughout different theories. For Gerald Prince a narrative is the "representation of at least two real or fictive events or situations in a time sequence, neither of which presupposes or entails the other."[8] In earlier writings he has claimed that three conjoined events are required. The first and third events are stative so that the third is the inverse of the first and only the second event is active. These events are organized in such a way that the first event precedes the second that in turn precedes the third and actually causes it.[9] Mieke Bal adds to this by defining an event as "the transition from one state to another state, *caused or experienced by actors.*"[10] Here is an important addition, because events or narratives themselves would contain no meaning if they did not happen to someone or were not caused to happen by someone. There needs to be someone experiencing the event for it to have significance. However, lot more complicated definitions for narrative exist. David Herman argues that a narrative consisting solely on transformations of events would not be a narrative and neither could a text consisting entirely of actions be called a story.[11] For Herman the minimum condition of a narrative can be defined as the "thwarting of intended actions by unplanned, sometimes unplannable, events, which may or may not be the effect of other participants' intended actions."[12]

Labov and Waletzky present us with a workable diagram about the structure of the narrative. The originating function of the narrative is reacted to with telling the originating section, which is followed into the apex of the narrative by the complication of the story. It is most often the evaluation that is the high point of the narrative where action is suspended. After that the narrative proceeds into its resolution and by the means of the coda returns to the point in time where the narrative was first elicited.[13] Labov and Waletzky's minimal narrative with a complication and a resolution is exemplified with "he hit me hard and I hit him back." The more complex the narrative is, the more likely it is to follow the pattern first described.[14]

The definition of a "basic narrative" is perhaps not sufficient when one undertakes to study the use of narratives in politics. Labov and Waletzky argue that a narrative that "contains only an orientation, complicating action, and result is not a complete narrative. . . . Such a narrative lacks significance: it has no point."[15] Perhaps the most famous—as well as the most simplified—narrative in the history of politics was Gaius Julius Caesar summarizing an entire military campaign in three words: "*Veni, vidi, vici.*" While this story is in its simplicity still more elaborate than it would have to be, according to the minimum requirements of the narrative, it is yet not powerful as a story. It only indirectly implies to the state that existed before Caesar arrived and indeed gave the reason for Caesar's arrival. Just as well, it only hints to the state Caesar created by conquering. Instead of including only the one necessary action to be qualified as a narrative, this offers three different actions: arriving, seeing, and conquering. But for the purposes of narrative political leadership, the stories told need to be more than basic descriptions of states, events, and actions; they need to be emplotted.

While a story and a narrative can be separated on the level of terminology by treating a story as an emplotted narrative, the separation of the two is only theoretical. According to Genette every narrative introduces into its story an "emplotting."[16] Paul Ricoeur echoes this view by claiming that a story is "made out of events to the extent that plot makes events into a story."[17] Plot governs a succession of events within any story and connects them to the story. For Donald E. Polkinghorne a plot is a narrative schema for organizing information. People explain their and others' actions by means of creating plots. Thus every event is understood to have been properly explained when, and only when, its role and significance in relation to some human project is identified. Events in a story can naturally happen by themselves, but unless they are connected to some human action or endeavor, they remain outside the plot, in the background of the story.[18] If narrative explanation of every event is configured among other events into a storylike causal nexus, a person is likely to account his actions in a narrative mode and events are explained by connecting them to their relations to other events. Plot is the factor that efficiently collects and organizes states, actions, or events and combines them into a more or less unified whole and makes a story out of isolated events.

A story emerges after events in the political arena, or any other part of human experience, are told so that they create a unity out of the plurality of isolated happenings. This emplotment will have to be to some degree performed or at least aided or suggested by the narrator. A politician is likely to guide the emplotment of what he tells by guiding the audience to accept his mode of thought and policies. The less he emplots what he tells in advance, the more confident he must be in his ability to enthrall the citizenry with his storytelling. It cannot be said that the more detailed in terms of its emplotment by the narrator the story is, the more political would its aspirations or intentions be. But one can say that a story with a highly detailed plotting by the narrator is more likely to have precise intended outcomes than a story that leaves a lot of the burden of emplotment to the narratee.

Polkinghorne further argues that a plot actually adds something into the narrative, because the plot can weave into the narrative historical and social contexts and thoughts and feelings of people. A plot is able to "articulate and consolidate complex threads of multiple activities by means of the overlay of subplots."[19] This reads that most political texts have several plots, which have to get interconnected in some manner by the narrator. Well-structured plots—whether by the narrator, or the story recipient, or by both of them—are often connected to other plots. To follow this thought, every storied narrative with sufficiently complex structure acts as a metanarrative, because within it are many different emplotted narratives, that is stories, and these have to be interconnected as well. The more complex the storytelling becomes, the more the stories told start to have the shape and structure of spider webs if one chooses to follow the storylines or plots and try to make sense on their interrelations. Along with other subplots, the text draws subtexts or sub stories to it. When the plot weaves historical and social contexts into the story, the stories told in the aforementioned contexts tend to get interwoven with the story as well and the result is a narrative network. As Barthes writes,

> To interpret text is not to give it a . . . meaning, but on the contrary appreciate what *plural* constitutes it. . . . In this ideal text, the

networks are many and interact, without any one of them being able to surpass the rest; this text is a galaxy of signifiers . . . we gain access to it by several entrances, none of which can be authoritatively declared to be the main one.[20]

A plot can act as a tool for combining different narratives together. As long as there is a unifying plot, many different storylines can be brought to coexist, and they are tied into a thicker strand of stories. With careful emplotting several smaller stories can be brought together to create a metanarrative. The storylines can intersect, interconnect, and intermingle, and the same applies to stories as well within the framework of the metanarrative thus forming what I later on will call a "story web." It should be the aim of any political narrator to create as many storylines as possible to build a story web, which enables him to choose the most fitting storyline for each occasion that arises in the fast-paced world of contemporary politics. The stories used in political leadership have to be established beforehand and already told into existence, so that they can be evoked instantaneously if the need arises.

To actually lead the people with storytelling, the stories need to be elaborately constructed and bestowed with minuscule detail and true talent in the telling. The stories must be as easy and simple or difficult and multifaceted as the purposes they are told to attain. In the discussion of the essential characteristics of a story, Sacks offers a good addition by claiming that a story always takes more than one sentence to tell, and that the initial challenge for a storyteller is to extend the story beyond that one sentence in order to create a full-blown telling of what he will communicate.[21] But to have any impact, a political narrative has to have some significance; it has to argue a point, and it cannot just be a long-winded yarn, if things are to be changed with the telling of the story. Labov and Waletzky want to add into the narrative structure the means of making its importance explicit. For them, the *evaluation* of the narrative is the part of the narrative that "reveals the attitude of the narrator towards the narrative by emphasizing the relative importance of some narrative units as compared to others."[22] The aspect of evaluation is to some degree emphasized in the political narratives, where the story of states, actions, and events may not suffice to clearly spell out the importance of the story. When the political narrator adds an evaluation section into his narrative, he can more effectively point out what is important in the narrative and make its meaning or "lesson" more explicit. He can guide the interpretation process of his listeners by including into the narrative he tells a "preferable" version of interpretation ready-made for the story recipients to accept.

For Todorov, a narrative begins with a stable situation that is disturbed by some outside force, and this intrusion leads to a state of disequilibrium. By another force that is directed into converse or opposing direction than the equilibrium, it is reestablished anew. The second state of equilibrium, or the end state, is not identical to the first, although it is quite similar.[23] Czarniawska allows that the only similarity between the initial equilibrium and the resulting one is that there indeed exists equilibrium. The latter may as well be a reverse of the first.[24] The end state of the story can be practically almost indistinguishable from the initial state, or alternatively so different, that the only thing in common is the state of equilibrium itself. The story of the American way of life that Reagan tells fits into this pattern very well. The initial state is the original sinlessness in which the American is in touch with his family, community, and God and is free to pursue his dreams as liberated to do so by the Declaration of Independence. The government causes the shift into disequilibrium by intervening on the rights and the freedom the citizen enjoys by limiting them. The policies of the Reagan administration politics will be the converse force that eventually will bring harmony into the society again. Herein lies the uniqueness of Reagan's political narrative, and yet it conforms well into Todorov's basic narrative. The initial state and the eventual state are not identical. There is a difference, and in Reagan's telling, the two stable states of bliss are different, because the latter somewhat surprisingly is qualitatively better. The tomorrow in Reagan's story is always better than yesterday. "And it's no exaggeration to say that we stand at the outset of a new golden age—a golden age of freedom that is sweeping across both the old world and the new."[25] Therefore the golden past is transformed into a more glorious future in the process of narration.

Claude Bremont sees all narrative sequences either as of improvement or of deterioration. An improvement sequence begins with a lack of disequilibrium and finally establishes equilibrium, which can either be the end of the story or the equilibrium may again be disturbed and deterioration follows. At each state the story may start a new period of improvement, or the situation can deteriorate until a rock-bottom stage is reached, and the story either has to end or improvement sequence must take place. In theory a story construed like this can go on forever.[26] The difference to Todorov is that the initial state is disequilibrium in this model, but this does not have to be an unsurpassed object. It is just a question of the point where to begin the process of storytelling. Bremont's model makes stories not circular but theoretically able to continue forever with improvements or deteriorations taking place and making the story linear but gradual, and the essential sameness of each period allows the narration to start at any moment without leaving the story lacking in credibility. The narrator does not have to go back in time to the very beginnings like the bad speaker, who begins his speech talking about the "ancient Romans." The politician can take any moment of actual time as the reference point of his narration and portray it as a moment of either disequilibrium or equilibrium. This is basically what Reagan does when he portrays every moment as "a Time of Choosing." In every moment lies the political choice for the citizens, and that choice determines whether the story gains a sequence of improvement or deterioration.

> In the days just ahead, whether we like it or not, you and I are going to write a page in history. It can describe the rise and fall of the United States of America or it can be a recital of our finest hour. Men will live a thousand years in the shadow of our decision.[27]

This lies at the heart of Reagan's policymaking. He gives at least the impression that the citizen plays an interactive role in the story, and that his decision will determine the direction of the story. In each moment lies the beginning of a new narrative path and a choice. Every decision made in politics is then a moment of closure, where improvement or deterioration commences or continues. These are the moments where the citizens are portrayed to make the decision whether to move toward the glorious future or, with a deterioration sequence, move further away from its actualization. These are the knots of the story web that allow for radically altering the direction of the story.

If the typology proposed by Kenneth and Mary Gergen were adopted, there would be only three prototypical narrative forms; the progressive narrative, the regressive narrative, and the stability narrative. Actual plots would then be composed by combining these rudimentary forms in various ways. In progressive narrative there is a goal and progress toward it is enhanced, in regressive hindered or impeded, and in stability narrative there is no change.[28] This does not sound meaningful in the specific case of Reagan's narration, since there is only continuous progress, and has to be, if the story is to remain meaningful. But the threat of regression is always there, since it is at the heart of political narration. "What a great moment we have before us, and, oh, how future generations will dishonour us if now in a moment of sudden folly we throw it all away."[29] While the threat of things going wrong with only one wrong decision is always there, the actual occurring of stagnation and regression must be avoided in the narratives told by political leaders. They are tools for the political counternarrator to use in order to supplant the previous occupant of a prestigious political position. The story cannot be allowed to pause and enter a moment of where progress is not made. The narration must go on and portray the politics as progressing constantly. At a time like Iran-Contra scandal, or rather at the time when Tower Board was investigating it, Reagan did not make many public appearances and avoided speechmaking; the story about moving to the future lost a lot of momentum and politics faltered as well.

How to determine where to start the telling and where to finish it? And what are the outcomes if the story of the mythical America theoretically can go on forever? Where exactly on the timeline are the golden past and the glorious future that politics move toward with improvement sequences? Aristotle's idea of a story is a combination of incidents that creates an imitation of an action that is complete and entire with a certain magnitude. In order to be entire, the story has to have a beginning, middle, and an end. By saying "entire," he means that the story ought to form a complete whole.[30] Aristotle argues that

> a beginning is that which does not necessarily suppose anything before it, but which requires something to follow it. An end on the contrary, is that which supposes something to precede it, either necessarily or probably, but which nothing is required to follow. Middle is that which both supposes something to precede and requires something to follow. The poet, therefore, who would construct his fable properly, is not at liberty to begin or end where he pleases, but must conform to these definitions.[31]

Another classical source, Horace, disputes Aristotle's assertion that the narrator should begin the storytelling at the beginning of the events. For Horace the narration should always begin *in medias res*, in the middle of the things it portrays. This is not easy. Choosing the place where to start the storytelling defines the narrative, and thus it is not always beneficial to start in the middle. Molly Andrews writes about the events of 9/11 as a beginning for a new story used to vitalize the national narrative. She notes that the shape the story takes is highly dependent on the starting point. If one begins telling the story from the moment the planes crashed into the World Trade Centre towers, the story is completely different than when it takes into account the American behavior globally during, for example, the previous ten or twenty years. A story that begins in 2001 requires no soul-searching, but allows a celebration of national identity, because those who participated in the massacre did so because they allegedly resented the freedom America stands for.[32] One could perhaps oversimplify by saying that if one starts to tell the story even before the events it describes are set in action, the story would be more comprehensive. But choosing the point of commencement for a story is a political decision and once it is done correctly, a lot of politically sensitive material can be excluded from the story and resulting story-world. The ability to choose the right time to initiate the story and at the same time to focalize the starting point of the story in the most suitable spot on the time line of the story is important for any political narrative, because it helps to create precisely the kind of story that will maximize the political gains.

Stories need to have beginnings and endings from the focal point of their recipients. There is a sense of disappointment, if the story is not brought into conclusion. Likewise, if the story starts at a point the audience deems "wrong," it does not matter how well the story is told, it still remains a disappointment and leaves the audience unsatisfied. Even the entire meaning or moral lesson of the story can be altered or even spoiled by failing to locate the most beneficial starting point. From the focal point of the author or narrator of a political story there is even more importance. The beginning and the end define the story in a very concrete manner. As Barthes has remarked, the beginning of a narrative is "an extremely sensitive point."[33] Beginnings and endings need to be chosen with a clear view of which story the politician wants to tell. The political strategy lies in making these choices.[34] However, there is more importance yet in the beginning, because the ending can sometimes be left open. If we take the tale of the Hansel and Gretel as an example, by switching the starting point of the story it can tell us of the inhumane cruelty children exhibit toward a hermit-like old lady as they fry her in her own oven. The huge metanarrative of the American experience starts most commonly either with the Puritans landing in New England or the signing of the Declaration of Independence. These are prestigious moments in American history and sources of many of the national myths. Either of these times is able to function as the golden past and also the point of beginning not only because of their prestigious meaning, but also because they are distant enough from the moment of telling to be easily endowed with mythical qualities.

In a political narrative all plotlines should not be tied up at the end point, because imagining a definite end may create a too-perfect satisfaction with the present and exclude the need for progress. Both Louis Mink and Hayden White agree that the world is presented to us "as mere sequence without beginning or end or as sequences of beginnings that only terminate and never conclude."[35] It is up to us as storytellers and story recipients to emplot these sequences, that is, to set the beginnings and endings into such places as best fit our storytelling. According to Louis Mink, "Stories are not lived but told. Life has no beginnings, middles and ends."[36] To create a coherent and plausible story these elements have to be placed at politically right junctures in the timeline of the sequences in order. As Andrews notes, "The lifeblood of politics demands constant movement; the narrative must always be unfolding, a perpetual process of renegotiation, reconstruction, and retelling."[37] In the particular case of Reagan's narrative politics this is exceptionally true. His politics were based on portraying every moment as a moment of choice, and the future would get better and better progressively. There could not be endings in his political story, because to narrate endings would have stunted progress and would contradict with Reagan's eternal optimism of things getting better and better.

Instead of an ending, the "closure" suggested by Jacques Derrida fits political storytelling. The closure is ever changing, and anything within it can continue indefinitely. Derrida argues that a book cannot end anymore than writing can begin. The closure is positioned at the end of the story but does not put an end to the story itself; it only causes the process of telling to cease. Once a story is put into writing the text excludes meanings and events.[38] To extrapolate this thought, one may argue that closures are important to political narratives, because there needs to exist some point in the narration where meanings of earlier events are formulated and evaluated, since politics traditionally aims at making things better in a teleological manner. The closure allows the story to continue after this evaluative moment and offers another advantage as well. It creates a nexus in the web of stories where it is possible to change the direction and even the function of story by switching storylines and plotlines. By avoiding the end, which is absolute in its nature, the story can take off again and at every closure there exists *in potentia* another expectable horizon for the story. In Reagan's narratives every political decision made by the

Congress or any other minor or major victory as an achievement or a milestone in the road to the glorious future can be seen as a point of closure, which opens up new vistas of things to achieve and choices to make. If the story would be narrated so as to have an ending, a fait accompli, there would be no need for politics anymore, since the ultimate goal would have been reached. By using closures a skillful political narrator can turn his narration into a never-ending story of political progress where the ending in form of something concrete is replaced with the elusive beginning of an age of glory. To ultimately reach the glorious future is to end the telling once and for all. Thus, to keep politics vital, the ending must be infinitely postponed with the use of closures.

> We've done our part. And as I walk off into the city streets, a final word to the men and women of the Reagan revolution, the men and women across America who for 8 years did the work that brought America back. My friends: We did it. We weren't just marking time. We made a difference. We made the city stronger, we made the city freer, and we left her in good hands. All in all, not bad, not bad at all. And so, goodbye, God bless you, and God bless the United States of America.[39]

As a farewell address to the nation this text can be considered to be the "ending" of Reagan's presidential narration. The telling of the story ceases, but the story goes on forever. According to Rabinowitz, there exists a widely applicable interpretive convention that sees these last presidential words as a "conclusion," which aims to sum up the entire work's meaning. Rabinowitz stresses the notion that readers assume that an author puts his best thoughts last actually crystalliz- ing or summing up his points.[40] Reagan's farewell address seems to work in the way of trying to sum up his administrations accomplish- ments. It is a point of evaluation and closure for a certain part of the story but not an ending.

Endings can be superimposed on a story later as well. Among Reaganites such an end often is portrayed to lie in the collapse of the Soviet empire as Reagan's ultimate achievement. Polkinghorne claimed the narrative framework itself creates meanings. Narratives dis- play purpose and direction in human affairs by configuring sequences of events and making individual events comprehensible by identify- ing the "whole to which they contribute." When separate actions are included in a story, they become significant as parts of the whole. "In this sense, narrative can retrospectively alter the meaning of events after the final outcome is known."[41] If an event can be linked to the sequence-chain, it will turn out to be a part of the something much bigger. In this way one single vote in the Senate can be portrayed as a part of the "struggle against totalitarianism." The collapse of the Soviet Union has been to a large part credited to Reagan, and thus his visions of the future, which many of political thinkers laughed at, have become important political choices. Meanings can be altered after the story has reached some kind of closure with a 20/20 hindsight. The retrospectively told story can be fundamentally different from the various stories told by the past actors, since the narrator does not describe past actions as much as he or she retells past stories with the help of the current perspective.[42]

> So, freedom's story is still being written. The brave defence of Fort McHenry by our patriot army was one of its first chapters. But the story will continue as long as there are tyrants and dictators who would deny their people their unalienable rights to life, liberty, and the pursuit of happiness.[43]

Connected with the endings of tales and political narrations alike is the spelling out of the purpose and meaning of the story. In many of the stories we tell, there is a moral lesson to be learned. Occasionally, the teaching of the story does not even reach for the moral plane but aims at giving a more down-to-earth lesson concerning the behavior and actions one should take in one's daily life. Sometimes the lesson may be subtle, and sometimes the face of the story recipient is rubbed in it. When Reagan spoke of the Soviet Union as the focus of evil in the modern world, the lesson was crystal clear, but the agendas of other political narrations may be hidden a lot deeper. Nevertheless, a large part of the political importance and effect of the storytelling lies in the lessons and teachings the narrative tries to convey to the story recipients. The lesson is often based in the entire narrative, and its existence is not necessarily tied to the ending or closure. The lesson can be taught gradually; each point of the storyline may add to the amount of "learning" instead of an ending that would draw conclusions.

Seymour Chatman makes an interesting argument about the Aristotelian notion of a story containing a beginning, middle, and an end. He claims that such a thing applies to narratives only, that is "story-events as imitated, rather than real actions themselves, simply because such terms are meaningless in the real world."[44] We have all felt the disappointment when at the end of an episode of our favorite

TV-series the words "to be continued" appear on a screen. We want our stories to have endings, clear and definite endings instead of things left hanging in the air. The traditional ending of a bedtime story, "and they lived happily ever after," is a definite *Endpunkt* of the story. Even when our story tries to convey actions, events, and happenings from the real life, we have to turn what we tell into a story, and thus give the events, actions, and happenings a beginning and an end. We have to turn the things from the "real life" and "real world" into narrative constructs within the storyworld. We have to "story" them in the telling. While the actual ending is not a prerequisite of a political narrative, especially when it is so intertwined with the life story of the politician as was in the case of Reagan, we still yearn for endings. Naturally a political narrator can sprinkle his metanarrative with smaller anecdotes and ministories that satisfy at least to some degree our hunger for clear endings, while allowing the large narrative to continue and continue. Because the metanarrative behind Reagan's politics is the grand myth of America and the American Dream, it must be narrated to continue unaltered from generation to another as politics will bring its realization for everyone closer and closer. Thus the closures must be confined to the more down-to-earth anecdotes the storytelling is sprinkled with.

An interesting aspect of the theory of Labov and Waletzky is its addition of the *coda* into the structure of the narrative. The coda takes place at the end of a narrative. Many narratives end with a resolution section. The resolution may as well coincide with the evaluation or be a separate part of the narrative. Usually the actual sequence of the states, actions, and events described in the narrative does not extend to the present, and a coda can work as a "functional device for returning the verbal perspective to the present moment."[45] In the simplest case the coda may tell us that "they lived happily ever after," but it would be a misunderstanding to view all codas as such uncomplicated punch lines. A coda is neither a description of events nor does it answer questions of what has happened. Reagan used many codas to tie his narratives of the past golden ages into the present of America. In his version codas, however, are used not just to tie the past into the present by bringing the story time up to the time of the telling. Reagan's codas typically create connections between the past and the glorious future, while only stopping briefly in the time of the telling to gain momentum into the future.

> And come January, when I saddle up and ride off into the sunset— [laughter]—it will be with the knowledge that we've done great things.

We kept faith with a promise as old as this land we love and as big as the sky, a brilliant vision of America as a shining city on a hill. Thanks to all of you, and with God's help, America's greatest chapter is still to be written, for the best is yet to come.[46]

Coda is not the only way to end a narrative, and it is not even appropriate in all occasions. Coda can be described as marking the transition from the storyworld into the real world. The story recipient exits the storyworld and is returned to the present with a coda.

REAGAN AND OTHER CHARACTERS IN THE STORIES

> Let's remember what we're all about. All of us, as Americans, are joined in a common enterprise to write the story of freedom—the greatest adventure mankind has ever known, and one we must pass on to our children and our children's.
>
> Ronald Wilson Reagan[47]

Now it is time to take a look deeper within the stories themselves and search for the states, events, and especially actors within them. The upcoming section discusses the roles given to the characters involved in the stories told; the inhabitants of the storyworlds, so to say. Who or what are the things that inhabit the stories, act, and live their lives in them? Greimas came up with the concept of "actants," which he organizes into four categories according to their functions; "subject," "object," "sender," and "receiver."[48] Actants are then the things that actually create a story as such. Later on Greimas adds to the four actants two "circumstants" of "helper" and "opponent."[49] The category of actants is actually wider than that of characters, since actants do not actually have to be living things at all. In the story by Hemingway, *Old man and the sea*, the sea itself is an actant and could be categorized as "opponent." Likewise, in Reagan's narration "America" is not just a circumstance or the locus of the story, but an actant and, depending on the particular story he tells, assumes different functions.

Stories are full of events, and these are things that the actants do in the storyworlds, or what is done to them in turn, or what just happens. Chatman argues that in the narrative sense "events are either *actions (acts)* or *happenings*. Both are changes of state."[50] If this is brought about by an agent, and is "plot-significant," the agent that causes it is called a "character."[51] A character is created only when it plays a part in some event described. One could say that a storyworld inhabitant becomes a character by acting or refraining from action and if the result of this is significant for the story might even become an actant.

We seldom refer to the dramatis personae or even actants when discussing any story but rather choose to talk about characters. Both the formalist and the structuralist viewpoints in general treat the characters within the narrative in a manner that is perhaps too limited.[52] They argue that characters are essentially "products of plots, that their status is 'functional', that they are, in short, participants or *actants* rather than *personages*, that it is erroneous to consider them as real beings."[53] I argue that in political narratives especially the characters are multifunctional from the viewpoint of the narrator. On occasion, like for example on the case of the creation of an "evil enemy," it is necessary to depict characters as merely functional and nonindividualistic and not as actual human beings. Here the Proppian definition of a character as "product of what the tale requires him to do," is fitting.[54] They only serve a function, that is, to manifest the enemy in an assailable form. In the building of a national identity the characters are rather portrayed as possessing immeasurably valuable inner qualities as humans. The Founding Fathers fit into this concept. Even in stories, they are more than the real people who once walked the earth. Reagan described the Founding Fathers, and through them the contemporary Americans as well, "Little minds and timid men do not build great societies; only a great people can do that and we are a great people."[55] The character cannot be always seen as either a functional concept or as a real-life person. It always depends upon the situation, the perspective, and the aim of the story.

Chatman argues for a theory of character that treats it as an autonomous being and not as a mere plot function. He claims that a character is "reconstructed by the audience from evidence announced or implicit in an original construction and communicated through the discourse."[56] Thus character is created in the interplay between the narrator and the story recipient, but it is the narrator, who holds the keys to the construction of the character. He can to a large degree determine what the "product" by the story recipient will ultimately be like. The narrator offers all the valuable clues as construction blocks, and if he is skillful in storytelling, he can shape the product to his liking, and the story recipient may not even notice that his "free thought" is in any way tampered with.

Alasdair MacIntyre notes that certain social roles in the form of "stock characters" are to be found especially in the United States.

They are culture specific and furnish us with recognizable characters, and the ability to recognize them is socially crucial, because knowledge of a character provides an interpretation of the actions of those individuals who assume a certain character. Character lays a moral constraint on the personality of those who inhabit them and define in a very limited way the possibilities of action for those persons. Characters become "moral representatives of their culture," because through them the moral ideas assume an embodied existence in the social and political world.[57] While Reagan was very adept in using the social roles or stock characters to the advancement of his politics, he seemed to genuinely enjoy the grandeur and the mythoreligious function of the American presidency. Even when Reagan had "true" stories to tell of real people, in the words of Wills, "he casts a mythic, even religious, aura over them and makes complex operations the story of one man."[58] People become mythic characters but the relationship goes both ways. In order for myths to become real to people, they have to see them acted out by actors in dramas of cultural significance.[59]

Individuals as stock characters are less likely to be seen as only themselves, since they are constituent parts of America. America itself brings infinity to individuals and individuals in turn to America. America is in Reagan's storytelling so otherworldly, larger than life and outside our scope of experience, that it is able to assume the stance of a divine being and link individuals to infinity. A fitting example of this is the stock character of the "American hero" or "unknown soldier." In the quotation Reagan shows how a social role can be imposed on a person; or rather a deceased person can be turned narratively into something that fits this function.

An American hero has returned home. God bless him.
    We may not know of this man's life, but we know of his character. We may not know his name, but we know his courage. He is the heart, the spirit, and the soul of America.
    Today a grateful nation mourns the death of an unknown serviceman of the Vietnam conflict. This young American understood that freedom is never more than one generation away from extinction. He may not have wanted to be a hero, but there was a need—in the Iron Triangle, off Yankee Station, at Khe Sanh, over the Red River Valley.
    He accepted his mission and did his duty. And his honest patriotism overwhelms us. We understand the meaning of his sacrifice and those of his comrades yet to return.
    This American hero may not need us, but surely we need him. In Longfellow's words:

So when a great man dies,
For years beyond our ken,
The light he leaves behind him lies
Upon the paths of men.

We must not be blind to the light that he left behind. Our path must be worthy of his trust. And we must not betray his love of country. It's up to us to protect the proud heritage now in our hands, and to live in peace as bravely as he died in war.

On this day, as we honor our unknown serviceman, we pray to Almighty God for His mercy. And we pray for the wisdom that this hero be America's last unknown.[60]

This case is a fitting example of the way Reagan turns actual people into character myths to use those myths to advance his policies. Barthes notes that the "myth hides nothing: its function is to distort, not make disappear."[61] The Unknown Soldier is no longer an actual person, he becomes part of a myth and specifically the signifier the myth requires. The Unknown Soldier is a representation of America.

The signifier has two aspects. One, that is full, is meaning, and the other, which is empty, is the form. The meaning is what gets distorted in mythmaking. For Barthes, in a myth "the meaning is always there to present the form; the form is always there to outdistance the meaning. And there is never any contradiction, conflict, or split between the meaning and the form."[62] Thus the person mythified may become unreal, but the core of the form is ever present should one choose to look for it. The Unknown Soldier becomes "everyman." He is at the same time not only a nameless unknown soldier but also every soldier ever lost in a battle. He becomes in Reagan's narration the universal missing son for every father and mother to mourn over, while at the same time he is only a body that could not be identified. He is everybody and nobody at the same time. The signifier turns into a definite "He" that compensates for every young man whose carcass could not be brought back. No matter whom the soldier actually was, with Reagan's narration he becomes a myth that can be applied to anyone. As W. Lloyd Warner writes, "The American Unknown Soldier is Everyman; he is the perfect symbol of equalitarianism."[63] An earlier version that Reagan used of similar stock character was the forgotten hero:

There is an American out there who has been a forgotten man, perhaps because he asked little of government except freedom. He holds the whole bureaucratic structure of government on his tire back and he works two and a half hours of each day just to pay its cost. . . . This forgotten American is black, he is white, he is all the shades in between, and sometimes he wasn't even born here, but he built this country and he can do it again.[64]

The Unknown Soldier, astronauts on the Challenger Shuttle, or George Gipp,[65] all these people are deprived of their history and changed into gestures. The form is not obliterated but not left as it was either. It also changes, because the concept needs its form. The soldier and Gipper remain in existence. They are, following Barthes, "half-amputated, they are deprived of memory, not of existence."[66] They are no longer what they once were, but they still have a form. Their meaning changes greatly but the form is altered in-between the lines of the narration as well.

Reagan's storytelling aimed at not making some glorious hero the focal point of identification for the people, but rather by the means of narration turning normal, boringly average people into heroes for people to identify themselves with. "The people [who] live on Main Street, U.S.A."[67] are turned into everybody and vice versa. John Doe becomes every American, and every American becomes one of the heroes Reagan constantly talked about: "And those who say we're in a time when there are no heroes, they just don't know where to look."[68] Reagan was always ready to assist his story recipient in feeling the heroism burn in his veins. Every single American could be a hero.[69] Reagan's everyday heroes were not only created for the purposes of feeling good but also to drive home his ideological points and vision of America.[70]

We don't have to turn to our history books for heroes. They're all around us . . . there are countless, quiet, everyday heroes of American life—parents who sacrifice long and hard so their children will know a better life than they've known; church and civic volunteers . . . millions who've made our nation and our nation's destiny so very special— unsung heroes who may not have realized their dreams themselves but then who reinvest those dreams in their children.[71]

Reagan's true originality lies in his ability to take and story *sjuzets* from the less exalted and down-to-earth areas of the daily lives of Americans and contemporary forms of folklore like movies or television. Reagan's heroes are "unsung," and often they are the true "salt of the earth." As Reagan said, "I am never happier than when I come across a story that reaffirms my belief in the capacity of our people

for great deeds."[72] Perhaps it is this ability to create heroes out of
the people that compose the mass of citizenry, and use the mediums
of storytelling most common to them, such as television, as sources
for his own stories, that enabled him at the same time to have mul-
timillionaire friends and still be seen by American's as "one of us."
Everyone is a potential hero inside, and the mythical America is all
about heroism.

> Heroes. You know, we seem to be in a kind of a cult. And the enter-
> tainment world is partly guilty of this, as well as other things. We
> seem to be obsessed with wanting to tear down our heroes. But you
> know something? We're a country of heroes. And the greatest unsung
> heroes in the world go unnoticed. No, they're not out there manning
> the parapets or riding to the rescue. They're getting up every morn-
> ing. They're sending you, their sons and daughters, to school. They're
> going to work. They're contributing to their church and their chari-
> ties. They're making this society run. [73]

Reagan claims constantly that America is a country of heroes. This
is evident in the type of stories he tells as well. For Reagan, the story
of America was always an epic saga, abundant with heroes who overcame villainy at home and abroad. His intention to put pride back
into America rested on the idea of communicating to citizenry, especially young adults, the meaning of their lives by relating them to
the "legitimate narrative of the society to which they belonged."[74]
Thucydides noted that it is not hard to praise Athens to Athenians,
and this principle certainly was at play, because who would not like to
conceive himself as a hero. Reagan helped the majority of Americans
to solve their value-related problems by giving them answers they
always wanted to hear concerning their characteristics.[75] It was
through everyday citizen heroes and their actions where America's
greatness begins.[76]

Reagan often used his State of the Union addresses to present
American heroes who were ordinary people who had done something
special. In the narration they became mythical American heroes who
exemplified the values Reagan wanted people to believe he stood for.
Presenting people such as Jean Nguyen, a former boat refugee who
graduated with honors from West Point, Reagan acted in the role of
the host. This was just like in his General Electric theatre days; only
this time marketing his own ideology. The ordinary people became
mythified in his presentation and some of the myth rubbed off on
him.[77] For Reagan, "The achievements and courage of individuals

provide an inspiring example of the essence of American spirit."[78]
Individuals are visions as well as narrator's creations, and their suitability to describe all of us is a central factor in linking us to the
never-ending story of infinity. They remove us from individual plane
into the region where all the rest of humanity is able to join us, or we
join them.[79] Again I resort to Reagan's words about the Unknown
Soldier: "We may not know of this man's life, but we know of his
character. We may not know his name, but we know his courage. He
is the heart, the spirit, and the soul of America."[80]

In a State of the Union address, Reagan's first following the assassination attempt of John Hinckley on his life, Reagan illustrates the
idolized meaning of ordinary Americans representing the entire
nation. "Sick societies don't produce young men like Secret Service
Agent Tim McCarthy who placed his body between mine and the
man with the gun simply because he felt that's what his duty called
him to do. . . . Sick societies don't make people like us so proud to
be Americans and so very proud of our fellow citizens."[81] Reagan was
able to take such a tragic event as the assassination attempt and narratively use it as an oration on behalf of America. Naturally Reagan
leaves out of the story the fact that the American society produced
John Hinckley as well. Hinckley is left out of the story simultaneously excluded from America. He is an aberration without a place
in Reagan's mythical America. It was quite a narrative feat to turn a
tragic event into something that once again glorifies America and, as
a byproduct, made Reagan a hero that was for a long time verbally
almost unassailable by anyone. McCarthy, Hinckley, and Reagan
himself became characters in the assassination story. Since Reagan
survived the assassination attempt with grace and humor, this created
a wave of popular support that Reagan rode as a heroic character.

James Phelan claims that a character consists of three components:
"the mimetic (character as person), the thematic (character as an idea)
and the synthetic (character as artificial construct)."[82] The relationship between these components varies from narrative to narrative.[83]
Reagan's use of character varies according to what his intention in
depicting characters is. Naturally characterization is not Reagan's
sole privilege just because he is the narrator. Characterization is an
ongoing process where ultimately the characters get their form from
the story recipient, and intertextuality is a strong aide in this. One
of the advantages gained by characterization is that, following the
thought lines of E. M. Forster, by creating characters out of actual
persons, we are able to know everything about them. Perfect knowledge about an actual person is always only an illusion, but about a

character, such as those in novels, we are able to know everything. Characterization banalises actual people into characters, which are both simpler and thus easier to understand. They become shallow and less complex, since some of their depth is removed. All that there is to know becomes equivalent to everything the story tells us. In general, the works of fiction and political narration as well "suggest a more comprehensible and thus a more manageable human race, *they give us the illusion of perspicacy and of power.*"[84] It must not be forgotten that the "god-view" provided by narrative politics into each political actor is nothing else than an illusion. Everything cannot be deduced about the actors, but the important thing is that the illusion can be created when actual people are taken out of the actual political world and inserted into the story.

Reagan's official biographer Edmund Morris extends his understanding attitude to Reagan's supposed short attention span and the rumors of dementia during the presidency. His explanation lies in Reagan being an actor, a person who moves from one production to another. An actor's life consists of entrances and exits, shorter or longer scenes, takes and retakes, and productions. Reagan forgot people with suddenness but adapted to new people at the scene just as easily. An actor lives for the future and remembers forward, not backward like most of us. Yesterday's scenes are in the can. Today is rolling inevitably and tomorrow is the main focus, because the lines of tomorrow have to be memorized today. Whenever Reagan gave a speech or any other public performance, it was a single shot within a large eight-year production of his presidency. That explains why he was so often so unfocused between the "performances."[85] Even Reagan himself once joked on the campaign trail about his future governorship: "If only I could think of it as a script that would run for four years."[86]

Reagan did not see actors as fakers but rather as people who were capable of transmitting noble ideals.[87] What they created was often better than the real thing in the same manner as Reagan's narrated America was closer to ideal than the real one. The storyworlds he helped construct, as well as the images and ideals behind them, were what needed to be communicated to other people. Reagan understood that there is always a strong element of stagecraft involved in statecraft, and that is why he built his entire political leadership on both the storytelling he used and the more visual dramatic effects his public personality radiated. Reagan was always as if he was in camera,[88] and his skills in acting enabled him more efficiently to become a mythical figure. Associates disillusioned with Reagan's 1976 unsuccessful campaign stated that he did not actually run his own campaign but treated it as a Hollywood movie and himself as a product to be sold by others. "He is an actor, not the centre of the action. . . . His act is completely natural; it has no pretence. He takes himself for real. He's been playing his role for so long, it seems real to him."[89] While voicing intense critique toward Reagan, this associate as a by-product reveals one of the strengths of Reagan. Whether his political performance was "the real Reagan" or just an act performed for the audience of Americans, he was natural in his role to such a degree that it became, if it already were not, the real Reagan. Reagan differs from the traditional narrators in the way he wanted to place himself as a character into his stories. He was not content just to remain the narrator but often wanted a part or a role in the story itself. Reagan was because of his acting profession a particularly gifted politician in assuming multiple and varying roles when escaping from the confines of his role as a narrator and entering his own storyworlds. These were not the type of "walk-in" appearances Alfred Hitchcock made in his movies but were crucial roles. Reagan often narrated himself into his stories in a heroic role.[90]

Reagan saw politics as acting, or in other words, performing a narrative by staging it in the form of an enacted play. As he said, "You'd be surprised how much being a good actor pays off."[91] His presidency was just another role for him and the status of the president allowed him the one freedom he had always craved for; the chance to write the script when he so chose to do. According to Reagan, "Politics is like show business. You have a hell of an opening, you coast for a while, you have a hell of a closing."[92] But then again, early on in his political career Reagan understood that the label of "actor" was something of a setback and commented,

> I had a feeling that my career theatrically was suffering because Hollywood was not looking at me like an actor. . . . Now, to turn around and find that suddenly—all of a sudden now that I want to be something else besides an actor, everybody is saying that I'm an actor. I'll tell you, I'll probably be the only fellow who will get posthumously an Oscar.[93]

In his public speeches Reagan denied ever attending "dramatic school" but very often mentioned his college degree in economics, supposedly to support his economic analyses.[94] Reagan frequently said to Edwin Meese III in private that he did not know how he could have done his job as a president if he were not an actor.[95] As Smith has argued, Reagan very easily mastered all the most important roles previous presidents had assumed; "the president as father of the country, as cheerleader for his policies, as heroic commander in chief."[96] Reagan did not limit himself to the confines of these roles but remained in continuous flux or a state of metamorphosis switching from one type of character to another. Hollywood had specialized in creating mythic American heroes ranging from lone rangers and sheriffs to citizen crusaders and soldier-heroes ready for the ultimate sacrifice for America.[97] Reagan had played them all and knew when to evoke a certain stereotypical character from his persona. Americans were forced during the 1980 and 1984 elections to render judgment not only on his qualifications and later achievements as a president but also on all the characters Reagan brought to life on the screen during his 30-year film career. It was not only Reagan but also George Gipp, Andy McLeod, Dan Crawford, Brass Bancroft, Jimmy Grant, Johnny Hammond, Web Sloane, and other characters that had to be evaluated, and Reagan consciously sought to portray himself as a real-life politician simulta-neously embodying all traits of action figures engaged in heroic acts of leadership on the silver screen.[98] Occasionally, this portrayal was not even very subtle. During his gubernatorial campaign before he arrived at a rally the public address system would blast the fight song of the Notre Dame University, attempting to initiate mental con-nection between Reagan and the Notre Dame football hero George Gipp he had played in a movie and ever since referred to himself as "the Gipper."[99] While George Gipp was Reagan's most prominent role, many of the B-films he starred portrayed him as a cowboy, and this was another role to exploit.

> I seem to remember a famous country and western song warning mothers not to let their babies grow up to be cowboys. [Laughter] The song forgot to say that cowboys can sometimes grow up and be President.[100]

Cowboy as a hero is tightly connected to a certain social strata as the prototypical American hero. Another stock character is the frontier hero, as exemplified by Daniel Boone or Davy Crockett. They occu-pied a middle ground in a civilization that still was in contact with its origins in nature.[101] The Western hero exemplified by the cowboy has even been argued to combine the most useful characteristics of the Old Testament God and the New Testament Christ to play the role of the redeemer.[102] The American mythic cowboy was a strong, moral, and a God-fearing character. While it is a popular metaphor for many other presidents and political figures as well,[103] Reagan heightened its suitability for him by spending a lot of time during his presidential terms on his ranch, the Rancho del Cielo.[104]

> Well, that's when the American people rounded up a posse, swore in this old sheriff, and sent us riding into town, where the previous administration had said the Nation's problems were too complicated to manage. Well, we said of course they are; so government should stop trying to manage them, stop putting its faith in the false god of bureaucracy, and trust the genius of the American people instead.[105]

Reagan certainly knew how to appeal to the compelling myth of the Western hero, basing his optimism on honesty, sincerity, and even innocence of this figure.[106] Knelman notes that in the age of vast technological progress, as was experienced throughout the Reagan era, the American hero of folklore, the cowboy, was replaced by another hero of the frontier, the astronaut.[107] Technology was all but neutral in the Reagan era, and space served not only as a new basis to "start Americans dreaming again," as Reagan claimed, but also as a guidance for the context of those dreams. Space was the new frontier, perhaps the "final frontier" to paraphrase the expression from the popular TV-series *Star Trek*. The hero of this frontier, where America could once again strive for its manifest destiny, was not the cowboy with his six-shooter but the astronaut, a new breed of an American hero and a new frontiersman. The importance of technological advances and especially those connected with space should not be underestimated when studying the storyworlds of Ronald Reagan. Knelman even proposes a new role for Reagan along his more common depictions—that of Buck Rogers, a comic book lone hero of the space.[108]

Reagan's use of American values actually both designed and reflected American popular culture. Reagan's bedrock values of family, work, neighborhood, peace, and freedom were reflected in many of the popular TV shows, such as "The Cosby Show." At the same time movies portrayed strong, often violent lone characters, fighting the injustices of the world such as "Rambo" or "Dirty Harry." Reagan was not only a reflection of the popular culture of his times but also the relationship was more complex. The Reagan presidency was one factor in creating the climate just as Reagan was an answer to the needs of the American public. The values Reagan espoused were incorporated into the national culture, but at the same time he was a direct response to the need of such values being reflected. Reagan was at the same time a product and the producer of the cultural climate.

When viewing Reagan's character one must acknowledge that it is not, following Jonathan Culler's argumentation, merely a collection of different features but instead a teleological set based on cultural models and transmitted intertextually. Reagan's speeches, as well as everything else told about him, cue us to construct a personality for him, but our formal expectations play a part as well. Characterization is a teleological process in such a manner that characters are not supposed to fit within stereotypes, but the mere existence of these stereotypical models cue the way characters are constructed.[109] The narratively created Reagan was fitted to fill a necessary role in the United States of the 1980s. He was an imaginary persona created, mostly by his own initiative, to fill a gap of leadership, and the need for a strong and consistent leader itself helped to create him after that image. After certain failures of the Carter administration, Reagan was conjured up narratively to be a "political messiah" to return hope and prosperity to America once again. The role he needed to fill influenced his persona as a president as well as his actual personality. Reagan may not actually have been the answer to America's need for leadership but was given shape and form by that need. He fits Uri Margolin's concept of "non-actual individual," which is a nonactual being who exists in a possible world, and who can be ascribed physical, social, and mental properties.[110]

When we attempt to understand the character of Reagan, we must take into account that presidential persona is more than the actual person cast in the role. Others participate in the creation of this character. During the Geneva summit Gorbachev made a tremendous impression for the media, and Speakes along with other White House media people was afraid that Reagan was losing the public relations battle. Speakes openly admits in his memoirs to drafting quotes for Reagan. News reported these quotes as having taken place off camera, and the Soviets never chose to dispute them. One of these quotes that got high media exposure was, "There is much that divides us, but I believe the world breaths easier because we are talking here together."[111] This was so close to the style of Reagan that he personally would in all likelihood not have disavowed this utterance, but it works as a good example that not all the stories "told" by Reagan were in fact ever actually uttered by him. Nathan writes that the presidency is much more than just one person. He is rather "congress covered with skin." He is a leader of a very large system.[112] But even more important is the way the political party groups itself around the one person they have chosen for candidacy to reach the intelligence of the crowd. The name of the candidate becomes a symbol, and all theories of the party are personified in him or her.[113] The candidate is no longer an individual but becomes the anthropomorphication of the party he or she represents. All theories the party has concerning politics and all its stories find a communicator and narrator in the candidate. Everything is personified in him or her, everything the party stands for becomes a part of his nature, and everything the party wishes to communicate becomes a part of his repertoire. If the candidate becomes the president, as Reagan did, he or she is a collective entity composed of many others as well.

We could treat the character of Reagan as a collective persona that consists of all the officials in his administration, who basically tell the same story, all the speechwriters and aides, and even the public that acts as recipients to his stories, and thus form a mental image of Reagan based on these stories and elaborating and extrapolating from them the imaginary figure of a leader who goes by the name Ronald Reagan. To borrow the words of Roland Barthes,

> The language produced and spread under the protection of power is statutorily a language of repetition; all official institutions of language are repeating machines: school, sports, advertising, popular songs, news, all continually repeat the same structure, the same meaning, often the same words: the stereotype is a political fact, the major figure of ideology.[114]

It is necessary to understand President Ronald Wilson Reagan as a fictional character that was created and recreated by stories of his own and others and to distinguish this entity from the actual historical personality to study him narratively. At the center of this study is then the dramatis, or rather the *narratis,* persona of Ronald Reagan, or Reagan as a character in his own stories. One can treat Reagan as a fictional personality that has only the characteristics endowed him by the story in the interactionary process between the narrator and the story recipient. I still wish to make a strong argument on behalf of the fact that Reagan himself played a major role in the narrative construction process of his identity. Since he was both a narrator and character of the stories told, he naturally was shaped by the story. But since his own life created a backbone for many of the stories he told, he shaped the stories simultaneously. The creation of Reagan's public persona was a self-feeding cyclical process. To a large degree his prepresidential persona influenced his political storytelling. The image dominated the narrative creation and fuelled itself. Reagan was then essentially Reagan, but only the narrated Reagan, and by the time of his presidency the actual, real-life Reagan had been engulfed by the story.

The presidential persona of Reagan was a character of his mythical American storyworld more than an actual human being. He was partially created in the narrative dialogue and storyworld construction, which took place between his narrations and the interpretations of the audience. What Reagan was to the American public was partially a result of how they wanted to interpret the stories he told, and he could infiltrate his stories partially, because so much of his storytelling concentrated on his own life experience and even his life story. So, is it fruitful to even study a president who is mediated to us as a *narratis persona*? Hannah Arendt has argued that "in politics, more than anywhere else, we have no possibility of distinguishing between being and appearance."[115] There is no way for a member of the general public to distinguish between the real person and his public image. The two are confused to such a degree that the appearance takes the place of the actual person behind that image. Reagan himself acknowledged the role of images and their creation in modern politics.

> All of us have grown up accepting with little question certain images as accurate portraits of public figures—some living, some dead. Very seldom if ever do we ask if the images are true to the original. Even less do we question how the images were created. This is probably more true of Presidents in our country because of the intense spotlight which centres on their every move.[116]

Reagan's media strategists noted that Reagan was the perfect messenger and decided that "governing was to involve the presentation of image—not of the self but a projection."[117] The Reagan team understood the power of images in the television age and produced pictures that were better than the real thing.[118] To a degree the public persona of Reagan was an answer to the needs, hopes, and wishes of the citizenry. The people demand certain things of their president, and he, or at least his image, is shaped by those demands and desires. Indeed, the president or other political leader needs to fit into the typecast given by the citizenry. However, the relationship is not that simple. Reagan gained the presidency after Jimmy Carter, and while almost anybody would at that point in time have been preferable for the voters, Reagan was not just an empty signifier. He had a long career of public speaking—always on political topics—behind him and could not have started anew, only as vocalizing the will and need of the citizens.

The imperative need of this nation at all times is the leadership of the uncommon men and women. We need men who cannot be intimidated, who are not concerned with the applause meters, who will not sell tomorrow for cheers today.[119]

Nevertheless, Reagan recognized the importance of the cheers and negotiated very carefully during the presidency between what he saw as best and what would be politically fitting. Reagan allowed the aspirations of the public to change his persona somewhat, but the essential core of values he had stood for remained intact. Reagan used his political storytelling as a tool to describe to the American public what his political persona was like and to manipulate with the stories the wishes of the public. Reagan was more than only an image projected from the common hopes of the voters, but it was a conscious decision he made as an actor to allow stories and the hopes of the public to recreate him anew with slight alterations to the original. Instead of being a mere marionette, Reagan was in charge of the narrative creation of his image, but the stories shaped him by shaping the image people held. While Reagan was not talking about himself, these words of his fit this situation as well:

There's a great deal of false image-making and an effort made not to dispute the views you really hold, but to invent some and hang them on you with the hope the false image will appear real.[120]

As Boorstin argues, there is strictly speaking no way to unmask an image. Every time an effort is made to debunk it, it only grows even more interesting. The creation of the image fascinates us, and just like a magic show, even showing us that the image is deception, we can still enjoy its pleasures.[121] Stories can be used in the creation of political images. Reagan's image was so strong that even on those numerous occasions he was proved to be making false utterances the image of an honest man still remained unblemished. A storyworld cannot be destroyed, only another better crafted and more intriguing storyworld can take its place, and the same applies to images. While many of Reagan's adversaries tried to take the role of an iconoclast, nobody was successful enough.

If it is a little difficult to view a political leader as a character in the drama of politics, a *narratis persona*, if you will, there arises another problem as well. How do we treat the collective of the citizens, be it a community or a larger society in a political narration? In other words, how do we handle the "mythical America" Reagan narrated into existence? Paul Ricoeur saw a problem with the tendency of history to deal with such social entities as societies, states, and communities, since these entities are composed of individuals and exist only by virtue of individual's sense in belonging to them and participating in them. These are not and cannot be a product of a historian's conceptual activity, since their existence is independent of him. In our everyday communication these entities are given personal subjects and viewed as genuine subjects of action.

Ricoeur calls these entities "quasi-persons" and events and actions they participate in as "quasi-plots."[122] A quasiperson of the state is an imagined community just because its existence is justified only if individuals believe in its existence and want to be a part of it. But these social entities are undoubtedly at least partially a product of political action. Political narratives are told to people precisely to get them to participate in these social entities. People are given a sense of belonging in these narratives. America is often personified as if it was an independent person in Reagan's narration, and indeed, it can almost become one. An example where Reagan almost anthropomorphises America is his statement that "Uncle Sam is a friendly old man, but he has a spine of steel."[123] Uncle Sam can on the one hand be interpreted as merely a jocular symbol of the United States of America as a nation. Seen like this there is no practical difference for example to the Russian bear or the British John Bull or any other way people create an anthropomorphic image of their country. On the other hand, this process of creating a fleshy manifestation of a country can be viewed as transubstantiation. Just as wine becomes the blood of Christ, the image of Uncle Sam becomes America. Just as creating an image of the entire nation in flesh profanes the nation or brings it closer and graspable for the citizenry, the process works the other way around. If the word becomes flesh, the flesh may become a word as well.

Peterson notes that the tendency of Reagan to use his perfected America as a standard and a characterization made him unable to address directly some deficiencies of the society such as racism, violence, and socioeconomic maladjustments. "The failure of such subjects to work their way to a significant place on the president's public agenda was the consequence of both what Reagan chose to emphasize and how he chose to emphasize it."[124] If we take Reagan's autobiography *Where's the Rest of Me?*[125] as an example, we can immediately see that the story itself has been severely distorted by what the teller wanted to communicate. The story is just too good to be true. There are no really hard times. All anecdotes have happy endings, and the climb from Dixon to Hollywood happens without any interruptions of discord. By creating narratively his Norman Rockwell–style America, Reagan simultaneously disabled himself. He was no longer able to include in his narratives anything that existed in the shades and not on the sunny side of "Main Street, U.S.A."[126] But essentially the small-town paradise myth was neither Reagan's invention nor has it sprung from experience. It is just the old Edenic myth, which for a long time has been among the organizing forces of American culture, one which arose with the discovery of America itself.[127] By trying to use this myth to his benefit, Reagan ran into a political cul-de-sac. By choosing to perfect his America, Reagan made it difficult for himself to address serious wrongs within America, because they would have violated his story logic and in the worst case scenario, crumbled the entire storyworld built.

The unification of the entire people of the United States into "America" was the goal of Reagan's political storytelling. He wanted to bring Americans together and unify them with a renewed nationalist and patriotic feeling. Once the individual subject of politics, the citizen, sees his own identity as a part of a larger whole, America, the object of politics can be transferred from doing what is good to them as individuals into doing what is good and right for America. Individual social problems vanish when individuals are formed into a collective. If the narration is seductive and successful enough, the individual is even willing to drown his own rights for the benefit of a collective. The quasiperson becomes an actual person with the consent of the actual persons themselves.

> America is in a danger of losing her soul. —Yes, in a manner of speaking, a nation does have a soul; the soul of a nation is the spirit of its people.[128]

It can even be argued that the most important character Reagan created was not "the Gipper" himself but the actant of "America." Reagan substituted the American reality with a fantasy America of a romantic storytype, teeming with opportunity and equality. In the words of Frye it was an idealized world where "heroes are brave, heroines beautiful, villains villainous, and the frustrations of ordinary life are made little of."[129] This is a good definition of the mythical America Reagan narrated into existence. And Reagan himself was a necessary part of that America, since political heroes represent mythical symbols, and Reagan became a symbol both for his age[130] and his mythical America as well. The America Reagan described in his stories arguably has never existed. It is a creation of myth.

The American people he told stories about were transformed into a mythical race of men in the course of the narration. One should not confuse the real American people and the collective character or actant that Reagan gives birth to. The people are endowed with all those qualities Reagan deems worthy in a person, and it is always this mythical community of people he addresses when speaking to Americans. The tie between the Americans and Reagan within the narration was complex. Both were connected so that whatever Reagan told about himself as a personal narration concerned America as well. As Ochs and Capps have noted, "Each telling reverberates across past, present, and unrealized time, yielding a more or less integrated logic of personal experience."[131] Reagan unified past and present in his narrations. In the process some things that have been unrealized became part of his personal reality and history, although they never have taken place in actuality. As Reagan noted, "In a single lifetime, my own, we have gone from horse and buggy to sending astronauts to the Moon."[132] Since things external to the narration have changed, the narrative needs to be different as well. But the essential superstructure of the mythical America as God's chosen country remained a part of the story. Reagan's storytelling was tied to his own life story but even more it emphasized the past, present, and future of America. One could say that he was narrating the life of his nation—the American life.

BEYOND AUTHORSHIP—REAGAN AS NARRATOR

> You know, some of you I'm afraid have been exposed to me before and you're going to discover, if you have, that I am a sort of "Johnny One-Note." I continue more or less hammering away at the same subject. The music is always the same, now and then a little re-wording of the lyrics, but it still comes out sounding the same.
>
> Ronald Wilson Reagan[133]

Besides blurring the distinction between the United States of the "real" world and the mythical storyverse of America, Reagan blurred also the boundaries between the internal and external elements of the story. As we saw, the author or the narrator could be story participant as well. This blurring of roles is an essential and particularly interesting aspect of Reagan's political narration. Here I will deal with the problem of the actual authorship of Reagan's stories and argue that in a political narration the narratorship is more important than the origin of the words that combine into a story by a performative act of the politician.

Barthes notes that the narrator as well as the characters within the narrative "are essentially 'paper beings' from our and the reader's perspective; the (material) author of a narrative is in no way to be confused with the narrator of that narrative."[134] He argues that there is historically a large mass of narratives without authors such as epics, folktales, and oral narratives. The person who speaks in the narrative is not the same person who writes in real life, and who writes is not actually who that person is.[135]

> Q: Do you enjoy being President more than being a movie actor?
> The President: Yeah, because here I get to write the script, too.[136]

During his entire career Reagan always had an interest in rewriting and reformulating the scripts to the desperation first of his producers and then of his closest aides in the White House. He wanted to be a part of scriptwriting in both movies and during his presidency when he had capable speechwriters. He spent a considerable amount of time rewriting, editing, adding to, and omitting from his speeches and choosing more suitable expressions and terminology.[137] But can Reagan be considered as the author of his speeches?

The narrator, author, and even the implied author have to be separated from each other. While the "hand mark" of the author can be seen influencing the text, the boundaries of the text must be transgressed. Author produces the meaning of the text, and narrator is a part of a model designed to account for textual operations within literary narratives.[138] In Reagan's speeches the actual authors (the speechwriters) tried their best to imitate the style of the narrator, who assumed the role of the implied author in the eyes of the story recipients. The distinctions become even more blurred, since the voice of the actual author is purposefully being drowned below that of the narrator. "It's typical, isn't it? I just quoted a great writer, but as an actor, I get the bow."[139]

Reagan often participated in his storyverse, but just as often hid behind the narrative, being only the teller with no part in the events portrayed. When Reagan chose to be part of his story portraying himself as both the hero and the narrator, he became what Todorov calls "narrator-character."[140] Reagan immersed himself into the storyverse, and thus allowed the recipients to start constructing a new identity for him in accordance with the story logic. Reagan was no longer an actual person. Once he started implanting himself as a character into his narration, Reagan's identity became narratively constructed and thus negotiable. To be a narrator-character is a strange combination at the first glimpse. But this is common in the genre of fiction in first-person narration, where the character acts as a narrator telling his own story. After all, everything Reagan tells about himself, he tells about America and the other way around. He is an actant in his mythical America, and indeed the America he depicts takes shape only in relation to him. All the political stories Reagan told were essentially stories about "American Life" to follow the title of his postpresidential autobiography.

Todorov emphasized the different stances the narrator can take. The narrative voice can be troublesome. The narrator can be omnipresent in the story intervening constantly or much more discreet. However, since the narrative itself enables making the narrator a figure within the fictive universe or storyworld, this is a totally distinct stance for the narrator to assume. The distinction does not lie in the narrator's use of the word "I" but in the actual level of intervention within the fictive universe. Todorov uses the word "narrator" only with regard to an explicit representation of the "implied author" in the general case.[141] There is a difference in narrative terminology between the two. Gerald Prince defines the latter as "the implicit image of an author in the text, taken to be standing behind the scenes and to be responsible for its design and for the values and cultural norms it adheres to."[142]

Reagan was not the author of the whole story, but still he wanted to portray himself so. Despite the fact that he wrote thousands of prepresidential speeches and took an active interest in the editing and rewriting of his presidential speeches and occasionally wrote them himself, he was assisted by numerous speechwriters, who authored the speeches he gave. Reagan made many additions and omissions to the speeches himself, and his earlier prepresidential speeches provided inspiration and guidance of his intentions for the actual authors. How can then one even discuss the stories and storyworlds of Reagan if he himself was not the author? There are numerous answers to this problem. The first is to consider Reagan as the implied author. It is sometimes hard to even make the distinction between the agency that organizes and selects events as the implied author, and the voice that recounts the same.[143] The speeches were authored by people who knew what Reagan liked to communicate in his speeches. Reagan is the implied author in every speech he gave, because they tell stories that adhere to his values and his worldview. No matter who originally wrote the script, it is Reagan that is being implied to as an author.

Reagan had long practiced being both an author and a narrator. Reagan's experience as a sports broadcaster before his career in

Hollywood or politics was a factor that contributed toward his mastery of narration later in life. Marie-Laure Ryan has called radio broadcasts a "factory of plot" that is constructed around three dimensions; the chronicle of what is happening, the mimesis of telling how the events look, and allowing the listener to picture the events and the emplotment of how things are connected to make sense of the events.[144] There is evidence of the personal importance of this for Reagan in two of his favorite stories, the job audition for radio WOC[145] when he had to "broadcast" an imaginary football game and the story he told when the wire went dead for several minutes during a baseball game and he had to invent consecutive fouls to keep the audience listening rather than admit that in the studio he had no idea what was going on in the game.[146] Another intriguing idea one may get from this story is that, as Reagan explained, he did not want to lose his audience and to avoid that, he relapsed instantly into a story that was pure invention. The implications of a politician's willingness to make such a choice without a moment's thought are fascinating, but broadcasting games from telegraph notes was a common practice at that time, and all the listeners knew he was only pretending to see the game.[147] Often the imagined and narrated game was just better than the real one, and Reagan did not want to interrupt the flow of his narration and stop drafting the storyworld for his audience. The same applies to his mythical America. As Lou Cannon has claimed, Reagan was "a storyteller who made the facts fit the story rather than building the story on facts."[148]

Naturally, the chronicle part of the narration is the most central to a sports broadcaster, but the real challenge lies in the emplotment of the broadcast by constructing characters, attributing functions to single events, and finding an interpretive theme that would link the events into a meaningful sequence.[149] Reagan was, by all accounts, successful as a sports broadcaster, and the use of radio as his medium enabled him even in later life make people "see what he sees." This in turn helped Reagan to communicate his visions of a mythical America, because creating an image into the story recipients' minds works more effectively than mere strings of descriptive sentences. These years were excellent training for Reagan's future as the great communicator, and his skills in producing vivid storyworlds long predated his use of index cards or teleprompter.[150] As a rhetorician and a narrator, Reagan acknowledged one shortcoming in himself and this was reading prepared material. During his speechmaking years Reagan wrote of still being no good at the first reading of a script. According to Cannon he overcame this problem by memorizing the

opening passage and repeating it out aloud before delivering it, and
so everything he read after that would sound spontaneous. The nat-
ural-sounding delivery he used in his political speeches came then
from practice.[151]

    Another important time was the years Reagan spent as a spokes-
man for GE. The GE years were a workshop for Reagan's political
narration to fully develop. He was the public face of GE for many
Americans and indirectly partially responsible for selling images and
the concept of technological progress.[152] Even later in life one characteristic of his storytelling was the ability to sell his views just like
any other product sold by a skilled salesman. It was during these years
from 1954 to 1962 that Reagan's vision or idea of America began to
turn toward practical matters of political ideology and policy. The
content of his speeches switched from Hollywood tidbits to political
matters advocating freedom. As Kengor notes, his speeches began
to be dominated by the theme of freedom, which in turn became
inseparable with God as a given right.[153] As Reagan described those
years,

> I know statistics are boring but reducing eight years of tours in which
> I reached all the 135 plants and personally met the 250,000 employ-
> ees, down to numbers, it turns out something like this: two of the
> eight years were spent travelling, and with speeches sometimes run-
> ning at fourteen a day, I was on my feet in front of a "mike" for
> about 250,000 minutes . . . I knew I had to avoid a set routine or a
> canned speech which, although it would have been easier, could have
> ruined the whole wonderful reaction we were getting. I was sure that
> one group exchanged notes with the others about what took place
> in these twenty-minute sessions, and it wouldn't do to have them
> discover I had one twenty-minute pitch which was turned on and off
> like a record. Besides, at fourteen times a day I'd get pretty sick of it
> myself. The answer was a brief greeting and explanation of why I was
> there, which of necessity had to be fairly pat, but then I freewheeled
> my way into a question-and-answer session and that really made for
> variety.[154]

During his GE years Reagan seemed to shy away from canned
speeches. He wanted to make a different speech to his every audience. Different audiences required different wording and topics,
and Reagan began to notice that he had to choose his words with
care. Ad-libbing became the best approach, but in the case of such
an experienced actor, even ad-libbing draws on well-practiced words
and gestures.[155] He assumed the same style he liked to use during his

presidency when giving informal speeches. A short introduction or a statement and a lot of room for questions became the standard script for his GE speeches and carried on into the presidency.[156] Naturally, some speeches were more tightly structured. During both of his presidential campaigns the speeches were in essence built around a certain frame, rhythm, and flow. Every now and then he told a different joke or spoke of his principal points in different order, but the framework of most of his speeches remained constant, and thus speeches were close to identical. The idea of ad-libbing goes a long way to explaining why in his later years, as biographer Edmund Morris has noted, Reagan seemed to be like a tape-recorder, which would turn on and produce a certain anecdote given the right stimulus; a certain word that connected things in Reagan's mind.[157]

During his first years of political speechmaking, Reagan talked about the joys of giving and the blessings of democracy along with answering questions from all walks of life. In time his conservatism grew and the tone of his speeches became more antigovernmental.[158] While his anti-Communism was evident from his years as the president of the Screen Actors Guild (SAG) onward, the antigovernmentalism was along with his own experiences at least partially a byproduct of the feedback he received from his audience. The members of his audiences told him of their own experiences, and some of these ended up in Reagan's speeches, and the amount of feedback kept growing. There was less and less Hollywood in his speeches and more about government. This same thought was expressed by Reagan himself in his 1965 autobiography.

> As the years went on my speeches underwent a kind of revolution, reflecting not only my changing philosophy but also the swiftly rising tide of collectivism that threatens to inundate what remains of our free economy. . . . The Hollywood portion of the talk shortened and disappeared. The warning words of what could happen changed to concrete examples of what has already happened, and I learned very early to document those examples. Bureaucracy does not take kindly to being assailed and isn't above using a few low blows and a knee to the groin when it fights back. Knowing this, I have become extreme cautious in dealing with government agencies.[159]

Already in the prepresidential times Reagan occasionally used the help of speechwriters. A good example is the "New Business Speech," which was drafted by William F. Gavin, but which received truly heavy editing and rewriting by Reagan himself.[160] Bill Gavin acted under orders from Peter Hannaford and drafted numerous similar speeches for Reagan. The common denominator in these speeches was that they required a lot of research into statistics. Still, it was Reagan who edited and gave the final shape to even these speeches.[161] Larry Speakes asserts that Reagan often wrote speeches when travelling aboard Air Force One and claims that he worked a lot on his major speeches only leaving the less important to the speechwriters, subject to his editing. This is an exaggeration, but it cannot be denied that he wrote his first inaugural address on a plane in shorthand on yellow legal pad.[162]

Reagan's speeches were his tools of leadership in many senses. He brought his old speeches to the speechwriters in the White House to enable them to write speeches along the same lines, in the same manner, and in the same style.[163] The most important people influenced by the newly authored stories Reagan narrated were the people working in his administration, since as Wallison claims, the speeches provided them with a sense of direction, which was ultimately reflected in the actions of the cabinet members.[164] A speech is a statement of policy and thus important, since the policy is words, and words are expressed in the speech. Probably no other US president has had such enormous experience as a public speaker as Ronald Reagan, and all his radio addresses and GE speech notes along with his gubernatorial speeches were able to provide guidance for the White House speechwriters.

Peggy Noonan was perhaps the most famous of Reagan's speechwriters, and after leaving the White House, she was called back to work on Reagan's farewell speech. Even she has become interested in Reagan as a writer only in retrospect. During her time in the White House she did not know the skills of Reagan in that area, and Noonan describes it as a shameful experience to later have read the texts Reagan had written in his own hand.[165] Noonan claims that Reagan was a great writer, evidenced by the fact that he had built his entire political career based on his original speeches but had not become a writer par excellence, because he had "turned his talent of writing into a talent for political communication. He had turned his art to the service of his beliefs."[166] Tony Dolan, another speechwriter who wrote the famous "Evil Empire" speech of 1983 agrees that the speeches consisted of Reagan's ideas, only expressed by him and other writers. In the words of yet another speechwriter Peter Robinson, who used Reagan's public issues from the 1970s onward, while researching forthcoming speeches, "He didn't steal from us, we stole from him."[167] One must not think that the speechwriters had completely free hands on their work. Besides the fact that the speech drafts were relatively widely circulated among the top level of the administration for approval, Reagan himself provided guidance to the speechwriters on several occasions in person as well. This guidance ranged from very concrete "shorter sentences & single syllable words whenever they can be used"[168] or "putting facts & figures in speeches"[169] to discussing "outline on planning major speeches for coming year."[170]

Another idea that supports the claim that the actual authorship does not matter is what Roland Barthes wrote about the death of the author that goes along with the birth of the text. According to Barthes the author loses his meaning, and the text and the narrator of the text become the central issues. The text is dedicated in the eyes and the ears of the audiences to the person who does the actual narration. Barthes notes that in primitive communities no single person is held accountable for a story except as the intermediary person between the author and the recipient. This person often was a shaman or a bard, who can be considered to have been narrators. For Barthes the voice loses its origin, the writer steps into his own grave, and the text begins.[171] The modern text is produced without a writer acting in the traditional manner by nurturing the text like father nurtures a son. Now, writer is born simultaneously with his text. Writing becomes a performative act that continuously creates new meanings and systematically evaporates old ones. A text is created of multiple writings from many cultures and this multitude is concentrated anew in one focal point, which is the reader instead of the author. The unity of the text is not in its origins but in its ending, the unspecified reader. And the birth of this reader has to be preceded by the death of the author.[172] Author, in other words, is not essential to Barthes, but only the narrator is as the conduit of the story when it is rebuilt and manifested in the reader.

> The text is not a line of words releasing a single theological meaning (the "message" of the Author-God) but a multi-dimensional space in which a variety writings, none of them original, blend and clash. The text is a tissue of quotations drawn from the innumerable centres of culture.[173]

This is a strong claim for intertextuality, and naturally, any writing or narrative cannot escape the influence of other texts. Nevertheless, the limits and scope of intertextuality vary depending on the knowledge of the story recipients. It is more than often possible to attempt to claim authorship for any expression or even an entire narrative if their origin lies in a lesser known text. In a political narrative the intertextuality works both for the benefit and the loss of the narrator. Some wonderful anecdote or expression, which truly moves people, can be separated from its original context and embedded anew in such a way that the great majority of recipients will not recognize its origin. Only a minority, whether educated, interested in the original text, well-read, or politically active, can spot the "stolen" words. However, some deeper meaning, which may move this minority, remains hidden from the large majority of story recipients.[174] A politician needs to be very careful in choosing his quotations so that some people are affected by the intertextual relations of his message, and for some others the lack of sufficient knowledge of linked texts will neither trivialize the message nor make it undecipherable. A careful balance must be kept within the narration to "touch" the intellectuals as well as the common people. Reagan did not always manage to balance on such a fine line. Many of his most memorable speeches, especially those given in defiance of Communism, mostly touched the nonintellectuals and even aimed at setting passions aflame mostly among them.

> Yes, let us pray for the salvation of all of those who live in that totalitarian darkness—pray they will discover the joy of knowing God. But until they do, let us be aware that while they preach the supremacy of the state, declare its omnipotence over individual man, and predict its eventual domination of all peoples on the Earth, they are the focus of evil in the modern world.[175]

I chose this quotation from the "Evil Empire" speech not only to exhibit Reagan at his most passion-exciting and anti-intellectual best but also to further illustrate the relationship between author and narrator. The expression "focus of evil" is another example of words or even storylines Reagan borrowed from somebody else. He had initially wanted to use this type of story in his Westminster address of 1982 but at that time refrained from doing so due to opinions of his aides, but the expression is included in the drafts of the speech.[176] The former communist who had turned on the party and become a conservative icon, Whittaker Chambers, whom Reagan admired and quoted on numerous other occasions, is the original user of the term in his 1952 book, *Witness*: "I see in communism the focus of concentrated evil in our time."[177] While Tony Dolan wrote the 1983 speech for Reagan, many of the finishing touches are Reagan's own. Originally, the draft of the speech talked of historians seeing Communism as a focus of evil,[178] but Reagan's ideology shines through in the fact that he moved the argument from retrospective vision to present tense and chose to stand among those who held that view of Communism. Dolan had tried earlier to include the part about evil empire into Reagan's speeches, but the State Department had always omitted them until finally Reagan himself demanded it to stay in the speech.[179] Reagan deleted 15 entire paragraphs and added 14 of his own in addition to cutting dozens on sentences and hundreds of words to be replaced by words of his preference and roughly 30 complete lines of text changes.[180] It was these editions that made the text as offensive against the Soviet Union as it turned out to be, and these very editions serve to remind readers of Reagan that he was more than a talking head. The message became personal. One of Reagan's intellectual and literary favorites, Alexander Solzhenitsyn, had talked to AFL-CIO in 1975 and told them that the Soviet Union was "the concentration of World Evil."[181] While the words of Solzhenitsyn and Chambers have drowned in the multiple voices of history, Reagan's use of these words lives. The authors of the texts have "died" in the Barthesian birth of the text. Only the importance of the narrator and the story remains.

The tone of the evil empire speech was nothing new in Reagan's storytelling. Already in 1981 he had characterized the Soviet Union to US Military Academy as an "evil force that would extinguish the light we've been tending for 6000 years"[182] and answered a reporter's question on Communism by stating it to be "not a normal way of living for human beings."[183] What is really intriguing is the fact that while Reagan himself buried the myth of the evil empire when he began cooperation with the Soviet Union under Gorbachev, the myth resurfaced again. George W. Bush resurrected the myth, only within a new context and under a different label. What else is the "Axis of Evil," but continuation of the Reaganesque storyline? Bush picked up the discarded mythical evil enemy and used the myth in his own story for his own purposes. The most important element of the "evil empire speech" was, however, not to only demonize the Soviet Union but in comparison to strengthen the ahistorical and oneiromantic vision of American and world destiny.[184]

Paradoxically the most important speech Reagan ever gave was none of the presidential speeches but was one given years before governorship or presidency. It was the speech in support of Barry Goldwater's presidential campaign in 1964, which was called "A Time for Choosing." In that speech Reagan made the case for modern conservatism, and the fact that private donors paid for its nationwide broadcasting launched Reagan's political career. It was referred to by all of those who worked for him as "The Speech"[185] Reagan himself quoted it occasionally when it suited his purposes. It is also noteworthy, that in wording, essence, and spirit it is the blueprint of almost every speech Reagan ever made.[186] All the ideas central to his politics were spelled out to great public in this particular speech. The importance of "The Speech" cannot be emphasized enough for Reagan's politics, but at the same time a full rendition of any of its multiple versions here would be useless. It was a skeleton of the speech, always to be edited and perfected and as such it had multiple shapes, but these shapes loom behind all of Reagan's public speeches. It was the one great speech Reagan spent his entire lifetime improving and recreating. The original version was one-hour long, and Stu Spencer among others was involved in trying to get Reagan to cut the speech into 20 minutes. Reagan himself understood the importance of brevity and tightness in speechmaking, and so the editing out was not the main problem but the adding back in. He was constantly field-testing new jokes, parables, and facts with his audiences using "The Speech" as the medium. When the response was good, new material got added into the speech along with some of the old and familiar lines Reagan just could not let go.[187] As Holstein and Gubrium argue, stories are "continuously shaped and reshaped as participants variously borrow from, keep separate, combine, individually formulate, or even suppress stories or construct differences and sameness."[188] "The Speech" was the one story Reagan reshaped continuously. He was always looking for new embellishments. "As a veteran of the mashed potato circuit— my name for the after dinner speaking—I'm always on the lookout for interesting anecdotes."[189]

Reagan was often during the second term of his presidency called a "lame duck," and this intensified during the long silences in his narratives and intermittent periods of narration connected to the Iran-Contra scandal. While Reagan detested this expression, based on his diary entries we can see that in the context of the authorship of his speeches, there was a certain ring of truth in this. There are numerous references to the actual writing of the speeches throughout the first term of the presidency, but as the second term begins there are only three references connected to speeches, and in these Reagan is involved merely in the editing of the precrafted speeches.[190] Naturally these diary entries cannot be considered to be a comprehensive description upon the work Reagan did on his speeches, since some occasions when he worked on them were naturally left out. An example is the statement after the Reykjavik summit with Gorbachev, which he drafted on the plane himself, but they still seem to hint that Reagan's interest on authorship was on the wane during the second term.[191] Reagan was first and foremost a narrator, and he was more than willing to argue that authorship was meaningless. "I communicated great things, and they didn't spring full bloom from my brow, they came from the heart of a great nation."[192] It was America itself that fuelled Reagan's narration.

"Now, some of you may be thinking, 'Well, he hasn't said a thing that's new.' I guess that's true. Some values shouldn't change."[193] Reagan himself is among the people who agree that there is not much new in his message. By saying this aloud he preempties the criticism that might be directed against him. Reagan's justification for not being original lies, as ever, in his deep-felt conviction that there really are core values that stay unchanged throughout the years: "I never thought of myself as a great man, just a man committed to great ideas."[194] It is the ideas that lie behind the stories Reagan elaborately narrates, which basically provide his message with its greatness. The situation is similar in essence to Milton's "Paradise Regained," which, as Frye declares, derives its greatness from the theme itself, which Milton passes on to the reader. The story itself does not have its origins in Milton, and while the rhetorical flourish he adds to it enhances the story told, it is by no means fundamentally his own.[195] The poet is besides being a licensed liar also a licensed thief. Reagan provides his listeners and readers with a skillful narration, but the idea of American Dream he discusses is the fact that turned his stories into important foundational myths for a large part of Americans. Reagan turned the old story into a new version by giving it his personal treatment. As Pope writes, "True wit is nature to advantage dressed; What oft was thought, but ne'er so well expressed; Something, whose truth convinced at sight we find, That gives us back the image of our mind."[196] Reagan's strength as a narrator did not lie in trying to invent totally new mythical narratives but in using existing schemata to his advantage and altering the old myths. In 1984 Assistant White House Chief of Staff Richard Darman wrote a memorandum for the presidential campaign where he skillfully characterized the essence of Reaganesque politics:

> Paint RR as the personification of all that is right with or heroized by America. Leave Mondale in a position where an attack on Reagan is tantamount to an attack on America's idealized image of itself—where

a vote against Reagan is in some subliminal sense, a vote against mythic "AMERICA."[197]

Reagan was turned to be the equivalent of all that people loved in themselves or their country, whether these characteristics were real or imagined. Reagan became a myth and blended with the mythic America in the process.

Reagan took a lot of care to portray himself to the story recipient as a reliable narrator. This can be defined as an author "whose rendering of the story and commentary on it the reader is supposed to take as an authoritative account of the fictional truth."[198] An unreliable narrator is one, who arouses suspicions in his story recipients as to the "truth" of what is being told. Rimmon-Kenan distinguishes as the main sources of unreliability "the narrator's limited knowledge, his personal involvement, and his problematic value-scheme."[199] All of these sources are evident and present in Reagan's narration, and sometimes they do considerable damage to his reliability, despite his efforts to appear reliable. His knowledge on some subjects was less than satisfactory, and his blunders caused considerable damage to his authoritarian narrator/speaker position. The personal involvement concerns naturally every political narrator, but the value-scheme is not necessarily as drastic as in Reagan's mythical narration. Nevertheless, the challenge to appear as reliable narrator is one that every political storyteller has to face if for no other reason, at least because of his involvement in the topics narrated. A politician wants to inflict a change, he tells his stories for a purpose and yet the narration should sound neutral to appear reliable. Reagan tried to create himself as a stock figure of truth who can be trusted and whose authority should be acknowledged both as an authoritative narrator and by using himself as a reliable and trustworthy character in the stories. His success was surprising, but mistakes happened. An excerpt from Reagan's speech to the nation explaining the Iran-Contra affair illustrates this point: "A few months ago I told the American people I did not trade arms for hostages. My heart and my best intentions still tell me that's true, but the facts and the evidence tell me it is not."[200] After something like this, it is a monstrous challenge for the narrator to regain reliability.[201] This was a serious blow to Reagan's credibility not only because he told a lie, but also because trading arms for hostages violated the story logic of Reagan's entire narrative and added an element of inconsistency to it.[202]

When the United States of America looks for a president, it is surprising to notice how much emphasis is put on his skills as a performer and a narrator as well. Nearly every major politician uses ghostwriters, and this is largely considered to be a necessary expedient in campaigning and governing. Voters do not respond to their president only as an individual, but as an institution as well. President Reagan, the object of the votes of millions of Americans in the 1980s, was not only Ronald Reagan as a man but "the Great Communicator" who spoke for the entire nation besides himself.[203] It was the voice of this larger than life persona that resonated in the American psyche, and sometimes this storyteller grew into a bigger institution than the man who articulated the words for it. Stephen Hayward complains that Gerald Ford's greatest inadequacy as a president was that "he was not equal to the supreme political demand of the television age—he was not a great communicator."[204] The president has to be the "chief articulator of collective aspirations, or he is not much. He is articulate, or he is inadequate."[205] The ability to spin words is seen as crucial to the institution of the presidency.

Audience as Storyworld Participants

Non satis est pulchra esse poemata: dulcia sunto et quocumque volent animum auditoris agunto

Horace[206]

Having determined Reagan's position both within the stories as a character and as the teller of those stories emphasizing the importance of narrating compared to the actual authorship, we will now look at the receiving end of the narration, that is, the audience. Reagan earned the nickname of the "Great Communicator," and it is the communicational aspect we will burrow into here. Telling stories is just not enough for a politician. He has to employ the story to communicate his message to somebody. The story recipients, or the audience, are a crucial part in making sense of the stories they are told and deciphering the political message contained within. While this ultimate meaning of a story is not solely in the hands of Reagan or any narrator, he had at his disposal tools to guide the interpretive processes of the audience. Even more importantly, the audience, especially when it consists of Americans, is turned into a part of the story as well. The audience not only mentally populates the storyverse with characters, actants, and circumstances with imagination, but through the role Reagan gives them in his storytelling, members of the audience themselves become storyworld participants. Thus, essentially the same blurring of roles that took place with Reagan as both the narrator and a character applies to his audience as well. The audience is engulfed into the narrative process, and they become not only characters but also part of the storyworld creation.

Reagan wanted to involve his audiences in his narration. He did not want to have the lights dimmed when he spoke in stark contrast to many politicians, who preferred a dark setting and a spotlight to focus on them. Reagan wanted the audience to have an ownership of the event and for them to make a mutual commitment. Reagan wanted to see their eyes and gauge the effect of his words. Mike Deaver claims that each speech was a "new adventure" for Reagan.[207] Deaver is often credited for creating the settings of Reagan's speech events in such a manner that would show the best of Reagan. Deaver in turn gives credit to Reagan. It was he who wanted his audience to be within "striking distance." Since he wanted eye contact, he instructed Deaver to situate the first row no more than eight feet from the lectern.[208] Reagan demanded such close contact with the audience partially because this enabled him to alter the course of telling if the audience response seemed to require it. But in this process the audience always became more active in shaping the eventual outcome of narrating. Any member of the audience was persuaded to participate in the story itself and encouraged to see himself as a central actor in any quest the mythical America chose to overtake.[209]

Again, we need to define what we mean by "audience" in the context of Reagan's storytelling. Political texts are always directed for a more than a "general" audience. A politician does not tell his narratives in the vain hope that someone, somewhere, somehow might read his story like a person stashing his attempts at poetry in a desk drawer might do. He always produces texts not only for the actual audience present at the moment of the narration (either live via television or radio) but also for numerous "authorial audiences" as well. These audiences are more or less hypothetical and can be reached by less direct "narrative by-paths," such as newspaper stories about the speech of the president. It is ultimately the authorial audience that the politician needs to embrace, and his authorial intentions are tied to this audience. He tries to create a change in the way of thinking of those not only actually present but also of all other citizens potentially listening/reading. The number of different authorial audiences can be finite, but this does not guarantee that the author would have "total control over the act of writing any more than the readers have control over the act of interpretation."[210] While any author, including politicians, can theoretically say or write what he wills and the readers interpret it according to their fancy, the crucial need for *communicating* the ideas limits the range of choices. The telling needs to be constructed keeping in mind the authorial audience, so that the story recipient will be able to experience the text in a manner the narrator wishes.[211] Riessman notes that story has a certain form just because it is told to a certain audience.[212] Since stories are told at particular times to particular people to affect them in a particular manner, they are given new forms and contents so as to rise to every occasion. Here is one limitation of Reagan's narration. He is often not able to transform his story enough to meet the preferences of various audiences. The stories told to the American public should be differently composed as those, say, to the Japanese Diet.[213] One of the less illustrious sides of Reagan as a narrator was to some degree his disability to speak convincingly to foreign audiences.

The narrator may wish to make his story accessible to any potential story recipient but some conception of the audience is important. Since the narrator cannot be sure all story recipients see eye to eye with him, "he therefore tries to define an audience. By assuming what it is that all men ought to be able to understand and agree upon, he creates a kind of humanity."[214] Reagan was, as noted, at his best when addressing mainstream Americans. As he put it, "There's an awful lot of rhetoric that is delivered for home consumption."[215] It is just because of his own personal certainty in the superiority of the myth of a golden future where freedom and the American dream will become reality for all people on the earth that he was blind to the existence of dissenters. He went to define all people of the Western Hemisphere as American, while this undoubtedly was not a source of pleasure for many people from South America. "The peoples of this hemisphere are one. In this profound sense, we are all Americans."[216] Reagan tended to automatically assume that each and every member of his audiences saw the world in the same manner he did. For Reagan, everything he spoke of was fundamentally true, and he was not open to other pluralistic views. In the American context the praise for America went down well, but with foreigners and dissenters Reagan had a communication gap. This might have been the source of European view of him as a trigger-happy cowboy armed with nuclear six-shooters.

It was America as authorial audience that Reagan addressed in his speeches, no matter what was the size and composition of the actual audience seated in front of him. Reagan wanted to address the "heroic America" he envisioned, but naturally the actual audience was more mundane. The timelessness of myth and the mythical America allowed Reagan to include future generations as potential audience. "I'm convinced that historians will look back on this as the time that we started down a new and far better road for America."[217] The politicking was made by the oral communication of Reagan's vision, but the written aspect of the narrative was used to convince the future story recipients. Reagan viewed his audience as a symbol and created agreement either with them or upon their values. Reagan picked one characteristic of the audience and used it to show that the audience in fact was emblematic of the entire mythical America. This was most apparent in his stump speeches where he made the audience feel that they are a special and unique part of the America Reagan loved and was proud of. The audience was given a vital role in all of Reagan's plans for America, since without them he could not "bring America back." Reagan's storytelling and his use of the concept of values united the narrator and his story recipients by showing that they essentially share the same values. It did not matter whether Reagan spoke to a small congregation of Elks or possible voters on a campaign trail. He created the impression that the audience was important to him because of some intrinsic value often based on those traditional American values Reagan was so fond of speaking about.[218]

> What is it that unites Americans of all faiths, creeds, races, political persuasions and ethnic backgrounds. What is the common denominator of Americanism? I believe it is a simple, single four-letter word. The word is *hope*. We who call ourselves Americans hope to see a better, more peaceful world tomorrow, and we expect to make steady, measurable progress toward the fulfillment of this dream. Now, it is not merely hope that defines an American. It is the habit of practical success in seeing our dreams fulfilled. It is this unique combination of aspiration and accomplishment, dream and deed that truly sets the American apart.[219]

Jari Rantapelkonen argues that audiences today are more diverse than ever before consisting of some many potential audiences along with the one actually present to hear the narration. In our age public speaking blurs the distinction of audiences, and already during the Reagan era his major speeches were broadcasted practically on a global scale. Thus a speech to the British Parliament was an excellent opportunity to spread the message about fighting Communism globally. This type of situation is to some degree under the control of the narrator, but even a speech of proportionally smaller influencing potential can present challenges to tell stories in a way that does not allow for misinterpreted perceptions in the global information system to affect the relationships between United States and other states.[220]

Barthes wrote, "On the stage of the text, no footlights: there is not behind the text, someone active (the writer) and out front someone passive (the reader); there is not a subject and an object."[221] The interaction between the writer or author and the reader is where the ultimate meaning of the text is born. Despite the intentions of the author, the meaning that gets finalized for the text cannot be completely predicted due to the participation of the story recipient in the process of interpretation. The better the narrator is the more likely he or she is to communicate his message in the intended way, and Reagan was the "Great Communicator." Barthes turned the writer-reader situation completely around by claiming "that writing is not the communication of a message which starts from the author and proceeds to the reader; it is specifically the voice of reading itself: *in the text, only the reader speaks.*"[222] Essentially the same approach has been argued by Mikhail Bakhtin who claimed that listener immediately takes an active and responsive attitude toward the text by agreeing or disagreeing, augmenting and applying it, and since understanding is imbued with response, the listener becomes a speaker.[223]

This approach is too radical to use for political narratives. In fact such a statement could deny the entire use of political storytelling. The reader is central in the interpretation of every text, but to give him full credit for the message in the text is going too far. If only the reader created meanings for political narratives, there would be no need to create politically charged texts but rather to work on the mind-set of the citizen through some other media. One could argue (to exaggerate and somewhat twist and elaborate Fredric Jameson's idea of political unconscious[224]) that a *zoon politikon*, a very politically motivated citizen, would read even a telephone directory in a manner that would impose political meanings on it. Thus there would be no difference in reading between "*Das Kapital*" and the phonebook, since the political implications of the text would come solely from the reader and not be even partially guided by the highly political process of writing a text to achieve particular political purposes.

Political narratives need to arouse passions and instigate a change or prevent the change from occurring in a particular moment of *kairos*. They do not need strict inner cohesion or story logic if they only manage their immediate purpose of influencing the status quo. Either the winds of change are blowing and the political leader using narratives needs to calm them down to stabilize his policies, or he has to act as the metaphorical butterfly that flaps its wings to create such a gale. The mechanism of arousing passion either to change or to prevent the change from occurring is the same. The passion is of momentary nature; it fulfills its role in a short time period immediately after the narration. It does not matter what a scholar publishes years later acting as a literary critic and shattering the vulnerable story logic, since the story by then has either affected the change it was created for or failed anyhow. However, as Reagan noted,

> Well, any motion picture or any drama or play is based on one thing: It isn't successful unless it has or evokes an emotional response. If the audience does not have an emotional experience, whether it's one of hating something or crying or having a lot of laughter, then you've got a failure out there.[225]

For political purposes the critics who praise the speech in their studies are inconsequential. The immediate response is what matters. Aristotle claims that when composing the poet should be an actor, since they are "the most persuasive and affecting who are under the influence of actual passion. We share the agitation of those who appear to be truly agitated—the anger of those who appear to be truly angry."[226] There is in political narratives the need not only to write a good story but also to narrate it with passion. This is more than mere rhetoric; it is the total immersion of the narrator into the storyworld of his own creation. Political narrating is more than speechmaking. It is rather acting out the story in the presentation. The more convincing the narration becomes, the more the narrator actually himself lives the emotions he is trying to communicate to his audience. Tzvetan Todorov has argued that "to speak is either to alter the feelings of which one speaks, or else to produce the feelings which one feigns in speech; thus, false speech become true and supposedly true speech becomes false."[227] Political leadership is at least partially about creating emotions, showing them, and hopefully managing to communicate those feelings to the audience. Truth is less important than what something feels like. The narrator has to be able to not only articulate but also to act out his emotions. A good and arousing political story has to be able to incite strong emotions for or against something. So, at its best as E. M. Forster argues, a story is able to

> transform us from readers into listeners, to whom "a" voice speaks, the voice of the tribal narrator, squatting in the middle of the cave, and saying one thing after another until the audience falls asleep among their offal and bones. The story is primitive, it reaches back to the

origins of literature, before reading was discovered, and it appeals to what is primitive in us. That is why we are so unreasonable over the stories we like, and so ready to bully those who like something.[228]

Essentially we are talking about the same passions Barthes discussed. Stories do not rely on our self-conception of ourselves as rational beings of the postmodern world but on our more primitive feelings and passions. That is why they are fitting tools for politics to use, especially during times of rapid changes. Story does not require its audience to think, analyze, and deduct but rather to feel and act, and the stronger and more immediate the feeling and the resulting action is, the more political the story and its telling are. Well-told narratives enable the politician to ignite political passions better than more conventional means.

The importance of arousing emotions and passions in the audience becomes a profound aspect of the entire story-based political leadership. If the audience remains in a cool and calculative state of mind, questions are more likely to be asked and suspicions are aroused. The audience ultimately makes the decision whether to accept and participate in the construction of the storyverse the politician tries to narrate into existence. When creating the American way of life and giving birth to his mythical concept of America, Reagan was dependent of his audience and whether they would choose to participate in this imagined community. But the audience, composed of individual story recipients, is a mass and as such has no personality; it has no common will or sense of its own. It is dependent on someone to tell it what to think and to have someone to lead it. The political narrator can exist and succeed only in cooperation with his audience. The audience provides him with justification, and he can attempt to create a unity among his audience and turn it into an entity with a common purpose. He has to be responsive to the wishes of his audience, and the power he wields over them is purely seductive. He can entice and seduce his audience but not coerce it.

Reagan's intense focus on his audience and its reactions enabled him to perform narrative editing on his narration based upon the changing mood of the audience or its reactions to what was being said. Even in retrospect the feedback of the audience was important, since Reagan kept editing "The Speech" constantly. He wrote very often in his diaries how his speeches had been received or how many people had called the White House switchboard to express support, or what his new approval ratings were after important speeches.[229] As an actor should, Reagan read all the "reviews" of his political

performances and considered them important. He never lost sight
of the fact that for a political narrator the audience and his ability to
capture and hold the interest of the audience are crucial. Reagan as a
man fascinated with stories chose to write about audiences that

> the basis of the dramatic form of entertainment is the emotional
> catharsis experienced by the audience. Our lives have lost a certain
> amount of excitement since we quit having to knock over a mastodon
> for the family lunch or keep a sabre-toothed tiger from having us for
> lunch. We've kept a little stardust in our mundane lives by identifying
> with make-believe characters in make-believe adventures in the house
> of illusion—the theatre. The house lights dim, the curtains part, and
> for a few hours all women are again beautiful and beloved, all men
> brave and noble of character. We laugh, cry, know anger, grief, and
> triumph—then go home at peace with our corner of the world.[230]

2

RE-CREATING THE MYTHICAL
AMERICA AS A STORYVERSE

We have it within our power to begin the world over again.

Ronald Wilson Reagan[1]

This chapter explores how Reagan was able to narrate into existence the mythical America, which had in fact never existed. Narrative has the power to create such worlds, imagined communities, or mythical nations, which on certain occasions can supplant the "real" world in the mind of the story recipient. I choose to call them storyworlds, and the following pages delve deeper into how these worlds are created and what their political function is. This section will deal with the creation of storyworlds, and how they combine into an actual universe of storyworlds that I shall label as storyverse. These concepts are created on the boundary or frontier of the internal and external structures of the narrative framework. They are not directly given birth to by the text itself, neither solely by the *intentio auctoris* nor by the interpretation of the text by the audience. Rather the storyverse emerges on the interface of the external and internal aspects of the story itself. The story itself interacts with the story recipient, his experiences, and worldviews to combine the elements within the story to everything situated outside the boundaries of the story. Each individual storyworld, and the storyverse as well, is a result of a play between the elements of the story and those of the "real" world and as such connects the fictional, or what is being told, with the "factual," or what the story recipient experiences in his everyday life. And the purpose of political storytelling is to create this membrane or boundary where the elements interact so permeable that the worlds blend together.

The manipulation of these multiple storyworlds is a crucial part of narrative political leadership, since by escorting the story recipients in and out of these storyworlds and blurring the boundary between real and fictional had many advantages for Reagan. I shall initiate the discussion with the development of the possible worlds theory into storyworlds and end up with my own theoretical concept of "storyverse." It is a conceptual tool for understanding not merely one story but multiple stories told and the manipulation of the different storyworlds they bring to existence. The concept of a storyverse is crucial in understanding how several slightly different stories within the same narrative framework can be used for the same purpose to fully exploit the benefits of storytelling for the political narrator.

For Hayden White narrative is not a neutral discursive form, but it always entails "choices with distinct ideological and even specifically political implications."[2] Narrative, instead of a neutral medium for telling what has happened, "is the very stuff of a mythical view of reality . . . which, when used to represent real events, endows them with an illusory coherence"[3] and meanings characteristic to dreams. It guides our view of the world and most of our encounters with the world, especially the world of politics, are not direct encounters. The world that emerges for us is a storyworld. The "realities" of society are meanings we create by sharing human cognitions.[4] In other words this could be expressed by saying that culture is an ambiguous text that is constantly interpreted by all those who participate in it, and thus language and narratives as vessels of transmitting world views interpersonally are parts of the creation of the entire social reality. Culture and reality are negotiated by all participants and in the context of a state, by all its citizens. Reagan offered his version and vision of social and political reality, the mythical American storyverse, which he effectively communicated in his narratives.

A. -J. Greimas wrote about concepts such as "semantic universe, which can be understood successively as a virtual universe."[5] It is a universe of manifested possible combinations and ultimately a discourse. The virtual universe of Greimas is purely textual in its nature. It is composed of words and texts and not concerned about the universe these words and texts bring to life. The universes and worlds discussed here are the possible worlds that are given birth by the stories and are created in interplay between the teller of the story and its recipient. A storyworld is a construct beyond a mere semantic universe that only has the textual ingredients to give birth to this higher construct on another, extra-textual level. But how exactly is a storyworld brought into existence? Seymour Chatman did not actually write about storyworlds as existing narrative constructs but only argued that plot details (and characters) have a world of their own *in potentia*, and these words can be actualized or brought to existence when necessary. "There is virtually infinite continuum of imaginable details . . .

which will not ordinarily be expressed, but which *could* be."[6] Such an idea conveys a storyworld that so far remains waiting for someone to activate these details.

POSSIBLE WORLDS AS PRODUCTS OF NARRATIVES

While narrative offers us a way to give meaning to our lives, we can also expand our "mental horizon beyond the physical, actual world— toward the worlds of dreams, phantasms, fantasy, possibilities, and counter factuality."[7] This is the idea of storyworld formation of the American dream. We are pulled away from the actual world we inhabit into alternate realities created by stories. Genette noted that the narrating itself creates a boundary; "a shifting but sacred frontier between two worlds, the world in which one tells, the world of which one tells."[8] The narrativity does not lie in only the structure and grammar of the text itself but also contains extra-textual elements as well. Marie-Laure Ryan proposes three criteria, which a text must bring to mind to qualify as narrative:

1. A narrative text must create a world and populate it with characters and objects. . . .
2. The world referred to by the text must undergo changes of state that are caused by nonhabitual physical events: either accidents ("happenings") or deliberate human actions. These changes create a temporal dimension and place the narrative world in the flux of history.
3. The text must allow the reconstruction of an interpretive network of goals, plans, causal relations, and psychological motivations around the narrative events. This implicit network gives coherence and intelligibly to the physical events and turns them into a plot.[9]

On the basis of this characterization of narrative, it is indeed possible to qualify the entire framework of Reagan's speeches as a narrative. The world-creating ability and tendency is omnipresent in Reagan's story. The intriguing aspect of this mythical America is its close connection and even partial similarity to the United States of the actual world, and the fact that one of the objectives and goals of Reagan's entire storytelling process is to convince the story recipients that no artificial storyworld has been erected, but that Reagan's narration refers to the actual world his recipients occupy.

Lubomir Dolezel initially brought new depth to narratology by claiming that instead of the more traditional views centered on a story as opposed to discourse, the "basic concept of narratology is not 'story', but 'narrative world,' defined within a typology of possible worlds."[10] Dolezel treated text as a "set of instructions according to which the fictional world is to be recovered and reassembled."[11] Paul Ricoeur argues that when a text is being interpreted what emerges in the process is a *"proposed world*, a world that I might inhabit and wherein I might project my utmost possibilities. This is what I call the world of the text, the world probably belonging to this unique text."[12] This world of the text creates a "distanciation that we can call a distanciation of the real from itself . . . fiction introduces into our apprehension of reality."[13] Ricoeur's most important contribution is the fact that this world can be "inhabited" by the story recipient, because a good story might "swallow" the reader and immerse him or her totally in its world. But what Ricoeur omits is the dialogic relationship between the story and its recipient. The world "proposed" by the text is a storyworld and not the same as the world of the text, because it does not solely belong to the text but is created in dialogue with the reader, the human who reacts to the text.

Dolezel argued that all worlds that we humans are capable of producing, or creating with the means of language, are merely possible worlds. There is no modern Prometheus, who could bring us such divine language that uttering words could bring the actual signifieds of those words into concrete existence. These possible worlds do not exist by themselves in a transcendental or metaphysical level but are constructed by human minds.[14] He divided possible worlds into physically possible and impossible worlds depending upon whether the natural laws of the actual world exist in them, and the conditions of existence and acting in the worlds depend on this juxtaposition of possible/impossible. While the fiction maker is able to "roam over the entire universe of possible worlds," historical worlds are restricted into the physically possible worlds.[15] The division into physically possible/impossible worlds did not separate history and mythology from each other as Dolezel wanted. In mythology things were accredited to supernatural beings that made their actionable contribution to the narrative, but in historical worlds no event can be assigned to divine agency, and human history is a history of natural agents.[16] Yet the majority of us still retain their faith in God. People tend to believe in divine interception and pray for it. Divine Providence and God's plan were common in Reagan's narration and even today have their place in American political rhetoric. When we had insufficient knowledge of the laws of nature in our world, sickness was a punishment from the gods. Rain was the tears of some Goddess falling.[17]

Another division Dolezel makes is within the sphere of literature more generally, but his division into fictional and historical worlds does not suffice either. All possible worlds are according to his thoughts fictional, and then there exists the true, historical world, which may exist even in texts if they were produced faithfully and avoiding fictive issues. I disagree. Creating such a true, historical world would demand that the text-producer is godlike and capable of absolute objectiveness instead of a mere human with all his fallibilities. There is no super narrator with capability to depict the world precisely as it ontologically is, even if we consider that such a world even exists outside the human sphere of experience. The real world can be understood as a possible or fictional world. Indeed, as soon as one starts to tell of the actual world and its events, the telling turns it into a storyworld.

There is a profound connection between these worlds as Bruner has noted. People allow stories to guide their decisions even in those times where a suitable theory or scientific evidence is available. He claims that narratives, "once acted out, 'make' events and 'make' history. They contribute to the reality of the participants. . . . Can anyone say a priori that history is completely independent of what goes on in the minds of its participants."[18] The real world is shaped after the possible one described in the story. Narratives have the power to change the world, and this adds to their political nature. It does not actually matter who tells a particular story about the way the world is. No matter how well constructed this narrative is, it does not initiate an immediate change in the world. The stories told to children that the moon is made of cheese do not cause this earth-orbiting lump of rock to turn into gorgonzola that cows jump over. The stories change the world in a more subtle manner. Mankind travelled to moon, not to find out if it indeed was made of cheese, but among other reasons to search for signs of life there as predicted (later on in the development of a child's personality) by science fiction stories. Stories affect the way people see the world they inhabit, and by guiding the way they see the world, stories inflict the way they try to change the world to be like. Stories contribute to the experience of reality people share, and the same people attempt to change the reality for the better. The world is changed when a narrative initiates the reaction to change the world. Therefore, neither does the "proposed world" that Ricoeur writes about remain contained in a merely semantic universe, nor is it content to remain on the level of stories , but rather even "everyday reality is metamorphosed by . . . the imaginative variations that literature works on the real."[19] Our reality is shaped by stories, but what is real?

Lyotard asserts that "realism is the art of making reality, of knowing reality and knowing how to make reality."[20] The same idea can be nevertheless borrowed and used in the context of political narratives. They are then realist even when they are future-oriented or mythical because of their power to make reality. If Reagan's vision of America's strength and greatness is first and foremost a vision, it is also realistic because as the president, he was able to change the world accordingly so that Unites States got the strength he called for. Chatman argues that a narrative will not admit events that do not belong to it and follow its laws.[21] This is one reason why in Reagan's political storytelling there are almost no failures in his administration's political goals. Reagan's optimistic worldview sets such a bias on the story that the story cannot admit within itself pessimistic elements.

At the same time it is worth noticing, as Chatman does, that what constitutes "reality" is "a strictly cultural phenomenon . . . [and] of course the 'natural' changes from one society to another, and from one era to another in the same society."[22] If we find, for example, within Reagan's narratives things that we just cannot assimilate to fit into our conception of the "real world," we must understand that we are living in another culture and era and try to change our mindset so as to better understand what mechanisms could have been in use at the time of the actual political storytelling in America. The problem with analyzing Reagan's storyverse is, as Chatman writes, that we make inferences "in terms of our ordinary coded knowledge of the world and our expectations about human society *as we know it*."[23] The storyworlds will not get created according to the same rules outside the cultural context where the stories originate.

Reagan spoke of an America that did not exist in the time of his presidency. In the words of Gary Wills, Reagan's ideas of America evoke an invented past, a heritage that never existed outside fables and Mark Twain novels.[24] One can debate endlessly whether the ideal society in Reagan's storytelling was based on Dixon of Reagan's boyhood years, but such an argument is futile. Reagan did not speak of the United States of America as it is or was but spoke of America as it could or should be. His focus, whether he talked of the past, present, or future, was always on what America could potentially be. Reagan's America was a dream, and the ones who criticize his vision of America fail to see that it is first and foremost a storyverse. The narrative aspect of Reagan's policymaking has to be taken into the context to understand what his mythical America is. It is fictional, based on stories told and retold, and its shape and meaning vary from one telling to another to suit Reagan's purposes.

Ryan has attempted to break the semantic universe of narrative into a realm of facts[25] and that of the possible worlds created by "the mental activity of the characters; the potentially actualisable worlds of knowledge, desire, obligations, anticipation, goals and plans, as well as the alternative worlds of pretence, dreams, hallucinations, and embedded fictions."[26] She goes further to argue that the intrinsic tellability makes certain plots produce new versions and is a function of the story's ability to "deploy a rich field of virtualities."[27] Out of these virtualities the American dream gets recreated anew with the telling of the story. The world where American dream was reality for all American's was the storyworld Reagan primarily wanted to create, and for him it was "real."

> I would ask you to join with me for a moment in a dream, not a fantasy or day dream but a practical dream.[28]

The politician should not appear to be a "day dreamer" who spins tall tales of possible worlds but a down-to-earth leader concerned only with what is actual events. Therefore Reagan took a lot of care in depicting his mythical America as the "real world." The multiple storyworlds and the real world are populated with the same people, while in storyworlds they are endowed with special personal traits depending on their function, and at least partially the same incidents and events tend to take place in all of the worlds. Thus the American dream is depicted as not fantasy but fact. It is narrated not as fiction but reality. It is a "practical dream."

POLITICAL MANIPULATION OF THE STORYWORLD

There is a long tradition of the American dream, and the concept is deeply embedded into the American culture. Palmer argues that storyworlds are constructed by language "through a performative force that is granted by cultural convention."[29] If Reagan's mythical America itself is a storyworld, created in the process of storytelling, it is futile to try to attach labels of "true" or "false" to it. It was enough for the world to seem "possible" and believable to fill the needs of Reagan's politics. Truthfulness and falsity are qualities that should not be attached to a narrative. The values it has to adhere to are credibility and plausibility. The same traits apply to the storyworld the narrative gives birth to. If people choose to believe in it and find it credible, it does not matter if it represents reality at all. While there is a world outside the textually created storyworld, comparisons and evaluations between these are futile. Evaluating the truth-value of the storyworld by how well it represents the real world is doomed to fail, since once the story enchants us well enough; it has the ability to alter our Weltanschauung. Our idea of what is real can be altered with the telling of a story about it. As Edmund Morris claimed, Reagan had an uncanny Daliesque ability to bend the reality to suit his purposes. "Imagination, not mendacity, was the key to Dutch's mind. He believed in both true and untrue things if they suited his moral purpose—and because he believed in belief."[30] Things became true for Reagan when he told them often enough or got himself suitably entangled in the storyworlds that had spawned them. The boundaries of "real" world and multiple storyworlds were so thin for Reagan, that he kept moving in and out of them continuously, and often was himself not able to locate his position vis-á-vis reality. If he managed to escort his listeners to his storyworlds and make them believe in their reality, he himself was at least as confused, which was the real world.[31]

David Herman defines storyworlds as "mental models of did what to and with whom, when, where, why and in what fashion in the world to which recipient relocate—or make a deitic shift—as they work to comprehend a narrative."[32] Storyworlds can be viewed as "global mental representation enabling interpreters to draw inferences about items and occurrences either implicitly or explicitly included in a narrative."[33] The term storyworld itself suggests that a narrative has a power to create worlds and has the ability to transport interpreters from the actual moment of narration or the space-time coordinates of the encounter with the text to the different here and now that constitute the deitic center of the world being told about. Storyworlds are then essentially mental models that are ultimately created on extra-textual, mental level with the aid of stories. According to Herman, to make sense of the narrative the interpreter must relocate into possible worlds more or less distinct from the world he treats as actual.[34] Both readers and authors shift their deictic center from the real-world situation to an image of themselves located within a storyworld. This fictional world may not contain the same objects, and objects may not have the same properties as in the real world. As Rabinowitz writes, "Every fictional world, like every real world, requires a history, sociology, biology, mathematics, aesthetics, and ethics."[35] It is only the nature and contents of these concepts that shift between real and fictional worlds. The storyworld becomes placed at the center of the conceptual universe, and the same natural laws need not exist in this universe of storyworlds.[36]

Jonathan Culler has written on the interesting concept of *vraisemblance* as the quality of a text that "attempts to make us believe that it conforms to reality and not to its own laws. In other words vraisemblance is the mask which conceals the text's own laws and which we are supposed to take for a relation with reality."[37] *Vraisemblance* can be used by the political narrator as a mechanism, which makes it harder for his story recipients to distinguish between the real world and the storyworld the politician creates. If this world exists, then following the peculiar logic of the stories told, the strangeness can be hidden from the citizenry with *vraisemblance*. It is the well-formedness of the narrative that naturalizes narrative events to facts and probabilities in the real world.[38] This is about the blending of the storyworld with the "real world." When the story is told well enough, things from the storyworld it evokes are transported into "facts" of the real world. Politically the interest and focus of the narrator should be to construct his storyworlds so that the transportation from one world to another is not only natural but also involuntary and furthermore nonnoticeable.

David Herman argues that story logic is the factor that gives a storyworld its internal integrity. No matter how far removed the storyworld is from actual reality it has to have *vraisemblance* to feel real and adhere to some logic. In Herman's writings the concept of *story logic* has two meanings to him. It refers to both the fact that the stories have logic that "consist of strategies for coding circumstances, participants, states, actions, and events in the storyworlds," and that stories constitute a logic themselves and provide a resource for comprehending experience and organizing interaction. The first kind of logic sees narrative as a product and the second as a process. Stories have a logic and are a logic themselves.[39]

Herman thus argues that the storyworld must be logical according to the internal story logic of the narrative itself. Then the narrator has more than adequate tools to guide the shaping of the storyworld to his personal liking or to fit the policy goals. The narrator has to adhere to this logic in the construction of the storyworld he tries to communicate, and within the boundaries of this logic he is free to provide story recipients with a plenitude of details about the storyworld. The addition of certain details into the storyworld makes the story recipients unable to add details of their own that would argue with the details already in place. The inner logic of the story dictates what can be inserted, and including something logically leads to exclusion of everything that would contradict it.[40] One problem that arises in storyworld construction is that, as Herman notes, there does not necessarily exist a "one-to-one correspondence between a story's textual format and the mental models that its form prompts readers to reconstruct."[41] Any textual format may evoke a variety of mental representations and vice versa. The role of the political storyteller is not to force the acceptance of storyworlds ready-made for his audience, but rather work in a way of "guides, who invite readers, listeners, and viewers to create, inhabit, and familiarize themselves"[42] with these storyworlds.

Herman argues that the construction of a storyworld applies to both fictional and nonfictional narratives and it sometimes is rather difficult and pointless to even try to make the distinction between those two in Reagan's narration. All narratives have world-creating power, and the type of narrative involved is the factor that causes recipients to use different evaluative criteria in their interpretation.[43] The political storyteller therefore benefits the most if he can tell a story that cues the interpreters to view it as nonfictional. If his stories are interpreted in any way as figments of imagination, the narrator is in trouble. He loses political credibility. He benefits only when he is able to convince the audience that however distanced his narrative is from the real-world events, it is still a plausible interpretation of the actual reality. Therefore the story must cue the relocation of the interpreter so that optimally he does not feel or realize his removal from the real world and insertion into the storyworld. The storyworld must be such an intricate construction that it imitates the real world to the smallest possible detail except for those that serve the politician's purpose by being added to or removed from the storyworld.

Dolezel claims that one can access a storyworld through semiotic channels by "crossing somehow the world boundary between the realms of the actual and the possible," and that the reconstruction of the storyworld "integrates fictional worlds into the reader's reality."[44] I differ from Dolezel thinking by claiming that the fictional worlds do not actually invade the reality of the reader, but rather the whole point is to make the boundary between actual and possible so thin that concepts can cross from one into another without great difficulties, and thus the story recipient/storyworld constructor is not able to tell where the division between actual and possible lies. The boundary between worlds is no Berlin Wall but rather a transparent foil that does not resist the attempts of the story recipient to cross from one into another. Language is the channel across this boundary, but the story itself has to have enough narrativity so that the storylines are followed through the membrane between worlds.

This involuntary and unconscious crossing between worlds is partially explained by Marie-Laure Ryan's "principle of minimal departure." This refers to the idea that when one has the position of the story recipient, he reconstructs a storyworld from the text led by the assumption that the storyworld is as close to the actual world as possible. Unless specifically told differently by the text, he assumes that the things not actually told in the story are constructed along the same lines as in his immanent reality. The story has to explicitly tell that something differs from one's day-to-day life to create the difference in the storyworld.[45] This means that to build a storyworld that radically differs from reality the narrator must explicitly point out and emphasize the differences. If Reagan had not portrayed the Soviet Union as a "focus of evil in the modern world" or the "evil empire,"[46] the recipient of the story would perhaps have seen the Soviet Union only as a competing superpower. If Reagan had not specified that daring to dream great dreams leads to greatness, the story recipient would not have included it in his storyworld, because it had not happened to him in reality. These are just isolated examples but enough to point out that the narrator needs to specify and point out those particulars of the storyworld his intention is to create that differ from the "real" world. Wills has compared entering Reagan's storyworlds, or, visiting "Reaganland" to visiting Disneyland.[47] Things are constructed to represent an embellished reality.

> Well, my fellow citizens, today we come together on historic grounds to write a new chapter in the American Revolution. We represent men and women of different faiths, backgrounds, and political parties from every region of our country—the people live on Main Street, U.S.A., and they're saying, "We love this land and we will not give up our American Dream."[48]

The use of terminology such as "Main Street, U.S.A." makes it clear that America itself is not only an imagined community but a storyworld. Reagan's mythical America is romantic, everything is essentially good and moral; the heart of America lies in the states in the middle of America's rural landscape and the small towns scattered there. Each of these towns has a similar Main Street, each of these towns is similar to others in all aspects, but they are narratively distanced so far from actual life that they have become just stereotypes that form the setting or staging of Reagan's America with its unifying American dream.

> You know, I've been accused, I know, of being a believer in Norman Rockwell's America; and that's one charge that, as a small-town boy

and a reader of the old Saturday Evening Post, I've always willingly pled guilty to that charge.[49]

The years Reagan spent in the small towns of the Midwest did not leave imprinted into his mind a strictly romantic picture. As he claimed in a White House briefing, "You know, those sleepy old towns where generation after generation lived. And the kinds in the Midwest left; there was nothing in those towns—Lord, that's why I left!"[50] This is in contrast with the claim that those years were of "rare Huck Finn-Tom Sawyer idylls"[51] as Reagan had depicted them. Reagan was able to create "little worlds," as Pemberton has noted, that existed only in his imagination. But he was able to use scenes from these little worlds to touch the hearts of his listeners and communicate his sunny visions to them.[52] One thing that proves just how strong these images are is that the description by Huck Finn of his childhood was not idyllic. Rather than a dream, it was a nightmare. Reagan was, with the aid of his imagination and storytelling skills, able to transform his own reality and life as well as Huckleberry Finn's into something that would appeal to millions of Americans. Reagan took stories and renarrated them into something different than the original version. But, as Wills wrote, with Reagan the perfection of pretense lies in the fact that he is not pretending. He was a sincere claimant to a past that never existed.[53]

Dolezel wrote that fictional worlds or storyworlds that claim a status of virtual and unreal worlds are always incomplete, since "finite texts, the only texts that humans are capable of producing, are bound to create incomplete worlds."[54] No one could hope to be able to specify every detail of his fictional world from the blades of grass to the shape of snowflakes, or even describe in detail every character that inhabits the storyworld. But there is actually no need to do that. Chatman wrote that since the world narrative creates is no more than "an evocation, we are left free to enrich it with whatever real or fictive experience we acquire."[55] The construction material the text provides is insufficient for saturation. It is not possible to create a storyworld with every minuscule detail described. But we do not need all building blocks, only the blueprint. Questions always remain and so do gaps and omissions. It is through gaps and omissions that a story becomes dynamic. When the flow of telling gets interrupted, we are given the chance to "bring into play our own faculty for establishing connections—for filling in gaps left by the text itself."[56] Shlomith Rimmon-Kenan argues that a gap in the narrative is a special point that enhances interest and curiosity but most importantly "contributes to the reader's dynamic participation in making the text signify."[57] A gap entices the mere reader to become a story recipient with an active role in producing a meaning and significance for the story.

Gaps in the narratives are as important as what has been narrated, albeit harder to study. Kafalenos argues that at best the gaps left in the places where information is deferred or suppressed offer us "windows" through which we can observe how narratives shape the interpretations of the events they represent.[58] The narrator of any given story chooses how much information he wishes us to have along with the content of the story. During the course of the narration we continuously interpret and reinterpret events from moment to moment, based on the information that has been made available to us by the narrator at each given moment.[59] By deciding where to leave gaps, either momentary, where the information is just suspended, or permanent, when information is denied from the story recipient, the narrator is able to guide the manner in which interpretations are made. In the flow of politics there are things that have to be suspended for a determinate length of time. As an example one can use the time prior to the presidential election where candidates try to leave certain policy matters outside their respective storyworlds (whereas the other candidate is more than likely to try to identify such subjects and try to bring them up in his story). Somethings tend to get entirely silenced as well.

We can argue that the crucial locus of narrative communication is the gap between the world of the narrator and that of the story recipient. It is the purpose of political storytelling to first utilize this gap and then fill it by communicating values in a manner that brings unity to both worldviews. On the one hand gapping leaves the storyworld incomplete, because all gaps cannot be filled. On the other hand, it actually helps to create elaborate storyworlds, because the story recipient's participation in the construction process grows bigger. He is forced to make assumptions, draw conclusions, and add the fine details. He is no longer a passive recipient but is coerced to participate in the creative process. With a very fitting term Peter Rabinowitz refers to this process as the reader's "license to fill."[60] Because things are not entirely spelled out to the story recipient, his own participation in building the storyworld adds credibility to it, since it is saturated with the details he has provided. The drafter of the storyworld relies on his story recipients to be cued to draw inferences and conclusions about the nature of the world being built. They supply information and insert it to fill the gaps in the narrative and make extra-textual deductions. The political issues the narrator wants to exclude from his storyworld do not even get the chance to enter it, if he is capable of manipulation of the way his recipients fill his story-world with details. Almost anything can be silenced and left out if the recipient of the story can be cued into constructing a preferred kind of storyworld. The evident incompleteness of the storyworld there-fore is an asset in political storytelling.

Marie-Laure Ryan claims that "we project upon [fictional] worlds everything we know about reality, and . . . make only the adjustments dictated by the text."[61] This relation between what is known earlier and what is told or dictated by the text is precarious. The more gaps there are in the narrative the more the recipient must saturate the text based upon his own knowledge and the less textual cues there are to guide this process of saturation. Therefore a political narrator must provide just enough information to sufficiently enable the read-ers to make the preferred adjustments to the text in order to some-what minimize the effect of recipients filling the gaps as they will. Unfortunately, the more he elaborates his narration the more the text itself is deprived of the "looseness" that is the main point of narrativ-izing politics. By storytelling the dreary world of politics is turned into something simpler and more comprehensible, and adding unnec-essary informational content into the narrative makes it gradually a more complex representation of the political reality and restricts the recipients free construction process of the storyworld and diminishes the tellability of the story. Narrative loses some of its narrativity and becomes "just" a description of states. Mary E. Stuckey noticed that Reagan only established themes, and when these themes reappeared in a broader context, "his audience of the faithful would hear what they wanted to hear, and would interpret it in a way consistent with their own political leanings."[62] Stuckey does not talk about story-worlds with my terminology, but the point remains the same. Reagan gave birth to storyworlds, and the audience created their storyworlds in a manner of their own liking after their political preferences, but these storyworlds still continued to work for the benefit of Reagan.

When it comes to filling the storyworld with details intertextuality plays a great role. As Julia Kristeva wrote, "Every text takes shape as a mosaic of citations, every text is the absorption and transformation of other texts."[63] The narrator needs only to refer to other peoples' storyworlds, and the details of those can be transplanted into the storyworld under construction. This process needs to be handled carefully in relation to the texts chosen. Naturally the story recipi-ents have their own favorite texts they use to fill the details whether the creator intends that or not, but similarly the narrator can choose some of texts used by planting cues within his storyline. This is most evident in the use of quotations or certain words or expressions that are known to lead some people to make connections to particular texts. To illustrate my point in connection to Reagan's narratives, examples of the former type are his numerous quotations from other presidents. Examples of the latter type are the biblical expressions and phrases used without reference, which only have special meaning to the religious part of the recipients, and thus work as exclusive cues. The creator of the storyworld is indeed not alone in his narrative task. There is no void empty of storyworlds or texts. The text is plurivocal; it is indeed a network woven out of other texts and other voices as Barthes claimed.[64]

Thus, to create a complete storyworld the political narrator needs to tell an elaborate story, manipulate the gaps, activate the audience to either fill them or ignore them, and use other texts and stories to his advantage. Only after all these things have been taken care of, can we view the storyworld construction as completed. But even when a storyworld is "completed" it does not remain exactly the same, never changing and unaltered. Far from it, a storyworld is remodeled, added to, reshaped, and reconstructed all the time with retellings of the story or just in the minds of the story recipients as they experience life. Alan Palmer argues that narratives cannot even be understood unless the storyworld is understood as a "complex, ever-changing intermingling of the individual narratives of the various characters in it."[65] Why then the need for separate and multiple storyworlds? My answer is because time is always of essence in politics, and in order to change the structure of the storyworld in fundamental ways, one requires too much time and too may retellings to simultaneously keep up the plausibility of the story. To distract the recipient from the issue under debate that causes the need to reform the storyworld on its basic level, it is more convenient to lead him into another storyworld through logical narrative paths. It is easier to use almost the same cues and storylines to create a new storyworld, or rather have one ready for future use, than trying to exclude something fundamental from one that already exists. To further use the metaphor of a story-world being constructed like a building and then furnished with the aid of recipients, one could liken this situation into one where one of the supporting beams is suddenly removed. The entire storyworld might crumble.

As we can see, one story does not suffice, since the political narra-tor needs to have multiple relatively similar stories and resulting story-worlds at his disposal. Thus, in the case of Reagan, we are discussing a web of interconnecting storylines that are told and retold again and refined and recreated in each telling. The story recipient does not wait until the end to understand the text. Although information in each of the stories is provided only gradually, according to Shlomith Rimmon-Kenan the data integration starts at the very beginning, and constantly the recipient forms hypotheses, reinforces them, modifies them, develops them, and maybe even casts them aside to be replaced by others.[66] Multiple storyworlds are created and modified to adapt to the changes in temporal, spatial, and factual conditions. For the storyverse creation to be effective, the stories told as a part of the story web, besides reporting the actions of the storyworld participants, also need to sketch out the acting situations. This is because virtual and unactualized states, events, and actions increase the tellability of the story, and all of these work as "virtual embedded narratives even while they remain unactualized possibilities."[67] These include "not only dreams, fictions, and fantasies conceived or told by the characters, but any kind of representation concerning past or future states and events; plans, passive projections, desires."[68] They provide the story recipients with extremely political promises of what the future will hold and aspirations to strive for. The most important embedded narrative in all of Reagan's stories is the American dream, which is pervasive to every utterance. The myth of America's past and future is omnipresent, and it affects directly the storyverse itself.

COMBINING STORYWORLDS INTO A STORYVERSE

The earliest theorist to write about anything concerning a storyworld or a storyverse was Northrop Frye. He noted that "the universe of poetry, however, is a literary universe, and not a separate existential universe."[69] It is unfortunate that Frye stopped his line of thought at that point. The universe of poetry exists only as a multitude of words on paper, but the reader constructs out of them a new universe consisting of several storyworlds, each evoked by a different narrative. I have taken this as my starting point to argue for an existence of something I choose to call a universe consisting of multiple storyworlds, or a storyverse. It is true that a storyverse is no more "real" in the existential meaning of the word than the universe of poetry, but it is precisely its *vraisemblance* to the actual, immanent one we inhabit that matters.

Alan Palmer claims that a universe must be brought to life and convey to the story recipient the sense that at the center of this universe there "resides an actual or real world, a realm of factual states or events."[70] So there is a universe of worlds, one of which is the world we exist in. The rest are possible worlds, created by narrative means. One single story may give birth to numerous storyworlds in the minds of multiple story recipients, and at the same time a multitude on stories told in connection to a particular storyworld may create reproductions of the original storyworld, which differ slightly. Every story is able to encode stand-alone storyworlds that cannot be falsified by virtue of their relation to other storyworlds. One story can build upon another so that this "successor-world" is preceded by the "protoworld" in time, and may feature different participants and fill in gaps of the protoworld, but both are not in contradiction to each other on the level of basic rules and organizational level of story logic. The storyworld refers at all times to only one of these worlds, and thus I use the self-coined expression "storyverse" to assess the multiplicity of these worlds, since it is not sufficient for political storytelling to have one story to merely fill the gaps in another to polemicize or complement it. There has to be a more intricate narrative construction, a combination of storyworlds loosely connected to each other within the entire storyverse.

It must be emphasized that the existence of multiple storyworlds is nothing new in itself. Marie-Laure Ryan seems to talk of something similar in her principle to "seek the diversification of possible worlds in the narrative universe."[71] The idea of a storyverse adds to the discussion, however, multiple simultaneous storyworlds that create multiple universes, with their different natural laws and logic. As Margolin notes, many postmodern novels portray ontologically multiple or indeterminate worlds where the "multiplicity is presented as an irreducible fact, not as competing hypotheticals."[72] Here lies the distinction. The postmodern novel as well as narrative theory portray the multiple and indeterminate nature of the worlds as a fact that cannot be avoided. The idea of storyverse-manipulation in politics proposes that these multiple worlds are presented as singular world, and furthermore simple enough in its structure to comprehend. The political narratives attempt to "hide" the existence of multiple worlds from the story recipients and exploit their indeterminate boundaries as means for transporting the story recipients between storyworlds at will. As Katherine Young claims, the boundaries of either the tale world, or the realm the story is about, and the realm of narrative discourse, or story realm, remain pervious.[73] Storyworlds are often unbounded, unless specifically built otherwise, and the lack of clear boundaries helps the often involuntary and unnoticed transportation of the story recipients from one world to another within the storyverse. The boundaries of storyworlds are at best semipervasive membranes. Characters or other elements internal to the story are not able to infiltrate from one world to another without being directed to do so by the narrator, but the membrane offers no resistance for the crossing of the story recipients.

Marie-Laure Ryan's interest in computer-created narratives and virtual reality technology offers us new ways of envisioning how storyworlds can blend together. One of these is the concept of "morphing." In computer graphics this is a visual effect where a picture is turned into another with the help of numerous intermediary frames in between that gradually alter one picture and transforms it in such a progressive manner that one realizes only retrospectively that the original form has been replaced with another. This excludes instantaneous changes that as a theme are as old as myths and narratives themselves. Naturally to speak of narrative morphing presupposes a certain degree of metaphorical displacement as the object of morphing has to be transposed from the visual to verbal domain.[74] Nevertheless, the concept or morphing is useful in understanding political narratives. Black can be whitewashed credibly only by progressive minute transformations, which enable the narrator, in this case Reagan, to make the ideological shift from calling the Soviet Union the "evil empire" to something one can reason with and share similar goals. The ability to avoid an instantaneous transformation allows the political narrator a lot of leeway. Other strategies must naturally be used when emergent situations cause an urge in politics that does not allow gradual change, but morphing makes the transformation more plausible for the story recipients when there is sufficient time to use it. While morphing allows on one plane the story to gradually change into another kind of story, on a plane of storyworlds, which can be seen as higher level constructions as compared to the stories themselves, another process of morphing occurs. One storyworld starts to morph into another, and this brings the multiple storyworlds that combine together to form a storyverse into play.

It must be remembered that neither the storyworld, nor a storyverse, is in all cases created solely by the particular story being told. Intertextuality and the life experiences of the story recipients play a large part in this construction. Thus, a storyverse actually controls the stories told about it or being added to it. Bruner claims that all stories of literary merit are about events in the "real world," but they render that world newly strange, rescue it from obviousness, and fill it with gaps that incite the reader to become a writer of a virtual text about the text they have read.[75] I differ from Bruner's argument, but only slightly. It is my claim that a truly great story assures the reader that it deals with the "real" world, while it actually incites the reader to construct along with the virtual text a virtual world as well, or in other words cues the reader to recreate his "real" world anew. It is in this process of recreation that the worldview shifts away from the "real" and toward a storyworld. The more subtly and unnoticeably the story manages this switching of worlds, the greater the story is. There have to be many different stories, each one existing at least in potential, or being embedded in the other stories, before a storyverse can emerge as the highest level of internal structure or organization within narratives. The crucial question we must explore is *when* the deitic shift between storyworlds needs to be initiated.

Since the purpose of Machiavellian concept of politics is to use ones virtú at the right moment to entice *Fortuna,* every moment becomes a moment of *kairos-time*, exceptional from normal chronological time. One has to sense the most beneficial moment to act and employ the opportunity given to him. As Reagan humorously put this,

> The problem of recognizing opportunities—it reminds me of a story about Moses. He had led the children of Israel out of Egypt. He got to the Red Sea. God parted the waters. Moses looked around and said, "Oh, Lord, just as I was going in for a swim."[76]

A politician at such a virtuous moment must be able to switch from one story to another and perhaps even denounce everything told earlier. If he switches to a completely different story, his plausibility evaporates, unless he is able to transport his story recipient into a storyworld very similar to the one used before. This new storyworld must lack those ingredients or building blocks that became the point of the whole political controversy that initiated the need to switch storyworlds. A credible political storyteller must have access to multiple storyworlds built so that certain story components are missing from each storyworld. Only then the issue of political debate can be silenced or excluded completely from the narration. These storyworlds lie parallel to each other and exist simultaneously so that multiple storylines serve as actual routes into them. Story recipients optimally can be cued to exit one via these routes and enter another without noticing the shift. For a single story, just one storyworld suffices. J. R. R. Tolkien built a single storyworld for his Lord of the Rings trilogy and added to it in his other works. Even the most intricate single story does not merit the creation of more than a singular storyworld, but in the rapidly changing world of politics the success may depend upon having multiple storyworlds to use as safe havens.

If a metanarrative is defined as something above singular stories, then we could say that a storyverse is something the metanarrative creates. A collection of storylines must exist and form a web of stories that are connected to each other at many juncture points where another storyline can be picked up. As discussed earlier, the points of closure in the narration can act as these points. Every moment of choosing in Reagan's narration is a point where the story potentially can take a new direction of a different storyline, and thus move fluently from one storyworld to another within the storyverse. Barthes writes about "the knots of the story."[77] These knots are usually points where it becomes possible "to think of something else," and thus abandon the telling of the whole story along the particular storyline followed thus far. In Reagan's narration, these knots are always situated at the peaks of crises and political choices. This positioning heightens their importance within the story web. The knot works as a closure or even an end of a particular storyline and provides a possibility to take a new direction for the narrative. "The knot closes, terminates, concludes the action in progress."[78] If the choice Reagan has spoken on behalf of, the story continues unaltered following its original direction otherwise a new storyline has to be adopted. The knots are the most important moments within any storyline, since each one is a nexus that allows switching from one storyline to another in the story web.

I use the expression "story web" to refer to the walkways between storyworlds. In other words, there are numerous storylines used in Reagan's political storytelling, and the task of each one is to ensnare the story recipient to enter the storyworld. Since these storylines are interconnected and overlapping, there is a big chance that the story recipient will start to follow another storyline even without noticing it. While each and every storyline leads into the storyverse, within it the numerous storylines create a story web that acts as the conduit within the storyverse from one storyworld to another. It would be tempting to describe the story web along the lines of a web spun by a spider, but this would be oversimplifying the matter. When enough stories are told that crisscross each other, the resulting story web is more or less as a Gordian knot or a ball an old lady has created by tying together pieces of string she has found. Within a spiderweb-like structure it might be possible for a talented narrator to unfailingly guide the process in which the story recipient wanders deeper and deeper into the storyverse.

This unfortunately is not true, since the story recipient may at each place where the storylines cross each other, or at each knot, take a more or less random turn or choose not to do so, all according to his or her personal preferences. All that the narrator can control is to try to tell all his stories so that the maximal number of storylines lead to the same "ending" of the story, which in the case of Reagan is the global freedom and the actualization of the American dream ultimately for every human being. If the ending of the story is depicted as the penultimate political goal, which is in the interests of every story recipient to see actualized, even storylines that emanate from totally opposite standpoints may blend together and exist (without even noticing it) in harmony within the storyverse. This political goal is situated as the central point of the story web, the place where all strands finally are tied together. To illustrate this, an important knot or nexus within the story web is the point where the totalitarian enemy of the Soviet Union is no longer in existence to hinder the American dream. Both starting points of "peace through strength" and détente with willingness to be flexible in negotiation table can lose their initial origins as their respective storylines proceed deeper into the story web and get connected together at this point. Nevertheless, since politics is a continuous process, the storyline must continue from this point of closure deeper into the structure of the story web and always, even with minuscule steps, proceed toward the elusive heart of the story web and the ultimate goal narrated to reside there.

The concept of a storyverse should be understood as a very important tool of leadership in narrativized politics. Only by creating a storyverse the political narrator is able to escape the restrictions imposed by the story logic within a single storyworld. When his audiences create multiple storyworlds, he can manipulate the members of his audience by transporting them from one storyworld into another. The concept of a storyverse can act in politics as a way of providing an illusion of unity when there is actually no such thing. The citizens as story recipients create their own storyworlds, and while they would be proved fundamentally different under closer scrutiny, they manage to provide a sense of consensus. In the next chapter I will take a closer look into how this can actually happen in the case of the American dream. People construct their own storyworlds based on such concepts as freedom, democracy, and the American way of life, and if the political narrator in a leadership position, like Reagan did, is able to manipulate his stories well enough to allow the construction of a storyverse, different storyworlds among individual citizens and the subgroups they form appear to project an illusionary sensation of unity. Thus a certain vagueness of political concepts, also communicated in storytelling, is a beneficial resource. After all, to gain political power and more importantly to hold on to it in the next election is one of the primary goals of any politician. In political narration the entire storytelling attempts to confuse the audience and distort the story logic when it is deemed necessary to do so for political purposes. A storyverse allows a politician to reach for a more universal support based on the illusion that the multiple storyworlds his story recipients have created is one unifying concept, such as the American dream or way of life.

The creation and especially the maintenance and restructuring of a storyverse is a demanding task, since besides requiring skills of narration, the actual drafting of multiple storyworlds is bound to take a long time, and thus the time span the narrator is able to spend in the spotlight of politics has to be longish. Reagan had a long stretch "toiling the political vineyards," and since narratives played such a vital role in his political leadership he upkept this process consciously and intentionally throughout his career, as was exemplified with the discussion of "The Speech." Reagan, and every politician, claimed that the way he portrays the world to his electorate is "realist." Reality and especially the concept of what constitutes the "real" can be altered by narrative means. By emphasizing the importance of one thing and leaving others neglected in this story and doing the opposite in another story, Reagan was able to focus the attention of the citizenry on, or divert it from, certain issues. When the storyworlds that create the storyverse are each very close to the "real" world the deitic shift is easy to initiate. By focusing on specific issues and downplaying others, the political narrator is able to manipulate the way people see their reality by supplanting them into one storyworld at a time and in response to the demands of the situation move them to others through the pervasive membranes of the worlds. So, it is the intention of the politician to build a storyverse and make it as elaborate and consisting of as many storyworlds as possible. It is a tool for politics, a mechanism that blurs the storied and the experienced and allows the politician to manipulate the Weltanschauung of his people.

In order for individual storyworlds and the resulting storyverse to be plausible, the story recipients need to believe in it. The mythical America is a storyverse, and there was a need to justify its existence. The beliefs of Americans need to be focused on the storyverse and make its existence an object of belief. Next we shall take a look at politics and religion as legitimizers and discuss their role in the storyverse-construction.

3

AMERICAN RELIGION

> Together, let us take up the challenge to reawaken America's religious
> and moral heart, recognizing that a deep and abiding faith in God is
> the rock upon which this great Nation was founded.
>
> Ronald Wilson Reagan[1]

According to John F. Wilson, American culture can be viewed as
characterized by religious meanings. Among this cluster of meanings can be found ideas of America as a perfected and pure society
where opportunity abounds and which is receptive to all the homeless and the deprived of the world. America is seen as "fulfilment of
the *dreams and aspirations* of the ages."[2] Occasionally this has been
evident in visions of America as the Eldorado where fortune awaits
for the migrant ready to take it. Or, as Reagan put it, "The streets of
America would not be paved with gold, they would be paved with
opportunity."[3] At other times America could be seen as synony-
mous to religious liberty and freedom. In both cases it was the "New
World," where men could start their lives over again, leave the history
behind, and see what opportunities would wait for them in this New
Eden. Multiple religious meanings set the foundations for all the narratives that describe this near-perfect society.

Culture is thus grounded by religious ideals, but the relationship
is reciprocal. Northrop Frye saw culture as ultimately the factor that
sanctifies both religious and political myths. Taken outside the culture where it was created, a myth, whether of Greek gods or a religio-
political one, will lose its validity.

> Culture interposes, between the ordinary and the religious life, a total
> vision of possibilities, and insists on its totality—for whatever is excluded
> from culture by religion or state will get its revenge somehow. . . . No
> religious or political myth is either valuable or valid unless it assumes
> the autonomy of culture, which may be provisionally defined as the
> total body of imaginative hypothesis in a society and its tradition.[4]

Culture is the factor that shapes our worldview and our beliefs. Culture is always in flux and under reconstruction. It is not stable and fixed, but rather a continuous and self-contradicting process that can and may be manipulated with both political and nonpolitical narratives. For Paul Tillich religion "is the meaning-giving substance of culture, and culture is the totality of forms in which the basic concern of religion expresses itself."[5] Religion plays an important role in any given culture while the role itself may differ in each case. It sets the forms for thought processes and condenses the values that guide the behavior of the individual. In that sense religion is a precondition for culture, and at the same time, culture becomes perceived in terms of a discrete phenomenon within it. Culture both acquires and maintains its legitimacy on the basis of a meaning system, which is at bottom religious. Wilson echoes Peter Berger in claiming that citizens exist in a dialectical relationship with their "worlds," and that these worlds exist only in the knowledge of them, that individuals and collectives share and reproduce.[6] Religion in a given culture is one of the primary shapers of these worlds. My addition to this argument is that this world can be a storyworld or a combination of them as a storyverse. Reagan managed to take a leadership role in the reproduction of these worlds and binding them into a storyverse.

It is harmful for religion to be used as a political tool to reach purely political goals. Some of the negative results of the combination process can be diminished by trying to narratively depict the goals of religion and politics to be the same. In his storytelling the politician must be careful not to emphasize one over the other, that is, neither to rally people behind his politics using religion, nor to wave the colors of politics in order to advance religion. The meanings of religion and politics need to get narratively blurred and intentionally made fuzzy, so that the citizen as a story recipient cannot be sure where religion stops and politics start, and vice versa.

SACRED PROFANITY—RELIGION AND POLITICS IN THE UNITED STATES

I'm only the head of a civil government, a secular authority. It's probably true that politics is the prose of a culture, but religion is its poetry. Governments are passing things in the long history of the world, but faith and belief endure forever.

Ronald Wilson Reagan[7]

It is possible for a poet to write fine poetry, and yet lead his society to Hell. The poet is essentially a seducer; woe to his people.

Mohammad Allama Iqbal[8]

This chapter will shed some light on the characteristics of religiosity involved in American policy, and the factors that have shaped this relationship. Politics is always connected to religiosity, and while in the United States this might not happen on the level of the "state church," it happens by religion justifying policies on a more subtle level of common beliefs, morality, and ethos. Emile Durkheim wrote that

> nearly all the great social institutions were born in religion. For the principal features of collective life to have begun as none other than various features of religious life, it is evident that religious life must necessarily have been the eminent form and, as it were, the epitome of collective life. *If religion gave birth to all that is essential in society, that is so because the idea of society is the soul of religion.*[9]

Durkheim wanted to use simple societies for his research of the forms of religious life and argued that they serve as basis for deductions for more complex societies. William James had a totally opposite idea, since for him the most fruitful objects of research are the people who have advanced the furthest in their religious life.[10] According to Durkheim religion is a social thing, and religious representations "express collective realities; rites are ways of acting that are born only in the midst of assembled groups and whose purpose is to evoke, maintain or recreate certain mental states of those groups."[11] Such a definition makes religion not only social but also a highly political thing as well. Religion is an expression of a collective. It is ultimately the thing that draws individuals together and creates unity among them, and even more importantly, through its rites and modes for action enables the unity to remain coherent. Religion creates a society. Max Weber admits that faith is an element always present in politics. A politician serves a cause while using his power. Naturally this cause may be a national goal, just as well as freedom and democracy for all people in the world. The politician "may claim to be the servant of an "idea" or . . . he may claim to serve external goals of everyday life—but some kind of belief must always be *present*."[12]

It is by no means my purpose to argue that only by thumping the Bible any politician could get his policies accepted, but in a more subtle way of storytelling that evokes religious feelings in the citizenry.

We are not discussing a religion per se, but evoking the general religiosity, the need of human condition to believe in something and seek for meaning for their lives from something higher. This can be God, country, state, or almost anything as long as the belief in a higher being exists, and preferably the object of belief can be depicted to be ethereal. Once something is physically there, once it can be touched and felt, there is no need for belief. In politically oriented narration the object of belief must be created so that it is not physically concrete in terms of its existence. In order to advance politics with the aid of belief, the object should be the nation itself as an imagined community and not just the state that has its tangible manifestations and institutions.

Our human condition seems to require a need to believe, and this legitimizes religion, but the more earthly world of politics needs to be legitimated as well. This is an important factor concerning the relationship of religion and politics. Religion itself does not need to look for support and legitimation from the world of profane, including politics. Religion, when it is born, has to be able to legitimate itself as a new apprehension of the divine. Politics belongs to the realm of the profane and often contains morally disputable acts. Thus, it needs a legitimating source of strength, and most powerfully this can be acquired from the symbolism of the sacred.[13] Even in the antiquity the sovereignty over their people of "God-kings" was established in connection to divinity. Nowadays democracy, ideals of human rights, and freedoms have altered our religious beliefs so that seldom the divine origins of any ruler are universally acknowledged. The legitimation of the rule has to be obtained in a more subtle manner. Even in the words of Reagan,

> Only in an intellectual climate which distinguishes between the city of God and the city of man and which explicitly affirms the independence of God's realm and forbids any infringement by the state on its prerogatives, only in such a climate could the idea of individual human rights take root, grow, and eventually flourish. We see this climate in all democracies and in our own political tradition. The founders of our republic rooted their democratic commitment in the belief that all men are endowed by their Creator with certain inalienable rights. And so, they created a system of government whose avowed purpose was and is the protection of those God-given rights.[14]

The idea of human freedom, which was given birth during the Enlightenment and has since evolved, might provide one connection, since from a religious viewpoint, it was in the political world that the

Creator left to man to exercise his intelligence and faculties. Freedom, as de Tocqueville wrote, "sees in religion the companion of its struggles and its triumphs, the cradle of its infancy, the divine source of its rights. It considers religion as the safeguard of mores; and mores as the guarantee of laws and the pledge of its own duration."[15] Freedom, or politics that emphasize it, and religion are not antagonists. Rather there is an alliance between them and both can easily adopt ideas from the other into their respective spheres of influences. While the Jeffersonian "wall of separation" may to some degree be a political reality, the human intellect is yet able to pass by such artificially created divisions, and the interaction between the systems may factually be rampant. Politics and religion remain intertwined at a deeper level than the superficial connection severed by the wall of separation. In the best of all cases, both are able to benefit from each other. Religion can just as easily be employed to caress and nurture the idea of freedom in a democracy as be exploited in a theocratic society. As Reagan saw it, "democracy is just a political reading of the Bible."[16]

Common to all religious beliefs is the tendency to classify the real or ideal things into two opposite genera: the sacred and the profane. The world is divided into two domains "one containing all that is sacred and the other all that is profane—such is the distinctive trait of religious thought."[17] Indeed, "there is religion as soon as sacred is distinguished from the profane."[18] But it has to be noted that nothing is sacred or profane inherently. Jonathan Z. Smith calls them "relational categories, mobile boundaries which shift according to the map being employed. There is nothing sacred in itself, only things sacred in relation."[19] In other words, to have something sacred, we have to *make* it sacred, and things excluded or set in opposition to the sacred are profane. The categories are a product of human activity. Narrativized politics does not need to abide by the rules of any particular religion but creates connections between the political and religious realm thus bridging the gap created between them by manipulating the need of the people to have something to believe in. It functions on the borderline of the sacred and profane realms and by making that borderline between these storyworlds more permeable.

The religious beliefs used in politics need not be Christian, or perhaps not even religious at all. As long as the mechanisms and structures of belief are there, political narration remains sound, regardless of the nature of the object of belief. Durkheim argues that there are rites without gods and indeed some rites that create or give birth to gods. Likewise there are cults that do not even attempt to unite or connect a man to deity. For him "religion is broader than the idea of gods or spirits and so cannot be defined exclusively in those terms."[20] Durkheim formulates a definition for religion: "A unified system of beliefs and practices relative to sacred things, that is to say, things set apart and forbidden—beliefs and practices which unite into one single moral community called a Church, all those who adhere to them."[21] Thus G. K. Chesterton's statement about America being a nation with the soul of a church is more than fitting.[22] Sydney Mead called a nation a spiritual society,[23] and in the political manipulation of peoples' religious beliefs for political purposes, the entire country is rallied into a moral community. The belief in the sacredness of something can unify individuals to such a community. Reagan claimed that "we are a nation under God. Freedom is not granted to us by government; it is ours by divine right."[24] Freedom itself gains the illusion of being sacred in repetitive tellings and thus can be a basis for religious belief just as well as the community of America itself. "That faith in freedom, that abiding belief in what the unfettered human spirit can accomplish, defines us as a people and a nation."[25]

Even democracy can take the role of a religion. Patrick Deneen argued that if faith is defined as belief in the unseen, "it may be that democracy is as justifiably an object of faith as a distant and silent God."[26] Indeed, the idea of "democracy" as well as that of "the nation," is something no man can experience for himself in a concrete manner. No one can visit the nation or speak to it directly. He can only do so to the representative of it. The objects of our faith are abstractions despite the fact that they are imbued with such a strong notion of reality that they give direction to our lives as a whole. These abstractions exist only in their own world.[27] To borrow the expression of Augustine of Hippo, the world they inhabit is the *civitas Dei.* While the two domains are considered entirely separate with nothing in common, a thing can nevertheless pass from one of these worlds into the other. When this occurs, the duality of the two realms shows clearly, since in order to pass from one into another, the thing has to undergo a true metamorphosis.[28] The depth and scope of the metamorphosis varies, but some change or alteration has to nevertheless take place. The profane has to be "sanctified" or the sacred turned into more earthly version of itself to pass from one world into another. Turning the worlds of the sacred and profane alike into storyworlds will allow a thing to move from one world to another more fluently.

While we tend not to allow the profane to infiltrate the sacred realm, the sacred world is inclined by its very nature to spread into the profane world. "While repelling the profane world, the sacred world tends at the same time to flow into the profane world whenever the latter world comes near it. That is why they must be kept at a distance from each other and why, in some sense, a void must be opened between them."[29] Durkheim sees the sacred as "contagious," and this principle allows for all rites of consecration, whether of people or things.[30] Aaltola writes about the intrusion of sacred into the profane and sees it as a practice where political leaders act as interpreters of extraordinary or sacred meanings.[31] Reagan interpreted the profane world as his mythical America where everything was extraordinary and endowed with profound meanings. According to Kelly, the Durkhemian notion of the contagiousness of the sacred does not work in the American context directly, because supposedly there is no drift of politics into religion or religion into politics because of an intervening area of morality.[32] I partially agree with him, at least in the notion that morality lays in-between politics and religion, but morality can be used to dissolve the border between politics and religion. Morality exists in both spheres of life and acts as the vessel that transports ideas between the two worlds. Morality is a passageway between the storyworlds, since it overlaps both of them. Politics is, after all, a theory and praxis of the "good life." Similarly, religion gives to believers guidelines how to live morally well. While the morality of religion is not the same as the morality of politics, it is relatively easy to shift doctrines of faith into political concept of morality.

No artificial separation of religion and politics can withstand the unification if it is done by narrating into existence such storyworlds based on these concepts that can create an illusion that things belong to both worlds. Mika Aaltola argues that "politico-religious practices can be used in a way that creates other modes of existence besides the concretely real one."[33] They assist in the creation of cultural meanings, and when these practices take the form of storytelling, such as preaching, they give birth to storyworlds as the other modes of existence. Thus Reagan's message about the interconnectedness of God and America seems less radical as a claim. Very often America is seen as a synonym for "freedom," and this concept gets a religious sheen. De Tocqueville noted the tendency of Americans to "completely confuse Christianity and freedom in their minds that it is almost impossible to have them conceive of the one without the other."[34] Freedom is what belief in America is about, and democracy and freedom are connected to the plan of God for mankind. God is pushed into the sidelines in this discussion, and these political concepts become part of the religious dogma if not, indeed, the object of faith.

Politics is the principal and ultimate control system in the realm of the profane; just as religion is in the sacred. While there is no need for the sacred to be considered as a part of the profane realm, it often is able to play a role in it as well.[35] This can happen through the Durkheimian notion of the deification of the society, where politics might offer another form of eschatological hope of salvation just like religion does, but in a more earthly form. It can happen following the Schmittian concept, where the members of the political leadership try to portray themselves as using God-granted powers as His earthly representatives. Even once the ancient cosmogonic politics are excluded, we know many political forms that claimed not only to regulate but also to embody the sacred. These reach all the way from Constantine Empire to the Third Reich.[36]

The basis of political theology lies in the argument of Carl Schmitt, who claimed that all significant concepts of the state are secularized concepts of religion because of both their systematic structure and their historical development through which they were transferred from theology to the theory of the state.[37] The omnipotent God was replaced with the omnipotent sovereign, the state. Thus, the study of politics is able to gain a lot from the insights provided by the study of religion. We live in an age characterized by the myth about "the Death of God" of which Nietzsche wrote. This causes theology to become factually atheology. Hans Blumenberg wrote how the modern man is deprived of the metaphysical guarantees God offered for the world, and how he constructs for himself a "counter world" of rationality and manipulability. We can treat this as yet another storyworld, albeit one that "unfinished," full of ambiguity and uncertainty.[38] It is this unfinishedness of the storyworld that forces man to "take part in its (hoped for but never realized) completion."[39] This provides politics with a drive to strive on toward a teleological goal. Later on, I shall further discuss the importance of not being able to "finish" the world, and the fact that the teleological goal of politics is depicted to be ever closer but yet is necessary to remain out of reach. Here, the importance is on the uncertainty itself.

The benefit of combining religion and politics is being able to give the impression that the presence of divine providence evaporates ambiguity and uncertainty. It imbues politics with a sense of purpose and meaning in response to the absence of God myth in the Western world. Still, there continues to be a huge impact of religion in politics. Nowhere is this more apparent than in the United States of America. For Reagan, God certainly was not dead or absent:

> A few years ago, it was fashionable in the media and the universities to say that America had no more heroes. Heroism was a thing of the

past, we were told, as old and dry as a fossil in Death Valley. Fashions often run together, and this one galloped side by side with the death-of-God vogue. I seem to remember that the argument was that if God was dead nothing anyone could do was important enough to be called heroic. Well, I've never believed that either God or American heroism was dead. This land of freedom was built, and is still being built, by men and women who, without chroniclers, without heralds, have brought a warrior's courage to the challenges of everyday life. America is a land of heroes.[40]

The relationship between politics and religion could not be more important. But the dilemma is how to bring them together for deeper study, since both have such an influence on each other that one could perhaps speak of contamination. As a result neither one can be "pure." According to William James, religion is collective entity, which cannot be separated into a category of its own. There is no object or action, which would be specifically religious and nothing else. Religiosity is a part of many different things but does almost never comprise the whole of anything.[41]

Durkheim claimed religion to be a "system of ideas by means of which individuals imagine the society of which they are members and the obscure, yet intimate relations they have with it."[42] God is merely an intangible representation of the ideals of society, and when the faithful strive to strengthen their ties to the God, they at the same time strengthen their ties to the society.[43] This is not very far from the Schmittian notion of the relationship between God and the society. God and society, which for Schmitt essentially meant the state, blend into each other. Durkheim writes about "society," and Americans as people create a society. A state is something removed from the people that could be defined as the machinery of governance. Perhaps Durkheim's ideas are even closer than Schmitt's to the policies of Reagan, who was very antigovernmental and emphasized the importance of the American people as the prime mover of both politics and social life. Schmitt wrote about the state embodied in the government, but Reagan abhorred the big governmental structure and saw it as something that obscures the will of the people. For him, people were closer to God than the state could ever be. State distorted the relationship between the practically divine will of the people and God's will imposed on them in turn. But the relationship of religion and politics is more complicated and multifaceted, and thus cannot be simplified to mere political rules of exercising divine judgment.

One could follow de Tocqueville, who wrote that "next to each religion is a political opinion that is joined to it by affinity. Allow the human mind to follow its tendency and it will regulate political society and the divine city in a uniform manner; . . . to *harmonize* the earth with Heaven."[44] All versions of religious belief are backed by some political way of thought and vice versa. Even atheism is a religion; the object of belief is that God does not exist, but since there is no proof either way, atheism becomes a system of religious belief, and is in close interaction with communist political thought where the focal point in not in a deity, but man himself. In a same manner in the Weberian interpretation Protestantism and Capitalism go hand in hand.[45] No matter how one positions oneself in respect to religion and how hard one tries to separate the realms of the sacred and the profane, there will still be some overlapping. If there is nothing else, at least the democratic need to create an ever more perfect society leads automatically to the process of perfecting the profane realm after an image of the sacred realm. Christianity offers us the utopia of an ideal society in the form of *civitas Dei*, and it is this originally religious vision that we try to reach in the profane political process. Taoism with its disregard for politics, or Hinduism with its ideas of rebirth, imposes a different way to govern than Christianity or other monotheistic religions. But any religion has its impact on politics, because each political preference is closer to some particular religious belief at least on the level of mores and ethics, if not in practical action.

In the Judeo-Christian political tradition teleological progress characterizes thought. Edelman argues that "so far as political beliefs are concerned, the most potent categorizations almost certainly are visions of the future."[46] Politics and religion are eschatological, and their goals lie in the future, in the glorious times to come. Both give guidelines how to live in the present and be a "good" Christian/citizen, but the rewards of the correct behavior today do not actualize immediately. Good behavior reaps rewards, but they are always tied to an eschatological vision of the future. Religion works as something seemingly nonpolitical that offers the political leadership means to curb individual autonomy. More specifically, those means can be summarized as "an afterlife that would reward faith and loyalty and punish heresy, a vision of a future utopia or of a past fall from grace."[47] It is a benefit that the eschatological use of politics does not actually have to provide anything instantaneously. We might not need bread today, if there would indeed be a sovereign who would let us eat cake tomorrow. The benefits of the future just need to be so extraordinary that the wants and needs of today can be suspended.

I've come here today to talk about where our country has been for the past few years and where it's going. And I want to talk to you about our vision of the future and the kind of America that we now have a dazzling opportunity to create.[48]

Future has to hold promise of great things, if not salvation. We cannot discount the role of millennialism or at least the millennial hope as a religious but at the same time highly political form of eschatology. Millennial hope is not always beneficial for politics, if it focuses on the coming Kingdom of Christ, but it can take the more earthly and profane shape of a future utopian society if certain political ideology is followed or manifest itself as unlimited economic growth. Rheinhold Niebuhr asserts that there is a millennial hope in play within every vital religion. While the promise of second coming and life everlasting is mostly a promise to individuals, "who can deny its relevance for nations and empires, for civilizations and cultures also, even though these collective forms of life do not have the exact integrity of the individual soul nor do they have as direct an access to divine judgment and grace."[49] In these words of Niebuhr the crucial word is "direct." A nation cannot be promised a life everlasting in heaven, but the nation can act as a vessel and create the impression that it will lead citizens into salvation. An individual's hope of salvation can be very important for a nation as a political tool to fulfill the nation's much more profane interests. A cynic might be in unison with Hegel and claim that the life everlasting of a nation lies in the fulfillment of its national interests.

Religion has always played a role in American politics since the Founding Fathers, but the shape of this religiosity has varied greatly. The founding of America was certainly imbued with religiosity, but all the talk of the deists concerning "Nature's God" or "Providence" shows clearly that to label it as a specifically Christian event, is a misstatement of fact. Hughes has even argued that the Declaration of Independence made Deism America's national faith.[50] Usually the people of today who see America's origins as Christian belong to the religious right.[51] This misstatement, however, evidences the power of myths. The fall of Lucifer, exile of Adam from Eden, the Exodus, or sin and redemption abound in old stories and myths, and these leak over into the American historical experience. The story of the fall from grace exists in the background so strongly that in this particular case it has managed to shape history. When Reagan chose to portray America as a New Israel, God's chosen land and people, he rearticulated one foundational myth. According to the Declaration of

Independence, America was not specifically exalted in its position but merely wanted to "assume among the powers of the earth the separate and equal station to which the laws of Nature and of Nature's God entitle them."[52] America wanted to be slightly different but just a nation among others, and it was this equal role to other nations in the world, which was its (Nature's) God-given right.

President Dwight Eisenhower once claimed that "our government makes no sense unless it is founded in a deeply felt religious faith—and I don't care what it is."[53] This quotation works as a good example of the functional approach to American religiosity by the political leaders. It is a very compact definition on the public and political uses of religion. Religion is justification for the political system in the United States, and while excluded from the political arena on the rhetorical level, it still offers some of the most crucial cornerstones of the American infrastructure. One could simplify things by saying that it does not actually matter, which religious doctrine or denomination one observes and believes in, as long as one believes in religion itself. Mead claims that in a religiously pluralistic America, whenever one talks or writes about religion, it has to be precisely this "religion in general," forced upon the people by the American experience.[54] The belief of a citizen provides the society with internal order and offers a politician a resource to tap into.

According to Phillips, Christianity in general, but especially Protestantism, has always been evangelical or of missionary nature with a streak of racialism. "Some message has always had to be preached, punched of proselytized."[55] In Reagan's case the message was for both God and freedom, and he spoke just as fervently for both. "This is a great time of year because it gives me an opportunity to get out and around and spread some gospel."[56] The mental association between the religious right and Reagan was easy to establish, since Reagan constantly spoke of revival and reawakening that are taking place in America. This part of Reagan's narration resonated well with the ideas of the religious right, who were worried that America is losing its spiritual characteristics and values.

> There is no need in our land today greater than the need to rediscover our spiritual heritage. Many nations in the past centuries have exchanged their gods for other gods, but no nation has ever exchanged its god for no god at all and lived to add further pages to its history.[57]

Great Awakenings and religious revivals have historically within the American culture been tied to periods of radical political change. In the words of William McLoughlin, "Awakenings begin in periods of cultural distortion . . . when we lose faith in the legitimacy of our norms, the viability of our institutions and the authority of our leaders in church and state."[58] For a country that prides itself for its pragmatic nature, it is surprising that spiritual, ideological, and religious factors have always been able to release enormous energies throughout American history.[59] The First Great Awakening started to bring politics and religion together, the Second started laying the foundations of evangelical Christianity and the myth of the Christian nation, but it was finally what some sociologists call the America's Third Great Awakening (but McLoughlin the Fourth[60]) that saw the return of Christian fundamentalism in a new wave. Moral Majority and later Christian Coalition led the infusion of new religious viewpoints into politics. This time it was not of their own particular creed they advocated but values that supposedly could be shared by all persons of faith.[61] Jimmy Carter rode on the crest of that wave into presidency as the first modern president to openly speak of being born-again.[62] In his due time Reagan called for an "awakening" and a "revival" and his era, besides being situated in the timeline at the time of the aforementioned awakening, was certainly a time of stress both militarily and economically and ripe for change.

> I came into office thinking that—for some time I was thinking that there was a hunger for a spiritual revival in America, and I think that has taken place. I hear from more and more people talking about the pride they have in country.[63]

In the communist world religion has sometimes been called "opium for the people," but while Reagan spoke of "revival" and "reawakening" of spiritual values and spiritual America, he used religion and freedom rather like amphetamine. Reagan wanted to electrify the nation, raise it from its slumber, imbue it with energy, and prevent it from falling asleep again. "At an important moment in our history, we set forth together to awaken our nation and rally her spirit."[64] Reagan's America should be "a nation forever young, forever bursting with energy and new ideas, and always on the cutting edge, always leading the world to the next frontier. This quality is vital to our future as a nation."[65] America is set for another "high," and religion is the propellant and catalyst for these hyper effective times. In his era, "in the past few years our country has seen a rebirth of energy and freedom—a great national renewal."[66] At the same time, to pursue the analogy, Reagan wanted the citizenry to share his vivid illusions of what America once had been, and how it could soar even higher in the future. While Reagan detested illegal drugs, this was one high that Americans should experience. And why not, since it is a part of his story logic that "I believe this country hungers for a spiritual revival."[67]

For Reagan only spiritual and religious values can bring about "rebirth of a nation, the revival of the independence, vitality, and resourcefulness that tamed a savage wilderness and converted 13 small struggling colonies into what Abraham Lincoln called 'the last, best hope of Earth.'"[68] Reagan claimed that a spiritual revival had taken place, because people were again talking about the "pride they have in country." In other words the revival he had in mind was first and foremost the revival of American pride in itself. For Reagan to believe in America is a part of believing in God and worshipping Him, because America is His Promised Land. Therefore, the pride people have for their country, patriotism, nationalism, whichever term one wishes to use, is religious by nature in the American context. This has to be understood to grasp the meaning of Reagan's political storytelling.

Reagan argued that "some suggest we should keep religion out of politics." But he added: "Well, the opposite is also true. Those in politics should keep their hands off the religious freedom of our people."[69] Church is strong enough to stand on its own, but it must steady the political structure. The way a person practices his religion is not of importance, but the same moral arguments, stands, and obligations should exist both in the private and the public life, which are influenced by religion.

> If you practise a religion, whether you're Catholic, Protestant, Jewish or guided by some other faith, then your private life will be influenced by a sense of moral obligation. And so, too, will your public life. One affects the other.[70]

The nondenominationalism typical to American religiosity makes it easier to blend politics and religion together in many senses. Since there are no sharp theological doctrines, the boundaries of religious sentiment are not clearly established either. The same applies in turn to the relationship between political doctrines, or the lack of them, and the political sentiments. At the same time two things happen. The two "guidelines to good living" blend and both religion and politics seek to compensate for the vagueness of the other by becoming more explicit themselves, while perhaps still remaining imprecise. Just as Durkheim wrote, the sacred tries to infiltrate the profane, but this goes both ways. That is why Americans have politically active preachers and preaching politicians. As Boorstin argues, "For those who find it difficult to express their political ideas, there is no reason why they should not expect the deficiency to be made up by their religious preachers."[71] Religion should play a part in shaping politics, but Reagan seems to deny the right of politics to shape religious belief.

> The churches of America do not exist by the grace of the state. . . . They have their own vantage point, their own authority. Religion is its own realm. It makes its own claims.[72]

The state has no say in matters of religion, but since religion is the basis of moral order, it should with its own authority speak out on political issues. It is not a state church Reagan called for but active participation by all religious leaders in discussion on faith and values that should guide politics.

> I believe that politics and religion are related, because I do not believe you can function in politics without some sense of morality. It is through our religious beliefs that our moral tradition in the West is descended. While a legislator or a President may not bring to his politics the specific tenets of his particular faith, each of us brings a code of morals to bear on our judgments. There is much talk in my country now of religion interfering with politics. Actually, it is the other way around. Politics . . . has moved across the barrier between church and state and has invaded the arena of religious beliefs. Most of Western civilization is based on principles derived from the Judeo-Christian ethic.[73]

Reagan's religiomythical message was able to create a religious master narrative that for at least the duration of the 1980 presidential cam paign totally dominated the religious storytelling. It is useless to evaluate which candidate was more religious, but it is a fact that Reagan managed to produce stories that touched the hearts and minds of the religious citizenry better than Carter.[74] The results in the 1984 campaign were even more stunning, since against Carter's vice president, Walter Mondale, Reagan won the votes of more than 80 percent of white evangelicals, 73 percent of white Protestants, and 55 percent of Catholics. In this election Reagan lost some Jewish votes to Mondale but only the black vote; both Protestant and Catholic remained in large numbers on the side of the Democratic candidate.[75] It is evident from these figures that Reagan's religious message only gained more acceptance and credibility during the first four years of his presidency, but he still remained unable to reach the black population with his stories.

Reagan was able to shape presidential campaigns and politics for years to come. It was to a large degree a matter of his support that his vice president George H. W. Bush got elected in 1988. Bush was able to consolidate his Christian-right support for the nomination against such a religious figure as Pat Robertson and later carried this support to the general election as well.[76] When Bush was beaten by Bill Clinton in 1992, William Safire observed that "never has the name of God been so frequently invoked, and never has this or any other nation been so thoroughly blessed, as in the 1992 campaign."[77] Ironically, Clinton has been called Reagan's best pupil, because he adopted so much of Reagan's style.[78] George Lakoff has argued that religion is the one thing the Democratic Party is not able to use to their advantage, and that the Republican Party repeatedly misuses it,[79] but in 1992 Clinton, a Southern Baptist, managed to use very Reaganesque rhetoric and storytelling. In his address at the Georgetown University he spoke of "a new covenant" between "the people and their government."[80] The "new covenant" became more or less a slogan for Clinton, and he also used the "great crusade" expression coined by Reagan. While he undoubtedly tried to reach the votes of the evangelical and fundamentalist Protestants, who rarely vote for Democrats, his approach astonished the Republicans, who have always been more adept to use Christian imagery to their advantage. This led the 1992 election to a veritable "Bible-race."

Herberg argued, using Eisenhower as an example that the fusion of political and spiritual leadership in the person of one national leader is not in accord with neither the Judeo-Christian tradition nor the tradition of the American democracy. Nevertheless, he acknowledges that since religion is the spiritual side of being an American, "why should not the President of the United States be hailed as the spiritual leader of our times?"[81] It certainly looks like spiritual leadership has increasingly become a part of what the presidency is all about. Reagan was just one of the most effective spiritual leaders, but essentially the path has been trodden by figures as unlike each other as George W. Bush and Bill Clinton. If America is indeed a nation with the soul of a church, there is a need for a "Pastor to the Nation"[82] to reside in the oval office. Reagan slipped easily into this role and was entirely comfortable acting it. Since growing secularism has paradoxically led to growing religiousness, a touch of religiosity is able to make the leadership aspect of the presidency more effective.

Reagan's Personal Faith and Beliefs

He was very spiritual and he believed in God, of course, and he prayed a great deal. . . . He prayed every time a plane took. He'd sit and look out of the window and he'd look lost in his thoughts but he was praying. And aides would come to him to say something and I'd wave them off, and let him have his prayers.

Nancy Davis Reagan[83]

We can never know anything certain about the inner religious life of someone else, since religious matters are never dealt with per se, but only as expressions and performances, written, oral, literal, or just acted out. These may have been carried out in just that particular manner for many purposes, some of which can be purely political. Religious faith turns into a story about that faith. That is why the creed of the president, or rather the denomination he belongs officially, does not give us anything unless we examine the story of that faith. As Ira Chernus claims, creeds do not matter for most conservative Christians, but the story does.[84] Being "born-again" relies heavily on the story itself and the power this story has. To be born-again one joins "a narrative tradition to which you willingly submit your past, your present and future as a speaker. [The truths of Christianity create] a world that is not merely evoked, but actually constructed by the story."[85] The shape of the religious belief becomes secondary to the story told about it, and thus the story has great power in shaping the storyworlds of faith that join together to form a storyverse. Storied faith becomes more crucial than the faith experienced.

Simultaneously religion shapes the life story of a person as well. Jerome Bruner argued that "religious instruction and other interventions in a life may often have such profound effects in changing a person's life narrative."[86] The autobiographical narrative is to a large degree influenced by the context in which the person lives. His religious affiliation or cultural connections may be raised almost to status of a "coauthor" or an "editor" of the life story. In Reagan's case his boyhood conversion into a Disciple may have shaped his life story profoundly. He was born-again and partially as a result dated the daughter of the local minister and even went to college in Eureka, a small community college run by the Disciples of Christ. Another such event of religious intervention was Reagan's survival from the 1981 assassination attempt after which he claimed to have realized that "whatever happens now I owe my life to God and will try to serve him in every way I can"[87]

Reagan used the mechanisms of belief as a political tool to provide more credibility to his narration. Therefore, this section deals with his religious convictions and other beliefs. It has often been questioned if Reagan had any faith at all, and that is why a short look into Reagan's faith is necessary. Michael K. Deaver, a close aide of Reagan for three decades, wrote his own memoir on Reagan and chose to call it "A Different Drummer." The title does not refer to Reagan himself, but the fact that, according to Deaver, Reagan was guided and inspired by "a profound spiritual faith that grounded him and left him with a nearly perpetual peace of mind. . . . His steady sense of purpose grew from him complete acquiescence to a drummer only he could hear."[88] Whether it should be called predestination, fatalism, or mysticism, Reagan felt called and ordained to be president, and this belief gave him a solid rock to stand on mentally and emotionally. We cannot hear the beat of the drum, and thus we focus on those beliefs Reagan chose to communicate to others.

Of all the radio addresses Reagan gave between the governorship and the presidency only a few dealt with religious matters. The same applies to his speeches before the governorship.[89] But what he focused on, according to Mary E. Stuckey's analysis, was "reaffirmation and purification of America and the American Dream."[90] It was only later when the two began to blend into each other. Reagan rarely publicly paraded his faith or merchandised it for political purposes outside a political office of governor or president.[91] Privately he was more vociferous concerning faith, and during the governorship when asked if he knew the Lord Jesus or only knew "about" him, Reagan replied, "I *know* Him." Reagan claimed that his faith is very personal, and that he had had a personal experience when he invited Christ into his life and made him a leader of his life.[92] While the governorship of California was Reagan's dress rehearsal for the biggest role in his life and a tryout for Washington, it was also a time when he began to occasionally express his faith publicly. In his Inaugural speech he quoted Benjamin Franklin's words about any man who would dare to bring the teachings of Jesus Christ into public office revolutionizing the world and promised to follow the example of the Prince of Peace but would not be so presumptuous as to imply that he would do so completely.[93] The same week at a prayer breakfast he said that "faith in God is absolutely essential if a person is to do his best. Sometimes we are afraid to let people know that we rely on God. Taking this stand just seems to be a logical and proper way to begin."[94]

The founder of Reagan's denomination, the Disciples of Christ, was Alexander Campbell, who is described by Kelly as "a man of great

scope and curiosity and a powerful and persuasive orator, . . . a cru-
sader, an educator, a theologian, a populist, and a patriot."[95] It is in a
way ironic that, while Campbell wanted to return all Christianity to
the presumed practices of the early primitive church and put an end
to the plenitude of religious denominations, he ended up creating a
denomination of his own thus further splitting the church. Disciples of
Christ is primarily a form of restoration Christianity. While almost all
of the new Christian movements have proposed a return into an early
or pure New Testament Church, the Disciples added their own touch
of downplaying the importance of the Old Testament. Reformers
chose names such as Christian Church, Churches of Christ, and
Disciples of Christ for their sects, and their modern descendants are
deeply divided among themselves, while the congregations remain for
an outsider difficult to distinguish from one another.[96]

The boom of the Disciples began in 1832, when a majority of
Western and Southern Christians blended with them under the leadership of Alexander Campbell. He was an Ulsterman, who had immi-
grated to the United States in 1809 and molded a set of distinctive
doctrines and practices for the movement. In the beginning it was
his father Thomas, who practically founded the Disciples movement
by writing and presenting a "Declaration and Address," as a constitution for them and a plan for achieving the unity for all churches.
His argument was that the New Testament was to be followed in
all it prescribed and to resist innovation in areas, where it offered
no guidelines. The Disciples should have no terms of communion,
except those expressly taught by Jesus. Later on the Disciples turned
this advice into a formula: "Where the Scriptures speak, we speak;
where the Scriptures are silent, we are silent."[97] One of the things
Reagan certainly shared in faith with the father of his church, was
the belief that the Bible was humanly written, but divinely authenti-
cated. Where their views differ probably the most, is in the fact that
Campbell advised Christians not to take an active role in politics,
because he considered it to be a corrupting practice.[98]

Campbell was a millennialist and had growing hopes for the coming millennial age. His idea of "millennium" was a thousand-year
period of great happiness for the church, but he did not believe that
this great age would be inaugurated by the miraculous return of
Christ. Like Reagan, he rejoiced of all examples of material progress
America made, and despite periods of disengagement from American
party politics, he remained an enthusiast for American democracy.
Hughes writes that the myths of manifest destiny and the millennial
nation were collapsed by Campbell into one unifying vision.[99] He

argued that Campbell typified the thoughts of a whole generation of Americans for whom the millennium would be "a golden age of peace and tranquility precisely because Anglo-American civilization, the Christian faith and the English language would dominate it."[100] Campbell was not a coherent dogmatist or theologian. He can be quoted for many different purposes, but usually he looked forward to religious, moral, and political reforms with the Anglo-Saxon civilization as the hope of the world.[101] In this matter he saw eye to eye with Reagan who repeatedly argued that America "still offers that last, best hope of mankind,"[102] and that this is the promise of future.

> America has already succeeded where so many other historic attempts at freedom have failed. Already, we've made this cherished land the last best hope of mankind. It's up to us, in our generation, to carry on the hallowed task.[103]

Campbell saw that a contractual sense of authority, obligation, and allegiance confirmed the cohesion of the society and enabled it to perform its duties, while the institution of civil government was legitimated. Politics was undergirded by an absolute dependence of the sacred sphere, but that sphere did not dominate politics; it merely provided authorization.[104] Except the need for authorization, Campbell wanted to keep the realm of politics separate from the realm of religion. In the early church the people patiently waited for the Second Coming and meanwhile allowed themselves the more earthly blessings of responsible self-government. Generally, in Christianity politics has been regarded as the "necessary buffering of the earthly city against chaos, a temporal space to be protracted as needed for the kingdom to come."[105] Reagan was not so naïve in his beliefs that he did not see the corruptive side of the political world. He once even remarked that "someone once said that politics is the second oldest profession. I'm beginning to think it bears resemblance to the first."[106]

While it would be tempting from the European perspective to label Disciples of Christ just as one of the multitude of American sects, already by 1950s the Disciples had established themselves as a respected church, indeed one among "the pillars of Protestantism."[107] The nineteenth-century Disciples often interpreted America's destiny prophetically. Their faith in the American nation was identified closely with their Christian faith. They often saw America's role as "a democratic mission to save the world from autocrats."[108] Herberg saw the Disciples of Christ as a group that "was entirely American, emerging in response to American conditions."[109] The Disciples of

Christ as a denomination had an impact in Reagan's future vision that connected religion and politics. Many themes of the Reagan presidency had been already discussed in the Disciples of Christ church for 150 years. The "shining" city Reagan spoke of, was certainly the same city and "beacon of light" Campbell had advocated as a "light unto nations."[110] These very same expressions were often used by Reagan to describe America.[111] For Alexander Campbell and Ronald Reagan alike, the moving speeches they made of the City on a Hill depicted the belief that God had chosen Americans to fulfill a mission on earth. Reagan was not even the first Disciple to become a president. In 1880 a former Disciples minister James A. Garfield was elected, as a pride for the church.[112]

It is probable that one of the greatest influences of Reagan's personal faith, his mother, had been later in life a convert into Disciples of Christ and thus born-again, like Reagan himself. There are arguments supporting it, like the fact that Nelle Reagan's proficiency in dancing would have been hard to obtain as a lifelong member of a church that disapproved of such an activity. More convincing are the records that she was baptized as a Disciple by total immersion in Tampico, Illinois on March 27 in 1910, less than a year before Reagan was born and undoubtedly had the ardor of a convert in her religiosity.[113] Reagan belonged to the same church as his mother, while his older brother, Neil, was a Catholic after their father.

Well, I was raised to have a faith and a belief and have been a member of a church since I was a small boy. In our particular church, we did not use that term, "born again," so I don't know whether I would fit that—that particular term. But I have—thanks to my mother, God rest her soul—the firmest possible belief and faith in God. And I don't believe—I believe, I should say, as Lincoln once said, that I could not—I would be the most stupid man in the world if I thought I could confront the duties of the office I hold if I could not turn to someone who was stronger and greater than all others. And I do resort to prayer.[114]

While he has in his private life and letters claimed to have been born-again, here Reagan evades the question by claiming that his "particular" church did not use that expression. It is clearly an evasion, since personal faith is a central aspect of the Disciples of Christ. They practice baptism by immersion, and usually these baptisms occur between the ages of 12 and 15. Therefore every member of the church needs to be born-again. Reagan joined the Disciples officially by immersion after reading a book called *That Printer of Udell's.*[115] It is often referred to by Reagan as his favorite book along with the Bible, and he himself claims that it was the book, which stirred the decision in him to join the Disciples of Christ and be baptized, and even further that its author "set me on a course I've tried to follow to this day."[116] Reagan remembers being immersed at the age of 12[117] but was in fact baptized at the age of 11. Later in life he claimed to have had the experience of "being born again."[118] This is not in the American context as spectacular as it may sound to a European. Jimmy Carter had already before his presidency claimed to have been "born again" and thus took the role of the first president of the United States of America to do so.[119] In the mid-1980s some 30 percent of American respondents to the Gallup Poll told that they had been born-again.[120] Despite his inner faith, Reagan did not want to take religion up as a subject in the campaign of 1984 because of the fear of affiliation with the political right-wing Christians. But he did not deny his faith either. Such a move would have been even more damaging than playing up the role of the religion.

One could speculate about the importance of childhood experiences in the development of personality if Reagan did not give evidence of the contrary himself. While the few years in Tampico were his "Huck Finn years,"[121] it was the years spent in Dixon, which provided Reagan with "faith [that] is unshakeable" and "peace beyond description."[122] The writings of Campbell were introduced to Reagan by the preacher father of his high school sweetheart Margaret Cleaver. Reverend Ben Cleaver emphasized God's plan for America and continued to be an important figure in Reagan's life until his death. Reagan called him "much responsible" for the fact that his "faith is unshakeable."[123] Reagan's relationship with the preacher's daughter started in high school, and by all accounts the relationship was a serious one. After high school both young people left for Eureka College, which was to become an object of lifetime affection for Reagan. The college was very small, underfunded, and academically not very competitive, but most important of all, it was a college of the Disciples of Christ. The college life left its imprints on Reagan and would shape the course of his life, but the relationship with Margaret did not last. It withered away after Reagan had graduated and was working in Des Moines and "Muggs" had become a teacher.[124]

When Reagan moved to Hollywood in the 1930, he joined the Hollywood Beverly Christian Church, which was also a Disciples church.[125] He did not constantly attend Disciples churches later in life but nevertheless listed himself as a member of that nomination.[126] Reagan chose to join later the Bel Air Presbyterian Church in Los

Angeles but was simultaneously a student of the type of Protestant sects that believed in and debated about prophecies, and that led to a belief in Armageddon and other phenomenal events.[127] He discussed with Billy Graham among others, whether the next great event of world history would be the second coming of Christ and believed that the founding of Israel as a state in 1948 was one of the biblical signs that the world is entering its last stage in history.[128] Reagan was introduced by his mother-in-law to Graham in the 1950s, and the two men became friends. This friendship was to remain all throughout Reagan's political career, and after Graham's disillusionment with Nixon, Reagan became his main contact in the political world.[129] Graham visited Reagan in the White House informally many times during the two terms and spent nights there as well.[130]

The senior pastor of the Bel Air Presbyterian Church Donn D. Moomaw was another minister in Reagan's life, but he seemed to have the role of a personal friend at least in the same degree as a religious figure. Moomaw was present and especially mentioned in many of Reagan's presidential public occasions such as the dedication ceremony of his presidential library, or his first inauguration. He was even given a role in a presidential committee for physical education, since he was an ex-footballer. Moomaw was a personal friend to Reagan and allegedly shared many moments of prayer and theological discussion with him. Undoubtedly, given this close relationship, Moomaw's ideas of Christianity and political and social issues had an effect on Reagan's narration. Indeed, Moomaw claimed that many of the illustrations used in Reagan's gubernatorial campaign speeches originated in his sermons.[131] Moomaw also claimed that he and Reagan "have spent many hours together on our knees."[132] Cardinal Cooke was another religious figure who was a close personal friend of Reagan. Probably one of the reasons was their shared zeal for pro-life causes. Their meeting in 1981 after the assassination attempt was perhaps the most important between the two men. Mike Deaver arranged the Cardinal to fly to Washington, and he had a one-hour conversation with Reagan in the White House. It was after this meeting that Reagan voiced his idea that

> I've always believed that we were, each of us, put here for a reason, that there is a plan, somehow a divine plan for all of us. I know now that whatever days are left to me belong to Him.[133]

Reagan had privately talked of the same conviction earlier, but this was the first public acclamation that God had saved him in the assassination attempt for a purpose. All his days belong to the Lord, and this is the new zest of Reagan's story. According to his story logic, God had a plan for him, and his survival only proved that his task is not done. He committed the rest of his life to pursuing the vision of global freedom he had so long advocated, and the mere fact that he lived was proof for the doubting Thomases that he was doing God's work under His protection. Reagan referred to a divine plan often in his speeches, and it is evident that in his storyworld God has a plan for every one of us. People were God's instruments. In his autobiography *An American Life*, Reagan made at least four references to the "God's plan" for himself.[134] This is not arrogance or self-centeredness, he simply believed that there was a plan for everyone, and his plan happened to include things like the presidency. All things happened for a reason originating in God. Reagan felt this more profoundly than ever after the assassination attempt.

> I'm also very aware that the Lord certainly was watching out for me on that day [of the assassination attempt]. And I guess—from now on my time is His time. . . . Well, yes. As I say, I think that He has the first claim on my time from now on.[135]

Reagan saw himself as advancing God's plan on Earth, but the details of the plan were to be understood through prayer and intellect. This great plan for humankind included freedom and liberty, but on a personal level, nobody could know the specifics of the plan. "It isn't given to us to know or understand God's plan for each one of us—we simply must have faith in his infinite wisdom and mercy knowing that he has a purpose."[136] Nevertheless, God's plan did not mean that everything was predetermined. During his Governorship Reagan told Oakland Tribune that

> there is nothing automatic about God's will. I think it is very plain that we are given a certain control of our destiny because we have a chance to choose. We are given a set of rules or guidelines in the Bible by which to live and it is up to us to decide whether we will abide by them or not.[137]

Everybody is free to make choices of their own. This suits the mundane realm of politics excellently, since if everything was predestined, there would be no room or even need for politics at all. God gives individuals only guidance, and it is finally up to them to act accordingly with His will and fulfill His plan. What then did this divine plan include for Reagan? Certainly the fall of the Communist system was a part of it. According to longtime aide William P. Clark, Reagan had fully expected Communism to fall in his lifetime, but no credit belonged to Reagan. His administration worked as a team to carry out the Divine Will, but they were mere instruments. Reagan had a certain Arministic twist in his thinking, since for him people will have to work together with God to improve the world according to His will.[138] How, then, was the Divine will and plan to be deciphered?

Alexander Campbell wrote that "the words of the bible contain all the ideas in it."[139] But human intelligence has to play a part, since "the words and sentences of the Bible are to be translated, interpreted and understood."[140] Thus the Disciple becomes a story recipient, with the responsibility on translating the God's will from the metanarrative of the Bible. Campbell saw the Bible as "to the intellectual and moral world of man what sun is to the planets of our system,—the fountain and source of light and life, spiritual and eternal. There is not a spiritual idea in the whole of human race that is not drawn from the Bible."[141] Reagan believed alike that the Bible was of divine origin and a source for wisdom and guidance.

> Can we resolve to reach, learn and try to heed the greatest message ever written—God's word and the Holy Bible. Inside its pages lie all the answers to all the problems that man has ever known.[142]

Reagan considered the Bible to be the complete set of guidelines for all of the problems one faces in his life. While he calls for everyone to study this "greatest message ever written," it must be stressed that according to his faith, the Bible does not read literally, but human intelligence has to be used in translating its meaning. For Reagan this translation produced for example a belief in creationism. He seemed to believe that if the world and its inhabitants were not created in six days, at least it should be taught in schools as a viable alternative to the theory of evolution.[143]

> I'm accused of being simplistic at times with some of the problems that confront us. But I've often wondered: Within the covers of that single Book are all the answers to all the problems that face us today, if we'd only look there. "The grass withereth, the flower fadeth, but the word of our God shall stand forever."[144] . . . It's my firm belief that the enduring values, as I say, presented in its pages have a great meaning for each of us and for our nation. The Bible can touch our hearts, order our minds, refresh our souls.[145]

Reagan quotes here Isaiah, who seems to be one of his favorite prophets. The quotation refers to people being as grass, because the spirit of the Lord bloweth on it and makes it wither, while the word of God is eternal and unchanging. The "enduring values" presented in the Bible have meaning for both America and Americans themselves, and some of those values have indeed been "Americanized" in Reagan's story logic.

> I believe that faith and religion play a critical role in the political life of our nation and always has. . . . Those who created our country, the founding fathers, and mothers, understood that there is a divine order which transcends the human order. They saw the state, in fact as a form of moral order and felt that the bedrock of moral order is religion.[146]

When Reagan was asked to reveal his favorite Bible verse, he quoted John 3:16 from memory.[147] Almost equally treasured was II Chronicles 7:14. Reagan quoted this verse often in his presidential speeches and had used this very verse in his inauguration, when the president places his hand on an open bible for the swearing in. The Bible used on the occasion belonged originally to Reagan's mother, who had written next to this verse the words, "A most wonderful verse for healing the nation."[148] Reagan further claimed that the verse "is ever present in my mind."[149]

> One of my favourite passages in the Bible is the promise God gives us in second Chronicles: "If my people, which are called by my name, shall humble themselves and pray and seek my face and turn away from their wicked ways, then will I hear from heaven and will forgive their sin and will heal their land." That promise is the hope of America and of all our people.[150]

Reagan's quote refers to King Solomon building a temple for God, and God choosing it as his house, so that His eyes and heart shall be perpetually there. Because of that God's eyes are open, and His ears attentive to prayers made in that place.[151] In Reagan's narration God will listen and hear and fulfill the prayers of Americans, if they only humble themselves in prayer, just because America has become the new temple built for God. America has become a sanctified shrine in the shape of a New Jerusalem, and all its citizens need to do is pray and cast aside their sinful ways, and God shall perpetually reside among them.

William P. Clark claims that Reagan's favorite prayer was the Universal Peace Prayer of Francis, and that he had often shared this prayer with Reagan during the presidency. "Lord, make me an instrument of your peace . . . where there is doubt, let me sow faith. Where there is despair, let me sow hope. Where there is darkness, let me sow light."[152] Reagan saw himself as a man of peace, and that was the gist of his favorite prayer as well. Prayer was not always a private issue for Reagan. In a speech fittingly renamed as "Time to Recapture our Destiny," given at the Republican National Convention when Ronald Reagan accepted the nomination for president, he was able to surprise everyone with the use of public prayer.

> I'll confess that I've been a little afraid to suggest what I'm going to suggest—I'm more afraid not to—that we begin our crusade joined together in a moment of silent prayer. God bless America.[153]

When quoted here, the text does not seem as radical as at the moment it was presented. Reagan led the Republican National Convention into a prayer with bowed heads that he ended not with amen but by asking blessings for America. The event was broadcasted on national television, and thus millions of Americans were shown how a presidential candidate turned his campaign into a "crusade" and linked his personal religious vision with the party's political destiny. Such a blend of religion and party politics was almost unheard of even in America. Reagan is the person who started among the US presidents the trend of leading the audience and the public in general into prayers in their speeches. As Mika Aaltola writes, the element of prayer lends a sense of introspection and mystical experience to these speeches.[154] Many other presidents had used prayers as part of their speeches, but leading the audience into prayer was a novelty that brought the element of crusading into presidential politics.

> America is too great for small dreams. There is a hunger in the land for a spiritual revival, if you will, a crusade for renewal.[155]

Just because America is so great, no small reforms in politics are acceptable. America's dreams must be gigantic, and they can only be reached with the help of God and by remaining true to the spiritual values. This scope of the dream and vision, and its profound nature as practically divine, calls for total renewal instead of just making changes here and there in the policies. This enables Reagan to use words like "revival" and "crusade" with all their religious connotations. Reagan seeks to evoke these connotations in his listeners. These words bring up strong images. What all revivals share between each other is a "sense of acute dissatisfaction with the current social and political order, and all rely on a common set of biblical stories."[156] Reagan's was a revival of old, faith-based, and time-tested values, crusading and fighting for the "right," for a Divine agenda. "Between us, we can wage a moral crusade—a crusade that we must wage, not for political victory, but because freedom itself is at stake."[157] A crusade means purely standing up proudly and doing God's work. It is fighting, but Reagan's storyworld is so far removed from killing the nonbelievers that the story is like the one of St. George slaying the dragon. American crusading is fighting against a force of nature, or a source of evil, that lacks all human characteristics.[158] Crusading is an idea of noble fighting on the side of God for the right values that has no evil intentions and no evil outcomes. In Reagan's narration crusades were practically given a new meaning, but America was to hear a lot of similar concoctions later on during the Reagan era. The number of public prayers by Reagan grew constantly during his presidency. While the number of Biblical references and mentions of God remained relatively constant, the rise in the number of public prayers during the second term as compared to the first was an interesting phenomenon. At the same time the fire and brimstone of crusading and revivals diminished. Prayer increasingly replaced other religious narratives and storylines as the "revival" proceeded.

Reagan believed in intercessory prayer that gave him "a strength that I otherwise would not possess."[159] He claimed to "have benefited from it. I have, of course, added my own prayers to the point that sometimes I wonder if the Lord doesn't say, 'here he comes again'."[160] Reagan saw prayers as having a meaning in a truly spiritual sense, but naturally he did not shy away from using narratives in the form of prayer to advance his policies as well. Prayers had a tremendous power.

> It is said that prayer can move mountains. Well, it's certainly moved the hearts and minds of Americans in their times of trial and helped them to achieve a society that, for all its imperfections, is still the envy of the world and the last, best hope of mankind. And just as prayer has helped us as a nation, it helps us as individuals. In nearly all our lives, there are moments when our prayers . . . help to see us through and keep on the right path. In fact, prayer is one of the few things in this world that hurts no one and sustains the spirit of millions.[161]

America is destined for greatness in Reagan's narration, but it can only be achieved through belief in God. He is the decisive factor that has brought America through every great challenge, because Americans have prayed for him in those times of great stress. Reagan both stresses that anyone should not be too proud to pray, for pride in itself is a sin, and that God certainly listens and fulfills the prayers of the American people. God has helped and continues to help America in a special way as the Americans try to reach the American dream.

> We have become too proud to pray to the God that made us. Well, isn't it time to say, "We are not too proud to pray." We face great challenges in this country but we've faced great challenges before and conquered them. What carried us through was a willingness to seek power and protection from One much greater than ourselves, to turn back to Him and to trust in His mercy. Without His help, America will not go forward.[162]

Often prayers are used to request for divine assistance in one form of other. The one praying asks for strength, guidance, or a concrete act. Petition is one form of prayer, and can take the role of a direct petition, in such a case where petition concerns oneself, or the larger community one belongs to.

> And because faith for us is not an empty word, we invoke the power of prayer to spread the spirit of peace. We ask protection for our soldiers who are guarding peace tonight—from frigid outposts in Alaska and the Korean demilitarized zone to the shores of Lebanon.[163]

Often a desired future event is narrated in a prayer, as when Reagan prays for strength and success in his upcoming summit meetings. These took place in public addresses as well as in the privacy of Reagan's diary. Just prior to the Geneva summit Reagan wrote down a simple prayer "Lord I hope I'm ready & not over trained."[164] Often the public invocations of prayer were more eloquent, but in both, the acceptance of the American agenda by the Soviets, can be seen as the desired event. When, as in the case of the "Evil empire" speech, Reagan prays for the Soviets, or later for Gorbachev, the prayer can be considered an intercession on behalf of the one prayed for. Third most common type of prayer is praise or giving thanks. In many cases the different types of prayer are combined into one, and the outcome of this is a more complex narrative to emerge from the act of praying. The narrative and the prayer interpenetrate, since narrative emerges through, and is inflected for prayer, and the prayer in turn takes on features of a narrative[165]

> America was founded by people who believed that God was their rock of safety. He is ours. I recognize we must be cautious in claiming that

God is on our side, but I think it's all right to keep asking if we're on His side.[166]

The choice of words is essential to note here. American's must only "be cautious in claiming that God is on their side." Reagan does not say that the claim should not be made. God is, according to his story logic, on American side in some issues. It is necessary to check and recheck that America does not stray from God's plan for it, but once righteousness is reconfirmed by this self-evaluation, such claims about Divine backup can be made. In Reagan's stories, God was unquestionably on the side of the settlers, and as long as America remains true to its original set of values and beliefs, He continues to provide safety for America. This is not typical political rhetoric but rather an attempt to draft new political theology.

An early attempt to articulate the relationship between God and America was made by Abraham Lincoln, who once told visiting clergy, that there was no reason to worry whether God was on his side or not, because "the Lord is *always* on the side of the *right*," and therefore his constant prayer was that "I and *this nation* should be on the Lord's side."[167] Lincoln at least expressed anxiety about his nation's position vis á vis God. Wilson claims that Lincoln profoundly articulated the moral dilemmas of the nation.[168] Reagan on the other hand did not see any moral dilemmas in his mythical America. Reagan asserts that as long as America is on the side of the Lord, all its actions are permissible, because it remains on the side that is right.

> They [the soldiers who died in Grenada] were not afraid to stand up for their country or, no matter how difficult and slow the journey might be, to give to others that last, best hope of a better future. We cannot and will not dishonor them now and the sacrifices they've made by failing to remain as faithful to the cause of freedom and the pursuit of peace as they have been. I will not ask you to pray for the dead, because they're safe in God's loving arms and beyond need of our prayers. I would like to ask you all—wherever you may be in this blessed land—to pray for these wounded young men and to pray for the bereaved families of those who gave their lives for our freedom. God bless you, and God bless America.[169]

The entire Reagan speech to the nation on prime time television, from which this quotation is picked out of, gives us an example of Reagan's storytelling at its best, combining patriotism and idealism with passion, and most importantly, prayer. The events in Grenada were some of the most important during Reagan's presidency in his process of creating public faith. This speechmaking and storytelling at the crucial moment was a powerful expression on behalf of the civil religion. Reagan combined patriotism and the sacrifices made and led the entire country into a prayer assuming the role of a priest. Moments like this when Reagan not only refuses to narrate the events, but also wants to play a more active role as a religious figure, are the crucial moments when the nature of his belief-based policymaking is most evident. In the Reagan metanarrative God is the basis for both American life and system of governance. God has blessed Americans by giving them among other gifts America, and therefore the people have an obligation to behave in a certain manner in return of these abundant blessings.[170]

In his presidential addresses Reagan often used expressions such as this "Prince of Peace," probably out of respect to those, Jewry in the forefront, who do not recognize Jesus as the son of God. For Reagan personally Jesus was not only a prophet, a great teacher, or a philosopher but also "the promised Messiah, the Son of God come to earth to offer salvation for all mankind."[171] In a similar manner Reagan used "God" in his narration. Any citizen could within his own church believe in the version of God he chose to, but when God was brought into the realm of public, it was seen as necessary that He could work as a unifying force and not be divisive.[172] When Reagan said "God bless America," he used a God that adhered to his own private faith, but more importantly each of his listeners or readers was able to define the God, whose blessings are asked for in accordance to his own preference. Reagan was careful in choosing his expressions so that this "insert-name-of-deity-practice" is almost always available for his audiences.

It has been argued in many occasions that Reagan was not a religious person, because he attended church so seldom during his presidency. According to Reagan his reluctance to attend church services derived greatly from the fact that the extra safety measures, such as arriving in a motorcade or having sniffer dogs search the church, would have caused discomfort for the other churchgoers. In the beginning of his presidency Reagan felt that some answer must be sought to the problem of not attending church.[173] But at the same time he wished for God to realize that he felt as if he was in a temple when being out in the "beautiful forest & countryside."[174] He reflects the same idea in a radio address claiming that "standing in one of the cathedral-like groves of [Redwood] trees is a moving experience and one can feel very close to God and very humble."[175] Reagan's ranch, Rancho del Cielo, was, according to Judge William Clark, "an open cathedral" to him, and Reagan said that "it casts a spell. . . . I think of a scripture line, 'I look to the hills from whence cometh my strength'."[176] The numerous times Reagan spent in his ranch during his presidency had a special importance to him. The ranch was a source of inner, spiritual strength for Reagan, not merely a vacation spot. It could be argued that the God Reagan believed in had at least some aspect of the Nature's God, but it is more likely that Reagan as a longtime outdoorsman just saw the beauty of the nature as one more example of the omnipotence of God.

There has been a lot of talk about Reagan's belief in astrology, which was revealed to the public by Donald T. Regan in his autobiography, where he claimed that practically every move and decision the Reagans made was cleared in advance by a San Francisco astrologer Joan Quigley, so that certain days were declared bad or dangerous and others favorable for action.[177] When confronted by the press on his beliefs in astrology, Reagan repeatedly claimed that it did not affect his policymaking or even his schedules as Regan had claimed. Reagan's explanation was that it was more or less Nancy Reagan's worry about him after he had been shot that she wanted to get over the traumatic experience and know "what does it look like now" occasionally. Reagan claimed that "we made no decisions on it, and we are not binding our lives to this [astrology]. And I don't mean to offend anyone who does believe in it or who engages in it seriously."[178] When asked directly, whether Reagan himself believed in it, the answer was direct but evasive; "I don't guide my life by it, but I won't answer the question the other way because I don't know enough about it to say is there something to it or not."[179] After Regan, many others started talking as well, old acquaintances as well as astrologers, and it is practically undeniable that astrology did play a large part in both scheduling and even creating the Reagan era politics. Reagan had dabbled with astrology for 30 years or more, and thus the claim of "not knowing enough" sounds incredible.[180] Larry Berman calls Reagan's relationship to astrology "more than a casual interest."[181] Reagan was inaugurated as the Governor of California at midnight. Personally he claimed that it was because he wanted the first possible moment to take over the governorship, and thus prevent his predecessor from burdening him with supposedly corrupt appointments. If the former governor Pat Brown had wanted to do that, he would have had over two months to make his appointments.

Other explanations Reagan used in different times to explain the odd hour of his swearing in were that there were several football bowl games on television, and he did not want to interfere with those, and that since the previous administration ends at midnight, he did not want to leave the state without a governor for even a few hours.[182] Many people, including the former governor Pat Brown, suggest the reason for this midnight ceremony to lie in the involvement of Jeanne Dixon, who was Mrs. Reagan's astrologer.[183] Wills argues that the timing indeed was due to recommendations from astrologers, but that originally the meaning was to startle by being sworn in as soon as possible. Thus Reagan could be seen "responding to new winds of inspiration but not to magi."[184]

There is no doubt that Nancy Reagan believed in astrology and found this belief to be sufficiently in unison so as not to collide with her religious beliefs. Perhaps Reagan found room in his religious beliefs for astrology as well. But it is more likely that his interest in the subject was less profound.[185] In his diaries Reagan vehemently denies the astrology allegations by claiming that "we have never seen her in our lives & don't know her [Dixon] at all."[186] In this case it might not do to believe Reagan, since Regan alleged it was Nancy who conferred with the astrologist, and Reagan did not have a good memory for even the people who worked in close interaction with him. But to understand what Reagan actually believed in, astrology cannot be left outside the equation any more than the fact that he genuinely believed the ghost of Abraham Lincoln inhabits the White House,[187] or his belief in extraterrestrial life that he brought up publicly in front of such distinguished audience as the General Assembly of the United Nations by declaring that "perhaps we need some outside, universal threat to make us recognize this common bond. I occasionally think how quickly our differences worldwide would vanish if we were facing an alien threat from outside this world."[188] It can be summarized that Reagan held strong personal beliefs concerning a wide variety of topics, and this concoction makes it difficult to pin down his beliefs. One can say that Reagan believed mainly in two things, God and America. They were the objects of his worship. If Reagan as a president was the pastor of the nation, his congregation consisted of all American who "believe as he does in family, work, neighbourhood, peace, and freedom—as he conceives of them."[189] The private and publicly expressed faiths of Reagan were two slightly different creeds, but love of America was the unifying factor in both.

AMERICAN CIVIL RELIGION

> There is something eternal in religion that is destined to outlive the succession of particular symbols in which religious thought has clothed itself. There can be no society that does not experience the need at regular intervals to maintain and strengthen the collective feelings and ideas that provide its coherence and its distinct individuality.
>
> Emile Durkheim[190]

As de Tocqueville has observed, what has long made governments prosper is religion; "there is nothing in the world but patriotism or religion that can make the universality of citizens advance for long toward the same goal."[191] Naturally, the combination of both would be even more effective. Thus politics needs to be able to combine the love of God and the love of country narratively in such a way that loving one means practically the same as loving the other as well. If one's own country can be narratively re-created as the kingdom of God on earth, or at least as something striving to actualize it in this world, the two great motivational factors work for the same purpose.

For Will Herberg, "being a Protestant, a Catholic or a Jew was understood as the specific way, and increasingly perhaps the only way, of being an American and locating oneself in American society."[192] To be American, one must be belong to one of these faiths.[193] He wrote that these are the "three great branches or divisions of 'American Religion'," and together they possess "an underlying theological unity."[194] The foundations of religious faith in America are essentially hospitable to democratic politics. If we ponder upon the limitations of civil, public, or civic religion, it is self-evident that it means and according to Herberg has always meant "the sanctification of the society and the culture of which it is a reflection. . . . Civic religion is a religion which validates culture and society without in any sense bringing them under judgement."[195] Civil religion sanctifies the culture and society by claiming that they constitute an uncontested expression of spiritual and religious values and ideas. This leads to the transformation of religion into *the cult of culture and society, in which the 'right' social order and the received cultural values are divinized by being identified with the divine purpose.*"[196]

This is why Robert Bellah, another influential scholar writing about civil religion, gave up on the concept. Bellah wanted to get Americans to "worship their nation's highest ideals—America as it ought to be—to counteract what he saw as excessive worship of the nation as it was."[197] But when we look at Ronald Reagan's narratives, his mythical America indeed was "America as it ought to be." His narration showed no doubt of his America being a living proof of the highest ideals of the United States. Reagan's mythical America was, in the words of Durkheim, *society hypostasized and transfigured.*[198] As Sidney Mead wrote, patriotism is often confused with idolatrous worship of the state, and my country, right or wrong, is the ultimate idolatry in politics.[199] Thus, while seeing civil religion all too often as misunderstood idolatry from a purely religious perspective, the ultimate and twisted form of national worshipping is crucial from the perspective of political studies. This is what American civil religion is from the perspective of belief-based politics as a way of narrative leadership. It sanctifies the meaning of being American to such a degree that the object of belief is the imagined, mythical community of America and its heroic inhabitants, the Americans. Wilson argues that the entire phenomenon of American civil religion should not be seen as much as a religious movement but rather as a latent political revitalization movement.[200] Political beliefs allow people to live within their political worlds and with themselves without strain.

Narrative is an effective way to produce and articulate meanings used to teach individual citizens "to live a distinctively imaginary relation to their conditions of existence,"[201] so that they will gain a meaningful relation to the social order in which they have to live out their lives. But this relation is nevertheless unreal. The entire social reality a citizen lives in can be both "lived and realistically comprehended as a story."[202] Dominant social groups can produce and control authoritative myths and ideologies based on these myths. There needs to be an adequate supply of stories to represent the reality to reveal its "true meaning." This helps to avoid the society entering a crisis caused by the loss of belief in the social system and the erosion of the possibility to lead meaningful lives within the social culture.[203] Stories become the vessels of transmitting meaning into the everyday lives of the citizenry, imbuing them with a little sacredness.

> There are only three words that are necessary to say. They say all we mean, all we hope for, all we believe in. They are: God *Bless* America.[204]

It is my argument that the American civil religion cannot be conceived as a stable concept, but it gets altered in time and, furthermore, each individual and subgroup of the society interprets it in a different manner. The politician using the mechanisms of belief needs to narrate his version of civil religion just as fluidly. The huge body of literature written about American civil religion can be divided into five different understandings of the concept as follows:

1. "Transcendent universal religion" as Bellah's idea of America as a bearer of universal moral values exemplified.
2. "Democratic faith" as a set of humanistic Enlightenment values (liberty, equality, justice, etc.) treated as sacred and distinctively American, with no reference to a spiritual or transcendent source.
3. "Folk religion" as exemplified by Herberg's American Way of Life. These are a set of beliefs and practices of the ordinary people as they define what being American means for them.
4. "Religious nationalism," where nation becomes the object of religious and patriotic fervour and
5. "protestant civic piety," where primarily protestant categories are used to articulate American nationalism.[205]

While this taxonomy helps us understand the treatment of civil religion within the academia, it does not help us decipher Reagan.

Mostly his civil religious narratives are focused on the concept of folk religion, but he blends all these different interpretations together in his storytelling. America was for him a standard of universal moral values. "For those who seek freedom, security, and peace, we are the custodians of their dream."[206] Likewise, the Enlightenment values had their place in the storytelling; "We are the keepers of the flame of liberty. We hold it high tonight for the world to see, a beacon of hope, a light unto the nations."[207] The American nationalism is just as often articulated in terms of Protestant Christianity's high values; "History is asking us once again to be a force for good in the world. Let us begin in unity, with justice, and love."[208] At the same time patriotic zealotry underlies Reagan's storytelling; "Now, you know, some people—and without wanting to flatter me—have referred to me as a super patriot. Well, I guess maybe I'm old-fashioned, but I don't think you can love America too much."[209] But, this is American civil religion, as Reagan articulated it, and there are practically as many civil religions as there are people trying to determine what it is.

There has been a debate whether civil religion indeed exists anywhere outside the academia, if it is a purely scholarly invention of a term for something that no one else calls anything. But Jonathan Z. Smith argues that the same applies to all religion. "Religion is solely the creation of the scholar's study. It is created for the scholar's analytic purposes of comparison and generalization. Religion has no independent existence apart from the academy."[210] I acknowledge that American civil religion, like any religion or even America itself, exists only as an imagined community; that is, only if people identify themselves to be a part of it.[211]

Ira Chernus sees the American civil religion "as a broad, dynamic field of contending forces rather than an imagined unified tradition."[212] All too often we overlook this pluralistic nature, which applies not only to American religions but also to American civil religion as well. There never was a version of civil religion, which would have encompassed all of Americans. Different subgroups of people have chosen as their points of belonging their own versions of what the American way of life means for them and what role it plays in their lives. Thus, the political narrator needs to narrate the contents of civil religion in multiple ways so as to be able to create a storyverse about the mythical America, and while the interpretations of what America means differ, the importance bestowed on it remains constant.

American civil religion should be understood as a cultural resource that can be activated by discourse for diverse and even contradictory political purposes.[213] It is an encompassing phenomenon to such a degree that practically anyone is able to insert anything within it. This makes the actual study of what form the civil religion takes, if not impossible, then at least fruitless. However, if we see civil religion as a dynamic field of contesting stories, the narratives used in the attempts to define it become politically interesting. Civil religion could, at least theoretically, work as an umbrella of belief, under which all Americans can take shelter and create a sense of community and shared values. Eck argues that E Pluribus Unum should not mean that one religion should be made out of the many. She denies that American unity would require a religious melting pot but argues that the *unum* should be civic oneness.[214] This could be possible by crafting a storyverse of belief in America that would automatically assume some religious trappings. It could be called civil religion but not understood as a religion practiced per se. It would rather be a general feeling of nationalist and patriotic belief as a guideline of behavior.

An American civil religion built entirely on narratives of commonly embraced myths, each citizen could construct a civil religious storyworld to his own liking, and due to the ambiguousness involved in the storytelling imagine that others actually think of civil religion in the same terms, while others, in fact, inhabit perhaps even fundamentally different storyworlds than his. The civil religion, or the American way of life, should not be spelled out in detail, but its characteristics should only be narratively referred to in order to allow people to design them to their own liking. If storytelling gives birth to the civil religious storyworlds, it would be possible to achieve this illusion of universality. Richard Madsen wrote about "contentless consensus" where certain expressions like "the American dream" or "common values" are not defined at all and thus encompass very different contents.[215] Reagan did not want to provide a very binding concept of American civil religion but allowed everyone to choose the storyline they found most pleasing and follow it deeper into "Reaganland." There was no unified civil religion, but an illusion of unity in the mythical America.

American civil religion is rather an attempt to label certain unnamed phenomena and pin them down for academic study. It is a field of diverse beliefs, constantly in flux and forever changing. The storyline I use to enter the story web is Herberg's idea of belief in the American way of life, and I develop the meaning of the American dream in it, arguing that both support and enforce each other. Multiple storylines create a web of various beliefs and interpretations of the American way of life and dream, and they combine into an elaborate storyverse about the meaning of being an American. Some scholars have argued that civil religion has never even existed. And they are right if we treat civil religion as a common set of values. But treating it as a storyverse and seeing the commonality as an illusion created by a Reaganesque crafty narrator opens new vistas before us. American civil religion is a master narrative that creates meanings within the culture, and even if the concept itself has become an empty vessel, the story still has considerable influence. American civil religion has been turned into stories about itself, and these can be put to use in the service of politics.

REAGAN'S VISION OF AMERICAN WAY OF LIFE

> There are many blessings in this good world, but surely the greatest is the one we all share: We're Americans.
>
> Ronald Wilson Reagan[216]

What could then work as a storyline of American civil religion? Herberg offers the answer that a "common religion" for Americans, by and large, is the system familiarly known as the American way of life, which supplies the society in times of conflict with an "overarching sense of unity." American way of life should not be dismissed as a "political formula or propagandist slogan" or an "expression of materialistic impulses."[217] Herberg's definition is suitable from the political standpoint Reagan occupied because of its functional nature. To decipher American civil religion as belief in the American way of life gives a politician the means to effectively turn it into his tool of leadership. The belief is essential, but its contents have to be manipulated, so that instead of living a good life according to the tenets of his faith, the believer should live the American life above all else. From purely religious viewpoint this tendency of religious pluralism degenerating into consistent homogeneity of the lowest level of shared belief is disadvantageous, since the outcome hardly even deserves to be called a religion anymore. Politically it becomes only more advantageous.[218]

Herberg describes the American way of life as "a spiritual structure, a structure of ideas and ideals, of aspirations and values, of beliefs and standards; it synthesizes all that commends itself to the American as the right, the good, and the true in actual life."[219] He uses the term "way of life" to underline "its religious essence, for one's ultimate, over-all way of life is religion."[220] Bellah writes that the civil religion "at its best is a genuine apprehension of universal and transcendent religious reality as . . . revealed through the experience of the American people. Like all religions it has suffered various deformations and demonic distortions."[221] At different times American civil religion has been more suited to describe the American experience or deformed into merely a political tool not consistent with the national collective thought.

I do not argue that Reagan's vision of the American experience was demonic, but a central aspect in his political leadership was distorting reality with storyworlds. How exactly did he attempt to manipulate the beliefs of Americans? In the case of Reagan's narration, the object of faith of the American people is not the state but rather the "imagined community" of America in the sense Benedict Anderson used the term.[222] Some writers like Zelinsky argue that object of faith of civil religion is the state itself as manifested in the government but in the words of Reagan, "We're turning America away from yesterday's policies of big brother government."[223] Paradoxically the story logic of Reagan distances the military and the police from the governmental apparatus by their function to protect the freedoms of Americans while rest of the government is narrated to curb these freedoms. Reagan built the American military strength to an unsurpassed level, and thus that segment of the government got as inflated as the national debt, which was the outcome of the buildup. But in Reagan's storyworld the strong military was not considered to be a part of the "big government." While he had long criticized all government spending and high taxes, there seemed to be no limit to the money he would spend on building up the military capacity.

A weaker America will not be a safer America; our program is peace
through strength. Peace through strength rests on a secure foundation of values. Don't let anyone tell you that we're morally equivalent
to the Soviet Union. This is a democratic country of free people. A
democratic country where all of us enjoy the right to speak, to worship God as we please, and to live without fear. We're not equivalent—we're far superior to any totalitarian regime, and we should be
darn proud of it.[224]

The reason for this apparent paradox lies in the special role Reagan
lays on the military. "Military strength is indispensable to freedom. I
have seen four wars in my lifetime, none of them came about because
the forces of freedom were too strong."[225] The heavy bureaucracy
and big government with its regulations restrict the freedom, which
is the birthright of every American in all of Reagan's stories. When it
comes to military, the uncontested strength of this part of the system
of governance is a protector of all the freedoms an American enjoys.
The effect of individual freedom is what separates the military from all
other areas of government as good. "The soldier, the sailor, the air-
man, and the marine in the United States and around the world are the
ultimate guardians of our freedom to say what we think, go where we
will, choose who we want for our leaders, and pray as we wish."[226]

Rest of the governmental and federal apparatus is portrayed only
as a false god and belief in it is misguided. "And it's not an exaggeration anymore to refer to the almighty Federal Government."[227]
Reagan raises the federal government to the status of a false divinity
by the use of words such as "almighty." Nevertheless, Reagan does
not claim that the federal government, or indeed the United States,
which it is a manifestation of, is in any way omniscient or omnipotent.
It just has raised itself to the status of a false idol or a demigod. In
the thinking of Mika Luoma-aho, a state is practically a God as an
object of political belief and is bestowed with the same divine rights
as God had in the premodern times.[228] This is exactly the idea Reagan
denies in his narration. "I am part of government now, but I am just
as fearful as I ever was of government's capacity for growth and government's appetite for power."[229] As little power as possible should
be delegated to that "great Leviathan" of the federal government.
It should be subservient to the people and their wishes. Instead of
believing in the state represented by the government, Americans are
guided by Reagan to believe in themselves, their families, and communities, and out of this web of belief emerges the mythical America
with its manifest destiny.

> The new patriotism is a positive force that unites us and draws us together—all of us—from every race, religion, and ethnic background. It gives us confidence because it's based on enduring values which we hold so dear—the dignity of work, respect for family, faith in a loving God, a belief in peace through strength, and a commitment to protect the freedom which is our legacy as Americans.[230]

Reagan's patriotism was directed at common values that build a society of Americans. "Together, with faith in each other, with freedom as our guide, there is nothing that we cannot do."[231] Patriotism, faith in each other, and faith in America are as necessary as the traditional religious beliefs. Reagan's society constructing stories were different and unusual, because he chose to strengthen the people's faith in an imaginary concept of America as a formation consisting of small communities. Families formed social circles, and they joined to create cities and other communities, and these communities formed states, which were only joined under the flag of the United States of America. Reagan sought to portray in his stories the relationships of people joined together in small communities and not people as part of the enormous machinery of the federation. Instead of resurrecting people's faith in government, Reagan attempted to get them to believe in themselves as a people. Reagan advocated the old values of the Founding Fathers and stuck to the quotation of "one nation, under God" and the fact that the Constitution grants rights to the government "by the people."

> But our most precious resources, our greatest hope for the future, are the minds and hearts of our people, especially our children. We can help them build tomorrow by strengthening our community of shared values. This must be our third great goal. For us, faith, work, family, neighbourhood, freedom, and peace are not just words; they're expressions of what America means, definitions of what makes us a good and loving people.[232]

People are the heart and soul of America and the factor that makes America not only a great but also a good nation. They create America's policy, which the government merely executes. This emphasis on the will of the people is, at least with its intensity, a unique characteristic of America, as Schmitt noted.[233] In the words of Alexis de Tocqueville, "The people reign over the American political world as does God over the universe. They are the cause and the end of all things; everything comes out of them and everything is absorbed unto them."[234] The same idea of the role of the people is evident in the narratives of

Reagan as well. Reagan found, or at least told he did, his inspiration and the ideal of democracy in the Declaration of Independence. This document set aside the American people in a very distinct manner. They are portrayed as the source of all political power.

> Policies come and go. Leaders will pass from the stage. The endur-
> ing sail and compass of our nation is "We the people." When the
> American people are strong and confident, when their leaders hear
> their voices, America, whatever storms it might be weathering, will
> make it through. It will survive, and it will prevail.[235]

It is "we, the people" who grant their power in the form of sovereignty to the state instead of God. Naturally, this should be the basis
of all democratic thought, but casting a vote every few years to determine who will govern you, is not the extent of power Reagan narrated
the American people to have.

> Here is the genius, the hope, and the promise of America forever and
> for all mankind: "We the People." In our Constitution, we the people
> tell government what it may do and what it may not; the people are
> sovereign, not the state.[236]

God's will is not the basis of government's authority to decree
upon the lives of individual citizens, but the will of the citizenry,
which endows the "powers that be" with all of their power. And
this power can supposedly be taken back at any time by "we, the
people." Everything in American political power emanates from the
people and ultimately returns to the people. The state is just a mid-
dleman, and despite Reagan's status as the president of the country,
he emphasized in his narration that all the power he wields belongs
to the people, and he uses it only according to the will of the people.
Since one of the tasks of belief-based narrative politics is to blend the
worlds of the sacred and the profane into almost undistinguishable
storyworlds, the relationship between God and the people is distorted in the process as well. The people take the position just below
God as the source of ultimate authority. Their will is turned into
something only a little less sacred than the will of God, and perhaps
even one can be deducted from the other with careful examination.
    "We, the people" is still a combination of individuals with their
own ideas and wills. Belief unified the individuals into a community.
When every American prayed as one and turned to God, a new unity
among multiplicity was born.

As thousands gathered in prayer in places of worship and encampments throughout the new land, the dispersed colonists found a new spirit of unity and resolve in this remarkable expression of public faith. For the first time, Americans of every religious persuasion prayed as one, asking for divine guidance in their quest for liberty and justice. Ever since, Americans have shared a special sense of destiny as a nation dedicated under God to the cause of liberty for all men.[237]

According to Reagan's story logic, being an American was such a unifying factor among the Puritan colonists that a feeling of unity and common cause was created among them. America's existence, and the fact of arriving there across the seas was a religious experience in itself, and as such experiences go, strong enough to convince even the doubting Thomases. While the dogmas between the religious denominations of the colonists were different and they were not such a unified whole as the term Puritan used to cover them all implies, Reagan tried to argue that in America they found such a unifying concept that "American" belief could replace for example Calvinist or Protestant belief. Americans could pray together as one for the blessings of God in their "quest for liberty and justice." Reagan picks these words from the Constitution drafted much later to cue the story recipient to believe that liberty and justice were since the dawn of America such values that there was indeed a quest to realize them. Therefore, what America stands for in Reagan's storyverse, is essentially the same as in the beginning of the colonies, and the values he advocated at the time of his narration are exactly the same as he claims to have caused colonists of different denominations to pray and believe in a unified manner. Unified belief in God was born along with the entire imagined unified community of America, and Reagan tried to offer belief in America as a superior object of belief that could accommodate different concepts of worship. Belief in God unites Jews and Christians, but belief in America unites all religious denominations, and the common cause or quest for liberty needs belief in both.

Ours is a nation on many heritages. Diverse religious, ethnic and racial backgrounds find unity in our common belief in the dignity of the individual and our national commitment to self-government.[238]

No matter what God one believes in and what country one's parents came from, there is, according to the story, still common ground for belief. In Reagan's narration the love of freedom was the unifying factor of all Americans.

There must have been a Divine plan that brought to this blessed land people from every corner of the Earth. And here, those people kept their love for the land of their origin at the same time that they pledged their love and loyalty to this new land, this great melting pot.[239]

Reagan failed to see that the metaphor of the "great melting pot" does not work for all Americans. The melting pot metaphor would work if there was only one single version of American civil religion. America is closer to a "salad bowl," where the ingredients are mixed together but do not blend indistinguishably from each other. Reagan's made a false assumption by trying to prove that his vision of the American dream is fitting for all cases. He tried to find common denominators among all citizens and had some success in this. He portrayed Americans as "special people from every corner of the world who had that extra love for freedom"[240] and emphasized the "shared values." There is no other aspect in Reagan's narration that would focus on inclusion of every American as the stories about the American way of life and what America "truly" means. In the past years, a new interpretation on Reagan has begun to emerge among scholars emphasizing the pragmatic, liberal, and inclusive themes in Reagan's rhetoric and policies alike.[241] But the metanarrative of America in Reagan's speechmaking is still understudied.

Reagan's vision of American civil religion was used to improve America's standing in the world and build it up to a superpower again. But the striking fact was his ability to connect with the mood of the nation. His message of the civil religion truly resonated with a majority of Americans. "I believe that faith in God, love of freedom, family, work, and neighbourhood are what made America strong and will keep her free."[242] Soft values, such as family, are tightly connected in his storyverse to other harder, even militaristic, factors such as the powerful army as components of the same plan to keep America free. The family needs to be as strong as the army, and according to the story logic one cannot be strengthened without the other. The value of family is practically a universally accepted norm, and no one would argue about enhancing its status, but its connections to military strength can only be explained with the concept of story web. Inbuilt into American civil religion is the need to keep one's nation strong and not allow it to decline, since, as Niebuhr wrote, "Those who make a god of their nation must despair when the might of their nation crumbles, as every creaturely and sinful might must."[243]

It does my spirit good to be among thousands of Americans from our heartland, people with *faith in God, the United States, and themselves.*

And despite the doomcriers that are abroad in the land, I believe that most of America shares your faith.[244]

In this quote Reagan reveals what the essence of his beliefs is. A new, more secular trinity emerges. One must believe in God, the United States, and Americans as people. To believe in God means according to the story logic that one automatically believes in America as well, since it was created by a Divine Providence, and to believe in America necessitates that one must have faith in its constituents, that is, citizens. There is something divine in each and every American, due to America doing God's work and performing the task of spreading freedom around the globe.

Herberg argues that there are dangers involved in the creation of a civil religion. In the worst case scenario the combining of religion and national purpose into an inseparable goal "generates a kind of national messianism which sees it as the vocation of America to bring the American Way of Life, compounded almost equally of democracy and free enterprise, to every corner of the globe."[245] This would ultimately lead to "the direct exploitation of religion for economic and political ends."[246] Bellah saw this as a grave danger as well. America itself should not be worshipped, and civil religion should be rather seen as a tool for interpreting the American experience. He stated explicitly that American civil religion is "not the worship of the American nation but an understanding of the American experience in the light of ultimate and universal reality."[247] In a sense both theorists are correct. Civil religion can be understood only as a means of grasping the meaning of being American and a guide into how an American should see his role in the greater scheme of things in the reality that encompasses him.

I stick to the definition of Herberg concerning civil religion because of its political potential. Bellah took Herberg's claims about civil religion and used them in totally opposite way. The definition of civil religion as a story web and a field of contesting stories, vying for more prominent positions in producing meanings, allowed Reagan the means to pick and choose characteristics of one of the numerous definitions and play with these meanings. Thus, it is possible to view the highly politicized version of civil religion not only as an interpretative tool of the American experience and its highest ideals in the sense Bellah calls for but also as a validation for the society and its politics without any judgment as Herberg argues. What one views as interpretation of the American experience can be seen as something completely different by another. But an elaborate storyverse where the American experience is not spelled out in detail can contain both interpretations and stories. The story web of inter-pretations that creates the storyverse can bring the narratee from Bellah's idealistic starting point into the realm of civil religion and end in unquestioning love of one's own country with the burning heat of a zealot.

If the American experience is narrated as "democracy,"[248] the American civil religion can be used on a more global scale. The world civil religion of democracy and free markets would be a fulfillment of the American civil religion and not a denial of it. As Bellah argues, a world civil religion "has been the eschatological hope of American civil religion from the beginning. To deny such an outcome would be to deny the meaning of America itself."[249] The spread of democracy, which began much earlier, was effectively carried out on the narrative level in the Reagan era. For Reagan, "The tide of history is a freedom tide. In the last 6 years, not 1 square inch of ground has been lost to communism, and a small nation—Grenada—has been liberated."[250] According to the story logic, freedom and democracy were spreading everywhere and the best showcase was Latin America. It was not so much that democracy itself would have been spread but rather the idea of spreading it by the means of storytelling. Reagan argued that what had begun was

> a new era of freedom: We see it throughout Central and South America—the great democratic awakening that in the last 10 years has brought 90 percent of the people of Latin America into the family of democratic nations.[251]

While the story logic supports this argument, in the real world the Reagan administration provided massive support to numerous totali-tarian regimes, especially in Latin America in both economic and military terms. This same process still continues, hidden between the strands of the story web. By spreading democracy, America is actually spreading both its influence and American civil religion.

> Our mission stretches far beyond our borders; God's family knows no borders. In your life you face daily trials, but millions of believers in other lands face far worse. They are mocked and persecuted for the crime of loving God. To every religious dissident trapped in that cold, cruel existence, we send our love and support. Our message? You are not alone; you are not forgotten; do not lose your faith and hope because someday you, too, will be free.[252]

While Reagan often assured foreign audiences that American mission is not imperialistic or threatening by nature, he still claims here that there are no borders that could stop this mission, since God's family knows no borders. If the mission was carried out in purely Christian terms, this might not seem threatening, since all Reagan seems to do is to advocate spreading the message of God to each and every inhabitant of this globe without artificial man-made restrictions such as borders.

However, since the message of God is about freedom, and America is the essence of concentrated freedom on earth, there is the imminent threat of spreading American values at the same time. This is a version of imperialism, whether only cultural or militarily aided. Hughes argues that the American myths can be used and indeed are used as a powerful force for good. The problem with them arises when the myths become absolutes, and then they can create an irresponsible empire within our global culture.[253] It is when the interpretation of the myths is absolutized, that they become metanarratives. They dominate the storytelling so that the voices of dissent and the suffering minorities cannot be heard. Naturally this type of dominant narrative is what narrative political leadership tries to create, but a certain sense of morality should be included in the story logic to avoid exploitation of the ones who cannot produce counternarratives.

> We have the power and the challenge to expand freedom in all areas of life; freedom of inquiry and thought, freedom for the practice of religion, freedom in commerce.[254]

Reagan's America sought to expand freedom domestically and globally. The problem is that many Americans believe in the universality of Americanism. It is like a super church that everyone can join and, indeed, every human being is a potential American. Thus, expanding freedom means expanding Americanism.[255] To understand Reagan better, he believed that it is only propaganda that depicts Americans as militaristic, while they are the "most moral & generous people on earth. We should be appealing to the world on the basis of morality."[256]

But what was the concept of America for Reagan? "In a very real sense all people who long for freedom are our countrymen."[257]This emphasizes the idea of America being an imagined community. It cannot be clearly defined, and the boundaries such as borders are artificial. For Reagan being an American is a state of mind or state of being instead of a state of being at. Being American and belonging to America is subscribing to a certain set of values, as they are defined and narrated by Reagan. Thus while nobody can become a German or a Japanese, everyone can become an American.[258] Already de Tocqueville noted while studying the Constitution that "the Union is an ideal nation that exists only in minds, and whose extent and bounds intelligence alone discovers."[259] America has never been a fixed geographical concept. It is a state of mind, a utopia to be fulfilled. It is the paradise on earth to come once its potential is in full bloom. "To all who yearn to breathe free, who long for a better life, we think of you; we pray for you; we're with you always."[260] It is worth noticing that, at least on the level of story logic, Reagan recognized that America is not such a culturally united block as often it is believed to be or even as he sometimes himself described it.

> It seems to me that America is constantly reinventing what "America" means. We adopt this country's phrases and that country's art, and I think it's really closer to the truth to say that America has assimilated as much as her immigrants have. It's made for a delightful diversity, and it's made us a stronger and a more vital nation.[261]

Since America is reinventing itself, we cannot allow the American way of life to be any more stable. It has to assimilate new ideas and evolve continuously and allow for the true diversity that exists among Americans.

> First of all, America is really many Americas. We call ourselves a nation of immigrants, and that's truly what we are. We have drawn people from every corner of the Earth. We're composed of virtually every race and religion, and not in small numbers, but large. . . . And this diversity has more than enriched us; it has literally shaped us.[262]

Reagan's America is pluralistic in its nature, but nevertheless unified into a singular concept. Reagan's America was not bound by a geography, indeed, before his presidency he had characterized America as "less of a place than an idea."[263] Everything the immigrants have brought and keep bringing into America supposedly recreates America anew. The diversity of cultures, customs, and ideas shape America, but in the actual process it is the American way of life or the dream, which conforms itself to match these new requirements. The immigrants do not have to give up their beliefs. They can continue to think in the same way, but the storyworld of the mythical

America engulfs their narratives within it, and the "small stories" of immigrants' individual dreams are turned into minuscule particles of the great American dream.

AMERICAN DREAM AS OBJECT OF BELIEF

Is a dream a lie if it don't come true, or is it something worse?
Bruce Springsteen, the River[264]

I don't see an American Dream, I see an American Nightmare.
Malcolm X[265]

In Reagan's storyverse, an integral part of the American way of life is the belief that it contains the possibility of the actualization of the American dream for anyone. The meaning and content of the American dream can be best transmitted in the form of stories, and this narratively constructed belief might be able to escape the traps set by the inbuilt exclusivity of the American way of life. Reagan's special emphasis on the attempt to "get Americans to dream again" was a result of his personal interpretation of America civil religion as the American dream, which simmered just over the horizon for each citizen. The dream is easier to use as an object of belief than the American way of life, since it has not actualized yet but always beckons one forward. Reagan's political leadership was about narrating the American dream into reality to supplant the way of life. Life was supposed to turn into a dream. In Reagan's mythical America dreams did come true, and boundaries between the storyworld of the dream and the real world and the storyworld of the proper way of life reality were ethereal.

What is the essence of the American dream? It is certainly more than the argument of Schurmann. He claims that the American dream is nothing but the nationally spread Californian dream of the house, the car, and the perfect individual.[266] That is only the materialistic, capitalist, and secular aspect of the dream. It is only a single moment of REM sleep, so to say. But Reagan seems to partially agree with this by claiming that "someone has said California isn't a place—it's a way of life. Well that is true, and it's a good way."[267] Since Reagan had been the governor of California, he could narrate himself to be at the zenith of the materialistic American dream.[268] Nevertheless, the American dream as a whole includes a spiritual side as well, and this side is the more dominant and able to persuade people of all walks of life better than the material aspect. Certainly the idea of "rags-to-riches" is a part of the American dream, but the dream itself is wider.

> The dream we share is a great dream—perhaps the greatest dream in all history. It's a dream of broad and open land that offers opportunity to all. It's a dream of a magnificent country that represents a force for peace and good will among nations.[269]

In Frye's words, "The union of ritual and dream in a form of verbal communication is myth."[270] A dream by itself is not communicable. It is only a system of cryptic allusions to the dreamer's own life, but in a dream there is always a mythical element that has a power of independent communication. Myth gives meaning to ritual and narrative to dream and acts also as identification of ritual and dream. Ritual is the archetypal aspect of mythos, and dream is the archetypal aspect of *dianoia*. In other words ritual is a dream in movement, and dream a ritual in stasis.[271] Myth unites the ritual and the dream, and in this unification dream gets limited and thus becomes more plausible and acceptable to the waking consciousness.

Frye goes further in his description of the dream and points out three things about it; first, the limits of the dream are not what is real but what is conceivable, second, the conceivable is the entire world of fulfilled desire liberated from all anxieties and frustrations, and third, and most importantly, the universe of the dream is entirely within the mind of the dreamer.[272] These characteristics of the dream help us to understand why they have to be communicated, and narrative is an effective means to free the dream from its confinement within one mind and spread it further in the social consciousness. As John Kenneth White has noted, in many aspects the American dream has assumed religious trappings, with the president acting out the role of the high priest. Voters have huge expectations that the president should make the dream come true for them, just as it has come true for the president himself.[273] Seen in this manner, it is the sacred task of the president to turn the American dream as the people dream it, into the American way of life for them to live it out. Reagan sought to turn the American dream into reality by using the same concept that arguably had given birth to the entire notion of the American dream. That was the American Revolution, which in a renarrated form would enhance the society. We can easily echo Muir who claimed that Reagan administration was organized to achieve a moral revolution to fuse together the fundamental axioms that Americans used to structure their lives.[274] The most important one was the American dream.

Well, my fellow citizens, today we come together on historic ground to write a new chapter in the American Revolution. We represent men and women of different faiths, backgrounds and political parties from every region of our country—the people who live in Mainstreet, U.S.A, and they are saying "we love this land, and we will not give up our American dream."[275]

Revolution changes form but remains essentially the same underneath. New chapters are continuously added to the saga of American Revolution, and the whole revolution is about the actions people must take to better follow the American dream. For Reagan, participating in the American Revolution is working for the American dream. Thus, all revolutionary work (naturally only in the American context and within Reagan's storyworld boundaries) is a practical way to worship and toil for the American dream. In Reagan's storyworld the concept of revolution has a modified meaning. It is no longer a process of "the King is dead, God bless the King," where one set of rulers is changed forcefully into another, as was the meaning of revolution in Machiavellian times. Reagan's revolution follows the storyline of the French Revolution in which revolution is a way for progress and changing the future for the better. Only Reagan's version is more suitable for the children; since there is limited, if any, violence, and the American idea of revolution does not devour its own children. For Reagan, revolution is a teleological process that gradually makes accomplishments in making the American dream come true. Franz Schurmann likewise saw that the American Revolution originates in "the teachings that dreams are more potent than reality. . . . There has always been a strong dose of mysticism, of reaching for and toward a higher plane, in the American revolutionary process."[276]

It is even more important to know the power, the glory, and the beauty of the real, the spiritual, the American Revolution. It is essential that we—the real revolutionaries—recognize that our freedom and our spiritual inheritance are inseparable—that only where the spirit of the Lord is, "there is liberty."[277]

In Reagan's America, the Revolution freed the Americans to live and to dream. The American way of life and dream are tightly connected to each other. Of course the dream is more intangible, but so it has to be to better serve as something to believe in. It is the ultimate fulfillment of the way of life. Mythical America gives a promise of life turning into a dream. Dreams give birth to ideas, and ideas become reality. There is a sense of almost magical transformation, and the relationship works both ways. Since the dream and the way of life enforce and support each other, it is a cyclical process. While it was the purpose of Reagan to turn the way of life into the dream on the level of the narrative, if not in the real world, simultaneously the dream becomes the way of life. It is within the dream an American should live in Reagan's storyverse, and the dream responds by turning into something solid. With dreaming, the dream can be actualized.

> Our system, tried and tempered by war and every kind of adversity, has been preserved by men and women of uncommon stature and common devotion to a dream. So dream your dreams and dream your ideas for this is truly Camelot.[278]

Some critics argue that the American dream has ended, and America has woken up. The American Revolution led to American civilization, which in turn gave life to the American dream, but with the aid of the dream, the United States of America has become more America than the United States it once was. America has become an empire, and this state of being is a causal stage of development, since the civilization still had the revolution in it. United States has outgrown its nationalistic period in which the dream originated and become a global empire.[279] Perhaps there is some truth to this. But empires dream just as aspiring nations do. At the time of the American Revolution the dream was different than it was in the Reagan era, which is again different from our contemporary conjunction. But dream by a definition is not even supposed to be stable and unchanging. Dreams, like stories, need to be retold and re-created anew when the need to alter them arises. It is the task of narrativized politics to rearticulate dreams and identities to fit the changing times.

The original vision of America as a promised land where dreams would come true was spelled out by John Winthrop to the Puritans of Massachusetts, who fused Christianity with civic doctrine.

> John Winthrop, who would later become the first Governor of Massachusetts, reminded his fellow Puritans there on that tiny deck that they must keep faith with their God, that the eyes of all the world were upon them, and that they must not forsake the mission that God had sent them on, and they must be a light unto the nations of all the world—a shining city upon a hill.[280]

Even after the most overtly religious overtones of Puritanism had faded, the idea of America as New Israel, a country with economic, moral, and political blessings, persisted. While many visionaries in different times have told new versions of the story of the American dream, changing with circumstances and taking different forms of appearance, the story itself will not vanish. Different creeds and interpretations of the American dream are, according to Erickson, "the several denominations of the American civil religion, . . . a potent set of convictions and visions that *translates history into mythology and life into a dream.*"[281] It is part of the American way of life that dreams are fulfilled, and the act of dreaming itself is crucial to being American.

> The poet Carl Sandburg wrote, "The Republic is a dream. Nothing happens unless first a dream." And that's what makes us Americans different. We've always reached for a new spirit and aimed at a higher goal. We've been courageous and determined, unafraid and bold. . . . As Carl Sandburg said, all we need to begin with is a dream that we can do better than before. All we need to have is faith and that dream will come true. All we need to do is act and the time for action is now.[282]

Interestingly what the American dream needs for its fulfillment is not intellect or skeptical analysis or even individual action such as hard work. What it requires first and foremost is belief; faith that it will indeed be actualized. For Reagan the only impediment to the fulfillment of the dream are those that America imposes on itself[283]—by not truly believing in the dream coming true. Such belief is passionate and religious and explains why the American dream acts as the object of faith that can be turned into a powerful myth. As Reagan put it, "All my life, I've believed in miracles. I believe that if you truly have faith, your dream will come true."[284] One of the reasons why Reagan was compelled to use the American dream as a basis of his political storytelling lies in the fact that a society, which becomes the substrate of religious life, cannot be the real society, which is full of flaws and imperfections. The real society is too mediocre, too base to inspire willing self-sacrifice from the faithful. The only society which could inspire such feelings would be a perfect society, in which justice and truth reign, and from which all evil was banished, or in other words the mythical storyverse of America that Reagan re-created. In the words of Durkheim,

> This society is not an empirical fact, well-defined and observable; it is a fancy, a dream with which men have lulled the miseries but never expressed in reality. It is a mere idea that expresses in consciousness our more or less obscure aspirations toward the good, the beautiful, and

the ideal. . . . The society can neither create nor recreate itself without creating some kind of ideal by the same stroke. . . . A society is not constituted simply by the mass of individuals who comprise it, the ground they occupy, the things they use, or the movements that they make, but above all the idea it has of itself. And there is no doubt that society sometimes hesitates over the manner in which it must conceive itself. It feels pulled in all directions. When such conflicts break out, they are not between the ideal and the reality, but between different ideals, between the ideal of yesterday and that of today, between the ideal that has the authority of tradition and one that is only coming into being.[285]

The mythical America has to be perfected. The society must create an idealized version of itself, and the narrator-politician can act as the spokesperson in this process. By turning the society into a storyverse, it is easier to avoid the real and the ideal colliding. It is politically beneficial for the society not to even attempt to create itself as "real," but rather aim for the ideal community, the mythical dream of America.

Boorstin contrasts dreams as visions, to which we can compare reality, with illusion as images we have mistaken for reality. A dream, especially a vivid one, reminds us of how different the real world is, but because illusion is what we would live in, we cannot reach for it or aspire to it.[286] The American dream embodied the hopes of men in America and was inspiring and exhilarating just because it was able to symbolize the disparity between the American possibilities and the hard facts of life. America has always been the land of dreams come true, but that was because "generations suffered to discover that the dream was here to be reached for and not to be lived in."[287] There is a danger in replacing American dreams by American illusions politically. An illusion may be powerful enough to be lived in, but the dream should always be there to aspire to. The fulfillment of dreams should in belief-based narrative politics be a source of inspiration, and not a fact of life.

The dialectical relationship of the way of life and the dream blurs dreams and illusions. Even the way of life is an illusion, because one of the reasons for creating a mythical America through storytelling was to make the citizens feel better about themselves and their nation. Reagan narrated his America so that the people could feel proud of living in that illusion, and the American dream was used to make people strive forward and not remain content within the illusion. Reagan's mythical America tended to turn both the way of life and the dream into illusions, because then one becoming the other was easier to narrate. It is an illusion that the dream is attainable, since in harsh reality outside the story logic the narrative is constructed to ensure that the fulfillment of the dream stays out of reach. Within the storyverse, however, there was nothing that could prevent the actualization of the American dream.

> The world's hope is still America's future. America's future is in your dreams. Make them come true. The only limits are your imagination and your determination.[288]

An essentially true expression coined by Richard Nixon is that it is the "great majority of Americans, the forgotten Americans" who "give lift to the American dream."[289] One has to believe in the American dream to raise oneself with enough diligence and energy from poverty. The same idea essentially applies to the poor inner-city black and the rich suburban white as well, but it is a question of packaging the dream invitingly enough for both types. Aggressive equalitarianism is an aspect of the dream, but one has to ask, whether in real life all Americans are in fact "created equal." Believing in the possibility of the dream coming true for everyone is a religious emotion, and certainly an act of faith. In Reagan's narration, only limits to the dream are given by lack of imagination and determination.

Reagan was skilled in finding the smallest common denominator among Americans, but even he should have burrowed deeper into the national consciousness. Reagan's intention was to set the Americans dreaming again, but the imaginations of all Americans were not equally free to roam. According to Wallace, Reagan's failure was in being the president of all the people that "perhaps he never fully understood *all* of America."[290] This deduction can be made, because the Reagan years were insensitive to the yearnings of the minorities. That is why the American dream Reagan spoke about was not able to win over the majority of the inner-city black population. Reagan was occasionally accused of discriminating against blacks, but close associates deny this. "Not that he was against them, but that he did not understand their problems, their hopes, their dreams, and could get no feel for what an inner-city black must experience," argued Speakes.[291] Reagan's exposure to blacks was relatively slight, and as a whole he did not seem to think that the color of the skin would be any kind of issue. Indeed he went sometimes so far as to argue that there was no racism in the Midwest he grew up in.[292] But the fact that Reagan could not understand the black experience, led to the involuntary exclusion of blacks from his American dream. Since Reagan could not understand that the black dream of America was fundamentally different than his own, he was not able to tell such stories about the American way of life or dream that would have included the blacks. Reagan ended up unintentionally telling a color-blind story, and this was precisely the problem. While Reagan was no bigot, his color-blindness did more harm than good by restricting the ability of his political storytelling to entice the black population. During his presidency Reagan enjoyed considerable popularity, but his opposition seemed to share hatred on an equal scale to his popularity. There was no neutral stance toward Reagan. This derived partially from his inability to get his vision universally accepted. The thoughts and values that form the basis of his version of the American dream were so far from those of his opponents that it bred strong dislike toward him instead of indifference. Nevertheless the complexity and plausibility of Reagan's multiple storyworlds were able to draw support from the majority of Americans and gained acceptance on large scale. The power of Reagan's elusive dreams and visions was the fact that he so fully believed in dreams coming true for other Americans, as they had come true to him. This was an aspect of both his narration and the view of Reagan as a person that all of his closest aids shared. In the storyverse of Reagan,

> Americans have shown the world that we not only dream great dreams, we dare to live those great dreams.[293]

A close aide, Michael Deaver wrote that sometimes Reagan's "simple belief that Americans can become whatever they aspire to be absolutely drove me crazy. Then I would remember where he came from and how inexplicable it is that someone like Reagan could become president."[294] It is easy to compare Reagan with, say, Lincoln. Both were men of the people, born in poor surroundings, and left the lower levels of American society to climb to the summit of power and prestige, the presidency. The Americans find themselves in such success stories, because they are symbols of the American virtues of equality and status. There is a lingering belief that there must be an equality of opportunity for all, and these exemplary men have fulfilled their potential. Everyone's opportunity for social mobility is the "fabric of the American Dream. . . . It does provide the motive power for much of what Americans do in their daily lives."[295] Zelinsky argues further that the power of the US presidency ultimately rests on the symbolism and image of his office.[296] The president of the United States is often in popular culture depicted as the "most powerful man on Earth," but it is a part of the democratic system that his power is restricted by the House of Representatives and the Senate. The president is a figurehead, a powerful symbol of the nation. The president as a leadership figure has to take the role of a living symbol of the American dream to touch the hearts and minds of the populace.

Reagan, as an ex-actor, was fascinated with theatre and acting. It is partially his past in the world of theatrics, which made dreaming so central to his politics. Some of this is explained by Lyotard's conception of the theatre as a dream. In his words it "fascinates and comprises a hallucination giving rise to identification. . . . It is dream intensified, the scene of the dream set on *its* own state, the figural space of fantasy installed in its figural space of representation."[297] Dreaming is central to Reagan's view of the political realm. Dreams have a power and can change the world, like he tells that the American dream can. "We have it in our power to start the world over again."[298] Lyotard elsewhere argues further that both art and politics function "to make people dream, to fulfill their desires (but not to allow their realization), to transform the world, to change life, to offer a stage on which desire (the director) plays out its fantasmatical theatrics."[299] This quotation could be Reagan's thoughts written down. In politics he was able to direct his own plays, and the similar nature of the theatre and his dream-centered politics allowed him to use his acting experience. Statecraft was turned into stagecraft. Like theatre, his politics made the Americans dream again. Wishes were fulfilled, but not concretely realized. The people were led to dream of things either unattainable, or of such oblique nature, that their fulfillment cannot concretely be measured.

> I've never felt more strongly that America's best days and democracy's best days lie ahead. We're a powerful force for good. With faith and courage, we can perform great deeds and take freedom's next step. And we will. We will carry on the tradition of a good and worthy people who have brought light where there was darkness, warmth where there was cold, medicine where there was disease, food where there was hunger and peace where there was only bloodshed. Let us be sure that those who come after will say of us in our time, that in our time we did everything that could be done. We finished the race; we kept them free; we kept the faith.[300]

By setting the goals of the policy that should be clear and concrete in an oblique manner and by creating illusions and dreams, Reagan's politics were able to change the world by altering the storyworld it had been replaced with. The storyworld is, after all, just a dream or an illusion crafted and spun out of words. Politics was the field in which Reagan was able to combine his skills as a storyteller and an actor in creating a fantasmatical stage used to create further dreams and illusions. Reagan's romance with the future and its concepts, be it the Strategic Defence Initiative (SDI), or any other vision of technological breakthroughs, was not focused as much on science as it was on science fiction. It was not a matter of rational argumentation of what could be seen as scientifically possible but rather imagining what science and America might ultimately be dreamed to achieve together.[301]

> But we are a people known for dreaming with our eyes open. We live our dreams. We make them come true. Our ideas and energies combine in a dynamic force. . . . And that force has always enabled America to overcome great odds, and it always will. We just refer to it as the American spirit.[302]

As Niebuhr argues, the American dream is not particularly unique, and every nation dreams similar dreams. But the big dilemma is what kind of political or other power could subject all individual dreams to the American messianic dream, which is informed by "true vision."[303]

> We had a vision to pass forward a nation as nearly perfect as we could, where there's decency, tolerance, generosity, honesty, courage, common sense, fairness, and piety. This is my vision.[304]

Reagan's own standing within the narrative discourse of the entire vision of the American dream was in the role of the narrator or the visionary. The president is an essential part of the dream since, as Fisher wrote, he as "the American hero is the symbolic embodiment of this dream in a single person."[305] He embodies the dream in a way no other public official can.[306] Thus it is of utmost importance that the president uses the "bully pulpit" to reshape, renarrate, and communicate the American dream. Naturally great athletes or rock stars can be embodiments of the dream too, but for narrative leadership of politics, the figure up front needs to be a politician in order to advance the national interests. The president has to be a hero. He must be "a visionary and mythic, a subject for folklore and legend."[307] It is his job to evoke the American dream, and Reagan was not even the first to bring the aspect of dreaming into American politics.

> Once, when Franklin Delano Roosevelt was President . . . he too spoke about dreams. He said one of the reasons the world gets better

so slowly is that too many young people lose their dreams as they
get older. In growing up, he said, they throw away their enthusiasms
and grow away from their ideals. And he said, "You ought to thank
God . . . if regardless of your years, you are young enough in spirit to
dream dreams and see visions. . . ." Hold fast to your dreams, he said,
America needs them.[308]

As a former New Deal Democrat, Reagan admired the politics and
ideas of FDR, and this is where he brought the concept of dreaming into his own narrative. The American dream consists of millions
of individual dreams and visions. America needs to be re-created
and renewed by dreaming. A citizen dreams of a brighter and better
future and achieving that dream in his own life. These dreams, big or
small, join together to create a more unified American dream, where
the objects to achieve are freedom on a global scale and realization of
the American dream in the society at large. The dreams of individual
success are turned into the great American dream where the individual characteristics disappear.

The American dream is a prophecy which yearns to be fulfilled
and, if not renewed, then at least refreshed from time to time. It is at
least partially re-created by the attachment of new individual dreams
to it. Story recipients are guided to dream along certain guidelines,
and they are responsible of many attachments into this storyverse
or the collective dream comprised of innumerable storyworlds of
individuals. Reagan just outlined the superstructure of living right
in freedom and individuals added their own infrastructure of more
detailed plans for success, where the minutiae are included. New
dreams can and need to be added to the American dream, because
only by filling in the minuscule individual dreams and hopes, the collective dream is capable of evolving with the changing times. While
the superstructure of the American dream is told in the same manner
today as during the Reagan or even Wilson presidency, the infrastructure of that dream world is much different because of the different
hopes of people at different times, and their ideas of how to make
the American dream come true to themselves. "We're a nation of
dreamers who've come here, as you have, in search of an ideal: respect
for the liberty and dignity of man."[309] For Reagan all Americans are
dreamers, optimists, and idealists. That is the core of being a member
of his mythical American society.

In a nation as diverse as the United States of America, it is not
possible to create a dream that everyone could use to reorient themselves. Thus one should not spell out the American dream explicitly

but allow everyone to create storyworlds of their own liking from a vast amount of protostories. Like Reagan, other presidents ought to offer a multitude of narrative building blocks for the citizenry. The task of the citizen is to build a storyworld from these blocks like Lego toys. Using some, discarding most, the dream would eventually emerge, and if the storyverse of the American dream narrated by the president is ambiguous enough, no one will be forced to question the legitimacy of their own construction. It is a demanding task to spin such a story web that the resulting storyverse could assimilate and accommodate all the possible storyworlds of the American dream citizens can oneiromantically come up with.

4

BLENDING THE MYTHICAL AND RELIGIOUS INTO POLITICAL

There is one other part of our national character I wish to speak of. Religion and faith are very important to us. We're a nation of many religions. But most Americans derive their religious belief from the Bible—the Bible of Moses, who delivered a people from slavery; the Bible of Jesus Christ, who told us to love thy neighbour as thyself, to do unto your neighbour as you would have him do unto you. And this too has formed us. It's why we wish well for the others. It's why it grieves us when we hear of people who cannot live up to their full potential and who cannot live in peace.

Ronald Wilson Reagan[1]

We have discussed the religiosity built into being an American, and how religion and political or civil religion interact in the society and sacralize what it means to be a part of the imagined community of America. Religious factors ground any story about what America is, and now we will burrow deeper into the connection of religion and narrative and point out that the relationship is complex. Jonathan Z. Smith has argued that there are two ways to study religion: to either view it as an exotic category of human experience or as an ordinary one.[2] Since it is an integral part of the American way of life according to Reagan, one must view religious materials, such as myths, as "common stories" to take them as objects of the study.[3] Grottanelli agrees when he argues that the books of the Old Testament should be studied just as any other text, and to apply to them "every new methodological approach that would clarify its entire semantic sense, its ideological intent, and its social and political value."[4] For him the biblical narratives should be compared to myths "for they share with mythical narratives the function of providing sacred warrants and perennial charters for behaviors, beliefs and institutions."[5] He argues that the Greek culture, just like the Hebrew, produced desacralized history along with mere fiction, but for some reason in the Hebrew context the stories about their ancestors and founding heroes were demythicized and rationalized and never became desacralized history or fiction.[6] Genette sees myth as a "type of narrative situated on an unsettled and shifting frontier of fiction."[7] If one chooses to accept a narrative that is religious in nature as a myth, then that also means to "accept it more or less by the same token as a literary text."[8] Religious texts can be considered as myths and treated in analysis like any other text. This holds true with the elements related to the founding of America as well. Some of the stories or myths still keep their sacred quality and function as foundational myths that provide an example to follow.

RELIGION AND NARRATIVE

> Fifty-six percent of Americans believe that religion can answer all or most of today's problems. In fact, only one in five doubts the relevance of religion in the modern world. And we'll get them, too.
>
> Ronald Wilson Reagan[9]

Vladimir Propp claimed that there was a natural connection between religion and everyday life and a similar connection between religion and the tales or stories told. *"A way of life and religion die out, while their contents turn into tales…the tale has still been studied very little on the plane of its parallel with religion and its further penetration into the cultural and economic aspects of daily living."*[10] Since his days the situation has not changed. If this notion is correct, then tales and storytelling are things that will outlast religion both in its sacred and political versions. Even if there is no longer such a unifying American civil religion as Herberg or Bellah described, stories are still being told about it. Independent of their subject's existence, these stories are able to penetrate "those cultural and economic aspects," which can be labelled as all political issues. Even if the civil religion cannot be resurrected, it can be exploited with stories. Just as a myth of gods degenerates into an epic story with time, it still has power to move the hearts and minds of some people, but differently. The story is left behind and still has power.

Religiosity is inbuilt to the structure and the very heart of every story told. Propp argued that "the tale at its core preserves traces of very ancient paganism, of ancient customs and rituals."[11] He claims that tales must be "studied in regard to religious notions."[12] The main focus of Propp's study was the Russian folktale, and we do not often tend to see these tales told to children as religious by their nature. But since there is something inherently religious in the tale itself, the multiple roles of religious beliefs in storytelling should not be excluded from analysis of other tales either, whether they appear religious or not. Nevertheless, the tale itself is never sacred enough that it could not metamorphose, and this gradual altering of the tale is the signature of the great storyteller, whether he is telling a children's bedtime story or a political story for consenting adults.

Religion is thus involved in the creation of narratives, but the relationship goes both ways, and narratives often have an influence on religion itself. The Judeo-Christian religious tradition that strongly affects the entire Occidental world, and especially America, is well adapted to the notion of the centrality of the concepts of language and narrative. This is because early Judaism itself established, in the second of the Ten Commandments, the preference of words and language over images as the realm where imagination and desires may play.[13] In Christian theology it was also "word," which was in the beginning, and that word was God. The factor that unites Islam, Christianity, and Judaism is that we are all religions of "the book." The Holy Bible or Quran lay down the foundations of our faiths, and these literary works are central in spreading or communicating it as well. The prominent religious scholar Martin E. Marty follows the classification of Judaism, Christianity, and Islam into the "People of the Book," because of the importance these religions lay on their respective (sometimes overlapping) texts. "They all became religions of 'the Word.' God, perhaps through leaders like priests or prophets, could speak to the believer."[14] In fact, as Alexander Campbell, the founder of Reagan's church wrote, "Unless words are understood, ideas and sentiments can neither be communicated nor received."[15] It is no wonder that the use of words and stories comes naturally to Reagan as a Disciple of Christ.

Paul Ricoeur argued that religious faith may be identified through language for inquiry, because whatever is the ultimate nature of religious experience, "it comes to language, it is articulated in language and the most appropriate place to interpret it on its own terms is to inquire into its linguistic expression."[16] Narratives that combine politics and religion often try to teach the way of interpreting, and to give a sense of belonging to a community, that can understand such narratives. They draw from the religious element to make the narrative persuasive, and often the religious language contains an authoritative instruction on how to interpret it.[17] The hermeneutical constitution of the biblical faith, according to Ricoeur, can then be summarized by saying that faith is never an independent experience but always mediated by the language it is articulated in. He links faith to self-understanding in the face of a text, so that faith is an attitude of one who "accepts being interpreted at the same time that he or she interprets the world of the text."[18] The relation between the reader and the text is two-directional, so that both are under the scrutiny of interpretation.

Durkheim saw another, often overlooked element of religion, which is its recreational and aesthetic element. Religious dramatic performances use the same techniques as drama and "they make men forget the real world *so as to transport them into another where imagination is more at home.*"[19] Durkheim asserted that there are story-worlds that can be entered by the means of religion. These combine into a storyverse where imagination allows the American dream to exist without restrictions. Any political narrator needs to be aware of this and like Reagan consciously create storyworlds to allow his people to escape the harsh realities of the everyday life into the storyverse. It is hope and our belief that makes us willing to allow the real-world to blur with the storyverse created for civil religious purposes. Unlike our real-world, imagination allows us to populate this storyverse with unlimited possibilities and yet it is so close to our real-world that the mental relocation may happen unnoticed.

Stories and their use is a part of religion. For Durkheim, "The truth is that there is poetry inherent in all religion."[20] There is poetry involved in religion and religion in the construction of stories. The powerful stories often derive some of their power from religious beliefs or religious protostories, even in the case that these have been distorted into mythical material and "common sense." In the same manner as myths and other stories, religious experience can be communicated to another person in writing like the Bible or orally as a narrative. Religion has to be tied down in words in order to communicate it from one generation to another. We do not know enough today of for example Zoroastrianism, because there is no written word, no literary product that would have been passed through the ages. Literature specifically and language in general are not only vessels for transporting the highly personal experience of religious phenomena, but also vessels for distancing belief from religion and creating myths with practically a sacred status.

In the context of Christianity there is, according to Ricoeur, no sacred text, because "it is not the text that is sacred but the one about which it is spoken."[21] The canon was put together or edited from separate texts, and the text that was produced is no longer sacred in the Ricoeurian sense of the word. Since the text is already altered, there is no blasphemy in altering it further, for example by such innocent means as translation, or even reading it intentionally and trying to find citations that back up one's political pursuits. Ricoeur's use of sacred implies to something so absolute in its unchangeable nature that he proposes the term "authoritative text" to refer to those texts that are fundamental to a community but yet can be reinterpreted and shaped.[22] A sacred text is one that constitutes the founding act of the community, and authoritative texts are excluded from this function, while they may have a very close kinship. While an authoritative text may talk about the same founding function, it "does not belong to the story of the way in which the community interpreted itself in terms of those [sacred] texts."[23]

In this Ricoeurian view the stories Reagan told were initially authoritative texts, because they discussed the founding of mythical America, but one of the accomplishments of "Reagan Revolution" was to elevate these authoritative stories into sacred ones even in the Ricoeurian sense of becoming unalterable. Reagan's stories complemented and combined the older ones and resacralized them while giving new form to the ways in which the Americans saw their society. For Smith texts become canon in a society as a limited number of them are fixed as immutable and authoritative.[24] But one of the objectives of Reagan's politics was to alter the canon and tradition by narratively altering the amount of sacredness bestowed to the texts of the canon. Some on occasion need to be more sacred than others for political means.

Ricoeur wrote about the sacred texts becoming "frozen." With this he implies that because of the fight against heresies, the interpretation of sacred texts was stopped, and with the rise of Protestantism, the text itself became sacred against the Augustinian tradition of free interpretation. The text was frozen and became immutable, and the process of changing it in the slightest manner, was a threat to both the text and the community.[25] There is a crisis of community because

> its own identity relies on the identity of the text, as distinct from both nonsacred and other sacred texts. . . . Preaching is the permanent reinterpretation of the text that is regarded as grounding the community; therefore, for the community to address itself to another text would be to make a decision concerning its social identity. A community that does that becomes another kind of community.[26]

The whole concept of identity in the context of a community relies on its "capacity to situate itself as being this and not that, but also as having this past and not that past."[27] This Ricoeurian idea interpreted means that Reagan can be said to have been successful in terms of altering and implementing ideas. New texts such as abolishment of all nuclear weapons as the ultimate goal of politics or supply-side economics to get the economy into recovery were included into the political "sermon." As the texts about the American identity got a very typically Reaganesque twist, the identity of the community itself transformed into something closer to the vision Reagan depicted in his narration. Reagan's interpretation of Winthrop's "city upon a hill" might serve as an example of this. For Reagan there was no doubt that America as this city would succeed in everything. His "shining city" would forever be the focus of human aspirations anywhere. The change in the contemporary perception of identity changed the history retrospectively as well. Reagan's vision of America extended also backward in time, and thus the stories of the American past got altered as well. Maybe there never had been a golden past to precede the "time of choosing" today to enter the glorious future, but it was resurrected or given birth to for the first time in the same process, where the way Americans saw their nation at the present moment was changed.

Mythology and religion go together, according to Durkheim. Mythology is not only important to the aesthetics and science of religion, but "one of the essentials of religious life. If myth is withdrawn from religion, ritual must also be withdrawn....Indeed the rite is often nothing other than the myth in action."[28] Myth has to be enacted. This is the purpose behind political ceremonies, whether Thanksgiving, Veterans' Day, Presidential Inauguration, or any ritual hallowed by the nation. But the myth has to be articulated as well, so that the symbolism of rituals does not disappear. When the myth is narrated, what happens is, as Northrop Frye asserts, "mythology projects itself as theology; that is, a mythological poet usually accepts some myths as "true" and shapes his poetic structure accordingly."[29] When one writes about myth, he chooses to believe in some myths and discard others, and these choices are politically interesting. Some myths have a position that are "considered self-evident," as the Declaration of Independence reads. But when the "self-evident" character needs to be spelled out, it automatically means that there are dissidents we try to convince. This is easy to discern in most of religiously oriented literature, which assumes the existence of God as one of the basic building blocks of the storyworld in creation. The text of the Declaration of Independence has become mythical. Michael J. Shapiro uses the writings of Jacques Derrida to point out that to "hold these truths to be self-evident" is not just finding a warrant for them but to constitute those truths themselves so that the truths mentioned in the Declarations are produced and brought about in the production of the statement. The Declaration of Independence bases the entire concept of American democracy on fiction and commits a "founding violence" by instituting a very exclusive "we, the people." The "we" in the declaration consists of only the free, white men and violates the plurality of the American society from its very beginnings.[30] Since Reagan's politics are to a large degree founded on this textual basis, it is hard to escape from the limits set by such a founding metatext.

De Tocqueville asserted that in order for a society to exist and prosper, the minds of the citizenry must be unified by "some principal ideas; and that cannot happen unless each of them sometimes comes to draw his opinions from one and the same source and unless each consents to receive a certain number of ready-made beliefs."[31] He managed to clarify two of the points that I am trying to make with one stroke. Old common beliefs exist in any society. Some are religious, some are mythical, and some blend both elements together. These beliefs and truths have to be resurrected and given a new semblance with differing retellings of the old stories and perhaps a glossing of ideological and cultural beliefs. Every society has told and tells stories about its own existence and there is a virtual library at the use of the politician. Mostly these stories are myths that get their original justification from the tenets of some religion.

RELIGION AS MATERIAL FOR MYTH

Myths reveal that the World, man, and life have a supernatural origin and history, and that this history is significant, precious, and exemplary.

Mircea Eliade[32]

Our world lives by so many myths, that these have to be studied for a better understanding of politics. It is not only American political life, which is shrouded in myths, but also the entire realm of politics. Myth is comparable to any metanarrative that shapes our existence. Narratives are evaluated by the story recipient and ultimately from this evaluation the recipient makes the distinction between what is a myth and what is a religious story. Religious stories are intentionally turned into or they become myths by losing their special sacred status in the course of time. The diving line between religious and mythical is drawn with a finger on the surface of water. The same applies to myth and "truth."

The story of Oedipus with all its different versions can be used to argue that in a myth (or a story) there actually is "no single 'true' version of which all the others are but copies or distortions. Every version belongs to the myth."[33] The importance of this is that there exists a metanarrative or a foundation myth, which acts as the ultimately "original" version of the story or a protomyth. This story shapes the tellings related to it. It cannot be identified as the "whole truth and nothing but the truth" of the myth but rather as a framework to guide the telling. It is neither solid and impregnably bounded nor easily defined, but nevertheless it exists, and every story and every version told about its constituent matter becomes part of the metanarrative as well. Just as the "ultimate" Oedipus story is a combination of all the versions, so it is with any mythical story. Each telling has at least the potential to alter the "original."

The first attempt to differentiate between myth and narrative was made in the second century by Aelius Theon in his *Progymnasmata,* which defined myth as "a false account portraying truth" and narrative as "an account descriptive of events which took place or might have taken place."[34] Another important early thinker on narratives was Origen. He used words like "enigma" and "parable," but they can be seen to mean essentially the same things as for example "myth" and "fiction." Origen wrote that where spiritual truths did not correspond to historical events, "the Scripture wove into the historical narrative what did not take place—at some points what cannot take place and at other what can take place but did not."[35] Origen then admitted that Gospels contain episodes that are not "authentic" in the historical sense, but at the same time "true" on the spiritual plane.[36] This idea provides even more legitimation for Reagan to narrate his story-verse of mythical America as it "should have been," because on a level of higher truth some things "rightfully" ought to have occurred.

If we cast Origen aside as an isolated example of a theologian, who admits that some mythical elements are inbuilt into Christian religion, it is a well-established tradition within Christianity to discredit myths and mythology and abolish them into a separate space of their own. There is a refusal to see a mythical figure in Jesus and myth in messianic drama. Most of the Christian churches want to separate themselves totally from all things mythical, but it is beyond doubt that mythological elements abound in the Gospels and other early documents of Christianity.[37] This has caused a deep divide between mythology and religion so that both "should" not be talked about at the same time in the Western context. Instead they should be treated as if they were totally different things, with myth holding a position of lesser value than religion. Naturally this idea was applicable only to Christianity, while tenets of other religions were commonly set in the category of "myths."

One scholar who wanted to bridge this divide again was Mircea Eliade. Eliade notes that during the nineteenth-century Western scholars have approached the study of myth from the viewpoint that they are not only "fables," "inventions," and "fiction" but also are in the archaic societies understood to mean a "true story." He defines myth as "a story that is a most precious possession because it is sacred, exemplary, significant."[38] Lincoln shows us that in its pejorative usage myth signifies "a story that members of some other social group (or past era) regard(ed) as true and authoritative, but that the speaker and members of her or his group regard as false."[39] The political importance of myths resides in the multiple meanings it created and perhaps still creates.

The ancient Greeks steadily emptied the mythos of all religious and metaphysical value, but it was finally Judeo-Christianity, which labelled everything not validated or justified by the two Testaments as "falsehood," something that really cannot exist. Eliade was interested in those societies in which myth is "living," in the sense that "it supplies models for human behaviour and, by that very fact, gives meaning and value to life."[40] In that sense Reagan was able to define his mythical America in the terms of an archaic society, since the myth of the American dream supplied Americans with a model for proper living and provided meaning to their lives. Societies, which keep myths alive, carefully distinguish them from fables or tales, which are "false stories." In general, according to Eliade, the "true" stories or myths deal with the holy or supernatural, and the "false" stories are of profane content. This distinction is important, since essentially both categories of narratives present histories, or, as Eliade writes, "relate a series of events that took place in a distant and fabulous past," but the difference is that myths concern the people directly, and fables have not altered the human condition itself.[41] "Living a myth, then, implies a genuinely 'religious' experience, since it differs from the ordinary experience of everyday life."[42] That is why Reagan wanted to mythify the American way of life and turn it into something extraordinary, so that the American dream blended with the way of life.

The way people actually live changes from one generation to another. In the course of time stories tend to change all by themselves as well. The modes of literature have a tendency to move from the mythical to low mimetic and at the same time approach a point of extreme realism meaning here a likeness to life.

> Myths of gods merge into legends of heroes; legends of heroes merge into plots of tragedies and comedies. . . . But these are changes of social context, and the constructive principles of storytelling remain constant through them.[43]

In the mythical mode where the stories are about gods who have the greatest possible power of action, there is at the same time present the greatest abstraction and conventionalization. Mythical fiction is therefore more stylized and less realistic of all modes of fiction. What once was told about the gods became first a myth, then it was told of the achievements of almost superhuman men, and then about heroes. Religious story then turns into a myth but the "truth value" remains. The Founding Fathers are an example. Myth can in time become a part of history. It can be reduced to legend, and legend is easy to reduce to exaggerated history.[44] Now we "know" the importance of Paul Revere's ride or that Washington confessed to cutting down his father's apple tree, just like we know that America is the "last, best hope of man." Myths create their own storyworlds as well as any other story. But there is a slight difference, which Boer points out: "Myth constructs or postulates world(s) whose truth will have been upon its completion."[45] He argues that such a world created by myth is a "powerful fiction of a completed truth."[46] For explicitly political myths this is important, because myth forces events to take place by creating the types of worlds, where the events will have occurred.[47] Thus, when myths are used in politics, the power of the story itself aids in the fulfillment of the myth. History creates myth, but the linguistic labyrinth of myth generates history.[48] Since myth can be only exaggerated history, history can be mythified as well. History has to be separated from time, that is, the timelines have to evaporate so that historic events are seen to paradoxically have happened outside time, and thus outside history as well. For the purposes of narrativized politics, time has to be mythified, and the historical events turned into stories.

There are no eternal myths, because myths are reality turned into speech by human history. A myth can be ancient but nevertheless has a historical foundation, because "myth is a type of speech chosen by history," and history is determinant of the lifespan of mythical language.[49] Any object can become mythologized, and any material be used in the construction of the myth, because "myth can be defined neither by its object nor its material, for any material can arbitrarily be endowed with meaning."[50] Mythical concepts are not fixed. They can come into being, change, disintegrate, or disappear completely just because they are historical in their nature. History can rise or suppress them at will.[51] Myths and other metanarratives are slaves of history. There are moments in the flux of history when these concepts do have an unquestionable, even a sacred status that no one argues against with their counternarratives. These myths can be found anywhere. The sun revolved around the Earth for a long time. Atom was the smallest unit of matter, which could not be split for ages. Thunder used to be caused by Thor rumbling in his chariot across the sky. These are just a few examples but from them we can make deductions. First of all, they were bound by the cultural context of their appearance. Indians had other explanations for thunder than this Scandinavian myth. Chinese astrologers not bound down by the dogmas of the Catholic Church could claim that the Earth was the body that did the revolving.

Second, they only existed for a certain period of time. New knowledge about the nature made possible the debunking of the story of primal nature of the atom. New stories supplanted older explanations for thunder. No myth or master narrative is eternal. They will always be replaced by new ones, but there is a time, place, and context, where they are the only "true" stories about the way things really are. Propp grants that myths indeed can change shape, when he writes that the tale "gradually undergoes a metamorphosis since real life, epos of neighbouring peoples, written literature, local beliefs and religion transform the tale."[52] The narrator has some leeway in reshaping the story. Even a myth can change, but this is "very rarely the product of personal or artistic creation. It can be established that the creator of a fairy tale rarely invents; he receives his material from his surroundings or from current realities and adapts them to a tale."[53] The elements that cause a myth to change its shape originate in the world outside the story. In political stories they are the rapidly changing aspects of political situations and realities, and the narrator reacts to these alterations and shapes his stories to better conform to them. Stories are at least updated in order to make them easier for the new generations to decipher. Time often erodes the sacred nature of a story. We no longer strictly abide by the conception that world was created in six days; it has turned into a myth for us, albeit a myth that we still consider to be "essentially true" and see the form as artistic misrepresentation. While some stories gradually turn more and more mundane in the due course of time, the process can be reversible as well. The ordinary can be mythified as well.

Times change, tempus fugit, and the stories used to communicate the true essence of those times change. Only one thing remains constant, the existence of some myth. "The mythical is present everywhere *sentences are tuned, stories told*...from newspaper article to political sermon."[54] The myths that have survived the pressures of history to the present day have to be placed under academic scrutiny to understand our political world better. But since they are to a large degree already naturalized into parts of our conception of the world, what is the way to do it? Applying the means of narratology and literary theory to politics could offer an answer and a toolkit to dismantle our "common sensical" beliefs and prove their mythic origin. Lincoln argues that myths, however foundational, are not stable taxonomies, since the relationship between social order and stories told about it is loose and dynamic, and this loose fit creates possibilities for rival narrators and counternarratives that modify aspects of the established orders.[55] At the same time this allows a politician to modify the myth and for the researcher to locate it.

All myths have been used differently in different times. Some myths are occasionally cast aside; some gain more importance. Especially during politically profitable times, when it is necessary to influence the idea Americans have of themselves, these myths need to be evoked and narrated anew. It is the narration of these myths that one has to alter to change the meanings of the myths themselves to suit one's political preferences. Myths are both stories and symbols, and as McLoughlin argues, "One way to describe an awakening is to call it a period during which old symbols are clothed in new meanings."[56] The creation of new stories on old plots or myths as retellings is the most convenient means of altering world views, and the political narrator is a crucial figure in recreation of the national image.

> You may remember that verse in the Bible that says, "Your old men will dream dreams; your young men will see visions." Well, I deeply believe that this is just such a time of reawakening in America, a time when our country is healing the wounds of the past and beginning to look with courage and confidence to the future. Yes, we are making a new beginning.[57]

AMERICANONIZED MYTHS OF US POLITICS

Ideas do have consequences, rhetoric is policy, and words are action.
Ronald Wilson Reagan[58]

Georges Sorel placed myth in its ideological context. He saw that social movements gained popularity and supporters by envisioning a struggle on behalf of an ultimately triumphant cause. The cause could just as well be the *Endlösung*, the world revolution of the proletariat, or the global spreading of the American way of life. It could be utopian or millennial, just as long as it was placed in the future. But Sorel claims that "myths should be judged as means of acting upon the present."[59] To make a crude interpretation, what is important in myths as political narratives, is their propaganda function in the present of their telling. Their effect determines whether they have been politically important, since they might have been used to attain completely different goals and purposes than the ones explicitly spelled out in the telling. The triumphant cause and even the struggle can be mere pies in the sky, as long as desired action takes place in the short run. The citizenry must be won over at the spur of the moment by the immediate impression the myth imposes on it. The myth acts in the moment for the benefit of winning a politically desirable future. It does not matter after Reagan's important address on radio or television that some journalist days later finds a fault in logic or even an untruism. What is politically important is that the impression had been made, and the action intended got initiated. As Barthes claims, no matter how much attention one pays to the reading of the myth, this "will in no way increase its power or its ineffectiveness: a myth is at the same time imperfectible and unquestionable; time or knowledge will not make it better or worse."[60] This brings us to the question how myths indeed are put to use in politics, and what is the role they play in political world. One of the great benefits of mythifying politics is that "it simply does not compute to say that fable of myth may be verified or falsified."[61]

Barthes tends to see myth as depoliticized speech, because the world supplies myth with a historical reality, and myth gives the world in return a naturalized image of this reality. In filling reality with naturality myth purifies and makes things more innocent by abolishing the complexity of human affairs and giving it the simplicity of essences. Myth organizes a world devoid of contradictions.[62] In this process supposedly the object of the myth is relieved from its political load and filled with hollowness. Some myths are considered politically insignificant, but only because they are not meant for us.[63] But to naturalize the world, and to make seem as if it was utterly devoid of contradictions, was of the main tools of Reagan's policies. The myth function turns a cultural interpretation into a natural fact, and this transformation of cultural into natural is highly political practice. Cynthia Weber claims that political power works through myths by appearing to take the political out of the ideological, which explains Barthes's idea of myths as depoliticized speech. When something seems natural it also seems apolitical, but "natural facts" are the most intensely political stories of all, not because they tell myths, but because they remove themselves from political debate.[64] By seemingly naturalizing politics with the myth function, in other words turning a thing into a myth to avoid its political implications, a politician is able to turn his policies into such naturalized facts that their political purposes get hidden.

Jerome Bruner writes that a "mythologically instructed community provides its members with a library of scripts upon which the individual may judge the internal drama of his multiple identities."[65] If myths are alive in a society, they serve as something the members of the society can build their identities upon. If the society wishes to see itself as heroic, as America often likes to do, there is a "library of scripts" to guide the identity construction. In this case it is not the society that "patterns itself on the idealizing myths, but unconsciously it is the individual man as well who is able to structure his internal clamour of identities in terms of the prevailing myth. Life then produces myth and finally imitates it."[66] The society with Reagan as its spokesperson uses myth to reconstruct itself, and the myth is carried on into the lives of the individuals, while they try to fit into the society by fitting into the mythical pattern. Myth becomes a living reality. When authoritative stories are reconstructed and myths modified, ultimately the society itself can be reformulated.[67] To change the way people see themselves and their country, is paradoxically the same as to change the people and the country, since they end up being changed in the process of changing the perceptions. The United States becomes the mythical America.

Richard T. Hughes writes about "American myths" and defines them as "stories that explain why we love our country and why we have faith in the nation's purposes. Put another way, our national myths are the means by which we affirm the meaning of the United States."[68] According to Hughes there are five monomyths that have given birth to other secondary myths like "Manifest Destiny." The central myths are that of the chosen people, of nature's nation, of Christian nation, of millennial nation, and finally of the innocent nation that draw their strength from the other myths.[69] One of the original purposes of Robert Bellah to write his influential article on American civil religion was to call for "new American myths" that would lead America into "a new balance of impulse and control, energy and discipline."[70] These new myths should have been the ones that indeed are considered self-evident by all Americans. There was even a promise that these new myths could be applied worldwide as well. While the project was doomed hopeless due to inner contradictions, Reagan took the rather more "shallow substitute for genuine religion"[71] that Herberg had argued to be the American way of life and built his mythical structure on this instead.

Northrop Frye writes that one major source of order in society is an *"established pattern of words."*[72] In religion this may be a scripture such as the Bible; in politics it may be the Constitution. While these patterns may remain unchanged for long periods of time, the meanings attached to them may change out of all recognition with the passing of the time. But it is the "feeling that the verbal structure must remain unchanged, and the consequent necessity of reinterpreting it to suit the changes of history, bring the operations of criticism into the centre of society."[73] What else could this established pattern of words be than an Americanonized myth about the society? Nevertheless, it has to be stated that in order to cloak policies under the guide of rationality, the politician needs to distance himself from myths. To openly admit that any policy is based on a myth, no matter how "true" the myth is deemed to be, is to open one to ridicule in the world of politics. The myth has to be denarrated. Even in the vocabulary of Reagan the word "myth" carries a very negative meaning.

> We're seeing a rebirth of these values, not to return to some mythical past, but to build on strengths for a creative future as we renew the quest for excellence at all levels of our society.[74]

So, paradoxically while myths may be a guiding factor for politics, they have to be kept outside the narration to such a degree that the entire term cannot be allowed to pop up to describe the goal of politics. Rather politics has to rely on the *meaning* of myth, as it was articulated in the beginning of this subchapter; an essentially true story. Myth has to be demythified and accepted as a part of the common knowledge that "everyone" shares. Only then, its true origin hidden, can the myth be a powerful motivator and catalyst for politics.

When it comes to defining the possible meanings myths may have on our society, one must notice that myths work and act on many different levels. Stories with mythical themes are told only for light entertainment, but the same themes appear in religious contexts "where they are accepted not only as factually true but even as revelations of the verities to which the whole culture is a living witness and from which it derives both its spiritual authority and its temporal power," writes Joseph Campbell and adds, "No human society has yet been found in which such mythological motifs have not been rehearsed in liturgies; interpreted by seers, poets, theologians, or philosophers; presented in art; magnified in song; and ecstatically experienced in life-empowering visions."[75] Myth, therefore, is neither confined necessarily to the sidelines of society, nor does it have to create the backbone of society. It can be put to use in anything, but it does not need to have to be of any value either. Why could it not be removed from the realm of purely aesthetic and used in the realm of politics? The stories of politics are fictional, and the politician can just well act as the interpreter or the seer, who gives it a new form in his vision.

Myths cannot be extracted from the political world, since they have an important function as a shroud. According to Jameson, if everything would be transparent, "then no ideology would be possible, and no domination either."[76] The concept of domination is crucial to political leadership, but in terms of dominating the political storytelling itself and being able to produce the dominant narrative. The narrator-politician needs to be able to put together a story, which is of such heightened importance that it gains mythic value as the "true" representation and severely restricts the opportunities of drafting a powerful and plausible narrative to contest its dominance. Contrary to Barthes, Jameson claims that our society is more mythified than any previous one, and any notion of unity presupposes a mechanism of mythification, which would make sense to seek latent meanings and interpretations of texts.[77] To understand American political myths we have to consciously adopt the viewpoint to "not aim to show how men think in myths but how myths think in men, unbeknownst to them."[78] The way people in a given society react to the myths within it has political consequences. Myths can enable us to understand human behavior by seeing it as myth-guided when clear rational logic offers no solutions. American political system evades critical self-examination through the myth function, or, in other words, by naturalization of politics. What is natural often does not need to be studied, indeed questions are seldom raised.[79] It takes a strange way of thought to question the obvious.

There is another reason why the concept of myth is necessary in the politics of our postmodern world. Our world is too difficult to understand, and we need to artificially divide it into more "digestible" units to comprehend. While according to Lévi-Strauss, myth cannot succeed in giving man power over his environment, it nevertheless is able to give him "the illusion that he can understand the universe and that he *does* understand the universe."[80] Mythology takes the place of science in providing a total understanding of the world around us. It is fitting, that our reality is constructed for us to digest with narratives, since in a society where myth is a living thing, "the World is no longer an opaque mass of objects arbitrarily thrown together; it is a living Cosmos, articulated and meaningful. In the last analysis, *the world reveals itself as language*."[81] The most suitable way thus to make the world reveal itself, is as a storyworld. We would not understand and appreciate the complexities of the society if we saw it manifested in its entirety in front of us. It is a requirement of the president, as Robert Ivie wrote, that he "creates political reality with a fantasy that cuts through the ambiguity and confusion, even inherent absurdity, of international affairs."[82] The same applies to domestic politics as well. The society or the world system has to be simplified, and once the myth function simplifies the United States of America into the mythical America can a citizen grasp its composition. Only this simplified version can be used for the citizen to inject it with purpose and emplot its actions in a meaningful manner. The following quotation from Reagan perfectly articulates my point. It is too difficult to contemplate the role the United States plays in global politics, but the mythified America can be explained in an oversimplification.

> This country isn't perfect. But, it is the best one in the world. And; as the saying goes, "that ain't boast—just fact." We have little to be ashamed of and everything to be proud of. If some psychotic African dictator or Latin American bullyboy or communist thug doesn't like us, who cares. Don't push anybody around, but don't let them push you around. The best way to avoid a fight is to show you're willing to fight if necessary. That is the wisdom of the street corner and the country store, the local barbershop and town meeting. Such wisdom may not get you a job in the state department. Some intellectuals may deride it as a psychological manifestation of inferiority feelings. And there are some congressmen who would faint dead away if you ever said such things to them. But that kind of wisdom has kept this country free for over two hundred years. It is the wisdom at the heart of the American people's desire for peace and freedom.[83]

The common man was able to understand Reagan and gain a glimpse of the world of politics and his role in it as part of the Mythical America. As de Tocqueville wrote, "only simple conceptions take hold of the minds of the people. A false idea, but one clear and precise, will always have more power in the world than a true, but complex, idea."[84] Naturally the story recipient, for whom the story has been oversimplified, is not able to grasp the nuances of politics, but this is of no great concern. He is liable to be used as a pawn in the political game of chess. Just because his conception of politics is dependent upon the stories told, he and his opinion can more easily be managed by altering the stories, than the actual policies those stories depict. As long as the story is altered, there does not necessarily need to be any change in the real-life. While the simplifications made Reagan's points and stories more personal and comprehensible, they also managed to place his message beyond argument.[85] When he made his arguments in narrative form, that is, as anecdotes and stories, the means of countering them were restricted. It is impossible to plausibly argue with rhetoric devices or rock-solid facts against a point made in a parable or an anecdote. And not many politicians could match Reagan in a battle of anecdotes.

The simplifications make good points that stick to the minds of the people better than longer elaborations of the status quo. As an example will suffice Reagan's description of the government, "I've sometimes compared government to that unkind definition of a baby: It's an alimentary canal with an appetite at one end and no sense of responsibility at the other."[86] In using simplifications Reagan follows the pattern set by Calvin Coolidge, his favorite of previous presidents. Reagan admired his clear articulation of political ideas. The simplistic presentation of ideology was similar for both presidents. While their use of words was not complicated or verbose, they both managed to discuss very complex issues in simple terms.[87] But while making such oversimplifications, Reagan needed to be able to at the same time narrate the political world to be complex as well, lest the difficulties inbuilt into his role are forgotten by the citizens, and to avoid alienating the more intellectual of politically aware segment of the citizenry. Again, this can be achieved by using storyworlds to take the place of the "real" world. Then each citizen can incorporate his knowledge of the world as part of his storyworld building. In other words he can see the world to be endowed with the difficulties he is already aware of, but yet accept the simplifications. If the world would be revealed to him only through simplification, he would become scornful of the naïveté. When the storyworld takes unnoticeably the place of the "real" world, he accepts the simplifications as a good way to make the "others" aware of the complex matters and functions that he can grasp.

A storyverse of the mythical America and its dreams is a whole web of storylines and meanings. Ultimately the metanarrative about Americans, their place in their mythical society and in the world emerges from this storyverse. Francois Lyotard argued that ever since the Second World War and the blooming of techniques and technologies, "the grand narrative has lost its credibility, regardless of what mode of unification it uses, regardless of whether it is a speculative narrative or a narrative of emancipation."[88] Supposedly these grand narratives have been overtaken with "little stories" told in their place with great varieties. There nevertheless arises an interesting question. Is post modernity something that only the intellectual elite even in our highly developed Western societies can afford to enjoy, and does the large mass of citizenry still live within the bounds of modernity? In American politics the grand narrative of "freedom" was in the days of Reagan, as well as in the days of George W. Bush, a legitimizer for all types of action in the eyes of the majority of the people. The political world is still able to rally its "armies" of the people behind the old flags of master narratives. Naturally there are contesting narratives, the "*récits petites*," which are told in opposition, but the master narrative still holds superiority over them. There supposedly is no longer belief in social and political teleologies or the great actors or subjects of history like the West or the nation-state. Lyotard wanted to bury the master narratives but for Jameson they are only just that, buried and seemingly disappeared but continuing as unconscious activity in the political unconscious.[89] It seems that the words of Reagan have a sense of truth in them: "Sometimes in the world of politics, it seems that our dialog hasn't gone much beyond 'Me Tarzan, You Jane'."[90] The world of politics has not moved into the postmodern age. As Vilho Harle has noted, religion and myths about religion were often the basis of justification for political organizations in the ancient world.[91] If we are not just as postmodern as we tend to view ourselves, is it really surprising to notice that the old myths and beliefs still have power to shape our politics?

There still exists the "unavowable dream the post-modern world dreams about itself—a tale that, in sum, would be the great narrative that the world persists in telling itself."[92] To extrapolate on this idea, it does not matter if there is no particular way to live or dream in America, since America still dreams and tells itself, with the help of presidents as narrators, how and what to dream. What does it matter that the great narratives have "obviously failed" from the viewpoint of intellectuals, if the world still insists in telling itself the great narratives. They have not become less powerful, since they are still persistently used despite the crumbling of their foundations, but, if anything, they have become even more political. To revisit the concept of narratively crafted American civil religion, since it gives shape to the way the members of the society perceive their existence, it is a master or a great narrative. As Propp argued, even when religion dies out or disappears, the stories told about it and the stories it has told survive. In the case of American civil religion, the American dream remains.

But the expressions "metanarrative" or "master narrative" carries too many negative connotations in our allegedly post-modern world. Perhaps we should talk of the concept of "Americanonized myth," seen as foundational or legitimizing myth in the American context that has become "canon" by gaining legitimation from being deeply ingrained into the "common sense" and also having religious connections in its mythmaking process within the American culture. America as a cultural context shapes the myth and together with the religious origins of the myth turns it into canon. These Americanonized myths are the little stories that help spin the grand story web for belief-based politics and ultimately take part in narrating the storyverse of mythical America and its dream into existence. Ira Chernus argues that stories shape our worldview even when they are not in the shape to tangible stories on paper or whichever distribution medium is in use.

> We can't even tell our most important stories completely in any detailed narrative. We take them for granted. We know them in bits and pieces, but the whole story is always there. Mentioning just one piece is like pushing a button that brings the whole story to life; the process unfolds largely unconsciously.[93]

Reagan thoroughly understood the structure of the grand national narrative archives of these Americanonized myths, what stories touch the people in a certain manner and why, which stories cause what kind of emotions. He was able to use all the foundational myths of the nation without having to narrate them at all. He could use only bits and pieces to conjure up greater parts from the memories of citizens to create greater visions, like a magician producing his tricks. A gifted narrator needs only subtly hint at other stories in the course of his narration and let intertextuality work its magic. The old stories need not be spelled out over and over again. There just needs to be a reference, to allow the new narrative to exploit them as well.

America is at the time of writing this undergoing another change in its self-image. It has reached a point when it no longer can claim to be an uncontested superpower in the realm of international politics. There is a need to rearticulate some of the old myths. Because of its multinational origins and the self-image as the last, best hope of mankind and other powerful foundational myths describing America as the fulfillment of human freedom and the nucleus of civilization itself, Americans tend to have a worldview that endows them with a special, hallowed task of keeping freedom and democracy alive in the entire world. This view of the role of the United States of America in the realm of international politics paves way for the argument that American domestic politics are a matter of global concern, or rather, that American politics view the international system as part of their domestic policy. As Reagan put it to the General Assembly of the United Nations,

> America is committed to the world because so much of the world is inside America. After all, only a few miles from this very room is our Statue of Liberty, past which life began anew for millions, where the peoples from nearly every country in this hall joined to build these United States. The blood of each nation courses through the American vein and feeds the spirit that compels us to involve ourselves in the fate of this good Earth.[94]

Mary E. Stuckey has noticed that the constant evocation of national myths is at least part of the legacy or imprint Reagan left into American politics. After his campaigning, with the increased role of the national media coverage, the national candidates must "increasingly reflect the national culture. They attempt to accomplish this through the articulation of national myths."[95] Mika Aaltola agrees by arguing that political power and legitimacy are highly dependent on the ability of politico-religious figures to draw from the cultural resources of the sacred.[96] This is increasingly true in our contemporary world, where myths seem to gain more and more power as legitimizers of policies. There is an entire "National Mythology," where historical experience of the nation provides metaphors and stories, which assume mythic proportions, and the resultant myth exercises a reciprocal pressure on succeeding generations.[97] But the balance of power in the world has shifted and US politics need to adapt to America's waning power. How to keep the Mythical America alive? Which myths to choose and which to discard? The power of stories has always been an important factor in shaping the American self. Especially the story of Christian America is so deeply accepted that it rarely is questioned. There may be yet unused potential in it, but in the multifaith America of today, a new version has to be produced of the narrative, and some of its basic tenets need to be reevaluated.

If Reagan's narrative resonates with the biblical scripts in the story recipients' memories, it is possible to directly interconnect the story told with biblical narratives in such a manner that it gets its inter-pretative techniques from hermeneutics as well. As J. Cheryl Exum writes, by telling and retelling stories instead of attempting to cre-ate a philosophical system, "the biblical authors bequeathed to us a multivalent, inexhaustible narrative world."[98] The Bible offers a rich bundle of storylines to follow. As examples might suffice the tale of Exodus, the parable of the Good Samaritan, the city on a hill, battle of good and evil, or numerous others. By taking these storylines and drafting new stories in new contexts, Reagan creates Americanonized versions of the old biblical and mythical stories. By using the biblical scripts, Reagan was able to use the authority of the Bible to back up his political stories. This allowed Reagan a more dominant role in the storyworld construction using the prestige of the biblical stories to minimize the role of the story recipient. This was because most of the elements of storyworld would be derivative from the biblical text itself, and the story recipient would be more willing to follow the canon of the text than his own interpretation. The authority of the Bible for Jews and Christians alike enable the narrator to add a coercive force. When a mythical story is blended with a biblical one, the resulting storyworld bears many characteristics of the biblical sto-ryworld, which is presented almost ready-made for the story recipient. Furthermore, a storyworld created in such a manner would automati-cally in its very essence be the type of "new promised land" Reagan portrays America to be. This may well be the case why Reagan's sto-ries managed to communicate the feeling of "Divine America" among the religious type of story recipients, and thus the storyworld created would be what Ricoeur calls "biblical world,"[99] where revelation is an essential characteristic.

EXODUS INTO THE NEW EDEN

> Since the exodus of Egypt, historians have written of those who sacri-ficed and struggled for freedom.
>
> Ronald Wilson Reagan[100]

For Reagan the view of Christian America was indeed the "true story." Even before the Founding Fathers, it was the Puritan era that laid the foundation for everything Americans still are hundreds of years later.

> I've always had a great affection for the words of John Winthrop, deliv-ered to a small band of Pilgrims on the tiny ship Arabella off the coast

of Massachusetts in 1630: "We shall be a city upon a hill. The eyes of all people are upon us, so that if we shall deal falsely with our God in this work we have undertaken and so cause Him to withdraw His present help from us, we shall be made a story and a byword throughout the world." Well, America has not been a story or a byword. That small community of Pilgrims prospered and, driven by the dreams and, yes, by the ideas of the Founding Fathers, went on to become a beacon to all the oppressed and poor of the world.[101]

Paradoxically Reagan denies that America has been made a story. He himself has taken the story and worked on it for his entire life, adding, editing, and elaborating. The words of Winthrop tell that either America will become a fulfillment of America's divine mission or a shameful tale of the failure and inadequacy of God's chosen people. Winthrop himself made the Puritans a story by a narrative act, and Reagan was another narrator who remade the story again in a very political act or performance.

The Puritans viewed themselves as exiles from the Europe where religion had been contaminated. Their voyage across the sea was an attempt to escape "Egypt" and find the "Promised Land." As Gutterman writes, the retelling of the Exodus narrative by the Puritans has become practically the official story of the nation's founding. It remains "a nearly hegemonic national autobiography. It is the story taught to generations of schoolchildren and preached by each president."[102] The Puritans are used as an example of people, who left the old world behind to seek freedom, but their idea of freedom was quite different to what America proclaims to stand for today. As Hughes wrote, the Puritans sought "freedom for themselves but for no one else."[103] Yet they have been storied to be the forefathers of all the freedom-loving Americans, so that they have become a myth themselves. The Puritans, however, were themselves very adept at using stories. They managed to create an inclusive story about the America and American identity that came to surpass all other attempts. The Puritans succeeded in telling "a focused, compelling, and convincing story that no other immigrant group could match. Nevertheless, it was a story with which many immigrant groups could identify."[104] Sacvan Bercovich wrote how Protestantism gave "modern culture its ethic, but Puritanism gave it the myth of America. And no culture, let me add, ever stood more in need of a myth."[105] It was the lasting legacy of Puritan thought in the American literary tradition that an idealized vision of America sprung up.[106]

The sacred story of Exodus was first adopted in America by the seventeenth- and eighteenth-century puritans in New England as their foundational story. After that storytellers who have used the same protostory have varied from Jefferson and Franklin via Abraham Lincoln to Ronald Reagan. America has been portrayed in these narratives most often as Canaan, a new Promised Land. Even today immigrants to the United States from outside the Judeo-Christian tradition are portrayed in a very Reaganesque manner as wanderers or sojourners searching for the new Israel.[107] In the beginning of the story of the American experience, the entire old continent was portrayed as Egypt. When America began to struggle for its independence, England was given the role of Egypt—this is most strikingly evident in a 1776 painting of George III as Pharaoh in his chariot. Finally during the Civil War America began to find Egypt within itself. This time the Northern states were seen by the South as the oppressors, and likewise the North depicted the South as oppressors because of their slaveholding.[108] In that sense both sides became the Egypt for the other side. The sacred story of Egyptian oppression has been used in the context of internal politics ever since as well. Naturally this has never been as self-evident as the case of King George III. The theme of Egypt just lies there, ready for connotations and denotations but rarely spelled out to support partisan politics. More often it occurs in foreign policy, and all totalitarian states can be depicted as Egypts of their age.

The Exodus narrative resonates well with the American political reality. It is easy to cast Reagan into the character of "God's humble servant" Moses, but several other presidents could be given the same role. Moses liberated the people from bondage, crossed the Red Sea, and made a foundational and conditional covenant between the God and the people at Mount Sinai. He led his grumbling and unthankful people that continuously disobeyed God's will for a generation through the wilderness acting as a mediator of God's will. He had to die first, and only then Joshua could reap the rewards and lead the "chosen people" into the Promised Land. The basic plot is simple, but it can be elaborated and twisted to fit numerous different versions even to such a degree that completely opposing stories can be told.[109] The Exodus narrative can be used just as well as a master narrative than its counternarrative. As an example, one could portray the collapse of Soviet Union as an event leading into the realization of the Promised Land on a global scale. Reagan would fit the character of Moses by not being able to see the Promised Land himself, since it was finally his vice president, who took over the role of the leader and ultimately led the chosen people, Americans, into this land of milk and honey. As Gutterman notes, the most common interpretation or adaptation of the story is the version where Americans are the chosen people living in the Promised Land, and the notion that God continues to bless America is difficult to exorcise from the national mind-set. Partially the history of America with its colonization from Europe, and the abundance of natural resources, has helped to depict it as a land of opportunity and of "milk and honey" as well. This national self-perception continues to justify both American glory and national shame. Occasionally, the "mission" of spreading freedom and democracy has been beneficial on the world stage, but at other times the "manifest destiny" has caused America to exploit the world as well. Belief in oneself as God's chosen people has justified numerous collective American black spots and politics of exclusion.[110]

Exodus narrative was certainly crucial in the earlier times when America first was populated or even in Reagan's time, but then only among the immigrants. After coming to America the exodus has been completed and the Promised Land reached. After that another aspect of the Exodus narrative must be used, and this is the concept of a sojourner in the wilderness. The Promised Land has been gained, but the promise remains to be fulfilled. As the vast continent spread itself in front of the new settlers this wilderness had a dual meaning as both the Edenic Promised Land and also as dangerous, uncharted land of which nothing was known. It was the original manifest destiny to tame this wilderness and turn it into the New Eden.[111] Understanding this dualism between the Promised Land and the wilderness is central in understanding the American character.[112] An explanation can be found in these words of Jonathan Edwards; "When God is about to turn the earth into a Paradise, he does not begin his work where there is some good growth already, but in a wilderness...that the light may shine out of darkness, and the world be replenished from emptiness."[113]

This interpretation of God's will tries to show that the emptiness, which America was prior to colonization, was the starting point where God chose to create His paradise. Ever since the time of the pilgrims and puritans, America has been constantly moving toward the final establishment of an earthly paradise, and away from its origins as a wilderness. Certainly an important part of belief-based politics and the narratives used even today is bridging this gap between wilderness and New Eden, so that America can be established and reestablished again as the chosen nation. The fulfillment of the American dream in every citizen's life could be seen as the point when each wanderer in the wilderness is finally permitted to enter the Promised Land. God promised the chosen land for his people, and they were immediately upon arrival able to make the best of it. In Reagan's storyworld the actual struggle is twofold. First a person must struggle and labor to get to America, the physical location of the New Israel, and then he must struggle to make the American dream a reality in first in his own life, and then globally.

According to Boer, the story of exodus is a powerful and motivating myth, and it tells a political truth. But the truth is not what has taken place. It is something we can claim "at some future point, this political myth *will have been*."[114] Therefore, the political truth of exodus and every other political myth remains to be realized. Myths can be used to define identity here and now just as well as the glory of the future. Myth can provide visions of the past just as well as aspirations of future greatness. There is a need to put political myths under scrutiny to get a comprehensive idea on how these stories affect the American reality today, since myth is not confined to history.

THE SHINING CITY ON A HILL

> Don't let America sink back into the boredom and mediocrity of collectivism, into the politics of envy, protest, and special interests. Keep America upward bound, on the move; keep her always that shining city, that inspiration, that "last best hope" to all the oppressed and helpless of the world.
>
> Ronald Wilson Reagan[115]

Reagan constantly told the creation stories of America involving the Puritan pilgrims and the Founding Fathers. These stories did not always get re-created in rituals. But speech itself is a ritual. It is a performance where the myth can be solidified, and this is what Reagan often did by renarrating over and over again the exceptionality of America so that ultimately it became what everyone "knows."

> We stand for freedom in the world. We see the gulags and the prisons, those places where man is not free to do work of his choosing and profit from his labor, places where the freedom to worship God has been extinguished and where souls have withered. But we're blessed by God with the right to say of our country: This is where freedom is. This is the land of limitless possibilities. And you don't have to travel too far in the world to realize that we stand as a beacon, that America is today what it was two centuries ago, a place that dreamers dream of,

that it is what Winthrop said standing on the deck of the tiny Arabella off the Massachusetts coast, with a little group of Pilgrims gathered around him, and he said, "We shall be as a shining city for all the world upon the hill."[116]

To describe a story fully, one has to "include both elements that are unique to precisely that story and those to be found in other stories as well."[117] Thus the researcher ought to have experience with multiple narratives in order to provide a description that includes contrasts and comparison both within the story analyzed, and between this and other stories. These comparisons can point out the "story's special figurational aspects in relation to the cultural stock of stories available to the teller of the tale."[118] The concept of the "shining city on the hill" Reagan so loved to speak of works as a perfect example. The "shining city" practically became a trademark of Reagan's narration, since it was the primary means of depicting his mythical America, but its origins are elsewhere. The Gospel of Matthew says,

Ye are the light of the world. A city that is set on a hill cannot be hid. Neither do men light a candle, and put it under a bushel, but on a candlestick; and it giveth light unto all that are in the house. Let your light so shine before men, that they may see your good works, and glorify your Father which is in heaven.[119]

Typically for Reagan a certain story or a thematic concept is picked out for further elaboration. In this case the origin of the story is in the Bible, but intertextuality connects it with a wide array of cultural and ideological stories as well. But ultimately the story is given a slightly new meaning.

I've thought a bit of the "shining city upon a hill." The phrase comes from John Winthrop, who wrote it to describe the America he imagined. What he imagined was important because he was an early Pilgrim, an early freedom man. He journeyed here on what today we'd call a little wooden boat; and like the other Pilgrims, he was looking for a home that would be free. . . . I've spoken of the shining city all my political life, but I don't know if I ever quite communicated what I saw when I said it. But in my mind it was a tall, proud city built on rocks stronger than oceans, windswept, God-blessed, and teeming with people of all kinds living in harmony and peace; a city with free ports that hummed with commerce and creativity. And if there had to be city walls, the walls had doors and the doors were open to anyone with the will and the heart to get here. That's how I saw it, and see it still.[120]

The above quotation marks the only occasion during Reagan's eight-year presidency that he tried to elaborate and further describe his vision of the "shining city" that became an essential myth of past and future America. Here is also an example of Reagan trying to narrate something in a way of showing with words what his vision is like and trying to insert the picture of his "shining city" to be a part of the storyworlds created by his listeners just as he wants it to be. The city is like a fortress, so strong that even the oceans cannot erode its faith-based foundations. It stands proud and tall, undefeated, indeed unchallenged, enjoying the blessings of God and peace bestowed on it. It is a city that abides to the rules spelled out elsewhere during the storyworld construction. It is an impenetrable fortress for its enemies, and yet welcomes in everyone who wishes to enter and live according to its rules. Yet, it is like the kingdom of God, because it requires "the will and the heart to get there." As a matter of fact Reagan equates the Kingdom of God and America so profoundly that to be an American, is to belong to the Kingdom of God as well. "Let us remember that being an American means remembering another loyalty, a loyalty as the hymn puts it, 'to another country I have heard of, a place whose King is never seen and whose armies cannot be counted'."[121] There is strong symbolism included. Shining city symbolizes America while at the same time it symbolizes the Kingdom of God or at least its earthly manifestation. "America is still a symbol to a few, a symbol that is feared and hated, but to more, many millions more, a symbol that is loved, a country that remains a shining city on a hill."[122] The storyline of America as a symbol of all the aspirations of the world creates it is a truly special place. It stands above the hubbub of the disorganized world, showing the world what they should attempt to become themselves. Depicting America as the shining city has a political purpose.

> We must present to the world an America that is not just militarily strong, but an America that is morally powerful—an America that has a creed, a cause, a vision of a future time when all people of the world will have the right to self-government and personal freedom.[123]

But ultimately within the storyline America is not merely an exemplary nation, but the new version of Eden. As Frye argues, Eden has almost always been placed on a mountaintop. The Promised Land is always situated above the wilderness, "its capital being Jerusalem, the centre of the world and the city on the mountain, whither the tribes go up." This is evident just as well in Milton as in Ezekiel's wilderness vision of dry bones in a valley with the prophet seated "upon a very high mountain."[124] When Reagan places America as his "shining city on a hill" he raises it above the wilderness that all the rest of the world creates. America becomes at the same time a place specially touched by God and a place from where the heaven can be reached. It is not only Jerusalem, or even the Garden of Eden, it is something connected with the divinity itself.

Alexander Campbell might have played a role in the fact that Reagan added the adjective "shining" to Winthrop's "city on a hill." Campbell wrote that "the light which shines from our political institutions will penetrate even the dungeons of European despots, *for the genius of our government is the genius of universal emancipation.* Nothing can resist the political influence of a great nation, enjoying great political advantages, if she walks worthy of them."[125] These words could just as well have been Reagan's and show how great an influence religion actually played in shaping his world view.

> And how stands the [shining] city on this winter night? More prosperous, more secure, and happier than it was 8 years ago. But more than that: After 200 years, two centuries, she still stands strong and true on the granite ridge, and her glow has held steady no matter what storm. And she's still a beacon, still a magnet for all who must have freedom, for all the pilgrims from all the lost places who are hurtling through the darkness, toward home.[126]

Life in the world outside America is comparable to exodus in Reagan's story. His "shining city" is a lighthouse that at the same time illuminates the darkness in the world and serves to draw and guide the wanderers in the wild to "home". America is the new Promised Land, but the tribe whose home it is, is not defined by race, such as Israelites but all who "must have freedom." Allegedly, according to this farewell speech to the nation, after Reagan's presidency the city still stands, and has grown stronger and therefore more secure and prosperous. But the problem, even without discussion about other religions and how they might view America, is that within the Judeo-Christian tradition Americans can be portrayed also in the manner of Abraham Lincoln or Martin Luther King Jr. as "God's almost chosen people." The people are still sojourners, still wandering the desert wilderness, still looking for the actualization of their Promised Land. Israelites were sojourners once and are likely to be sojourners again, and the same applies in these modifications of the story to Americans as well.[127] There is strong inherent irony in the fact that the people of Israel are continuously by their prophets like Isaiah, Jeremiah, and

Micah told to treat the badly off sojourner well and generously, but this aspect is hard to find from the American domestic or foreign policy. The role of the Good Samaritan is one America chooses to perform very seldom.

Jonathan Culler argues that when one chooses to study myths, the mechanisms used should be somewhat different from the more conventional literature, and it takes a lot of effort to put together.

> The cultural context that provides clues to the nature of possible codes, and we start without a firm sense of meaning which would enable us to evaluate the description of myths. This requirement produces a spiral movement, in which one myth is used to elucidate another, and this leads on to a third which, in turn, can only be interpreted when read in the light of the first, etc.[128]

This structure is clearly apparent in Reagan's web of interconnected stories, where a certain storyline cannot be followed logically unless other storylines have previously been accepted, or shall get accepted in the process of reading. The idea of a "shining city on a hill" is absurd at a first glance, but when one delves deeper into the structures of Reagan's storyworld and the foundational myths America lives by, and discovers the crisscrossing storylines that give support to each other, can one begin to understand the concept. At the same time the spiral movement takes us on a mythical time travel through American history—mythified, of course. One has to travel back to the days when the Arabella landed on American shores and start following the creation and elucidation of the myth toward the present to understand how America can see itself as exceptional. One myth is built on top of another, and only by mythifying the entire American history and following that spiral, can one unravel the elaborately interwoven mythical story web. Just creating a storyworld version of America is not enough, but rather America has to be understood as a storyverse where this spiral elucidation of myths takes place with separate stories under the same story web, creating multiple Americas fused into a storyverse.

UNIFIED PAST, PRESENT, AND FUTURE IN MYTHICAL AMERICA

> The time is now, my fellow citizens, to resolve to recapture our destiny, to take it into our own hands.
>
> Ronald Wilson Reagan[129]

Joseph Campbell claimed that the hero of old myths is dead in our modernity. The society people live in is no longer grounded on religion but increasingly secularizing sociopolitical constructions. The society no longer aims at creating "a heaven on earth" and mythologies are supposedly understood as lies.[130] The mythical America is a society where myth is alive and tries to fulfill its promise of being the New Eden. Likewise Reagan's political storytelling is highly future-oriented and in a very Campbellian sense wants to allow the promise of a glorious future to become reality. There is a bind to the past, the past of New Deal, of the Founding Fathers, of the Puritans, and naturally the past of the Biblical times. This bind however exists only on the level of attitudes and beliefs. Reagan wanted to revive the old religious beliefs, myths, and heroes and to bring them back into the American discourse of his era. Myths and beliefs are so essential to Reagan's narratives that the society must be brought to believe in them and in an America endowed with mythical qualities.

So, a return into the times long ago is advocated by Reagan but only as the groundwork on which to build the tomorrow. America's meaning is to be found as much in the future as in the past.[131] Some of this future-orientation has its roots in Reagan's religiosity. Religion, at least in the Western three major religions, sees time as an arrow and history as teleological process, working to reach some destined end point, and not cyclical, like many of the Eastern religions. The teleological conception of time causes the Western religions to look into the future and believe in progress, and this belief was at the core of Reagan's politics. Wallace Martin writes that our Western world has lost "its devotion to the biblical plot of life, death, and rebirth, it finds earthly substitutes for God and a divine plan: empire and nation become objects of devotion."[132] In the case of Reagan's mythical America, this is not entirely true. In Reagan's storytelling the biblical plot runs on a parallel path to the more secular plot concerning the perfection of the American society toward its dream. They act as separate storylines, with their own hooks to catch the story recipient into the tangles of the entire mythical story web.

Our self-conception as a society can be achieved through the use of a unifying, foundational story that connects our past, present, and future into a teleological process leading toward a future perfection. This mythical metanarrative of the society can be composed of innumerable different stories, but under the umbrella of the metanarrative they have to be connected and understood as a single unfolding and developing story. In the words of Polkinghorne, the self "is not a static thing nor a substance, but a configuring of personal events into a *historical unity which includes not only what one has been but also anticipations of what one will be.*[133] Myth provides people with a sense of importance and direction as well as a communal focus for individual identities.[134] Reagan was able to provide his people with a unified view of themselves with an idea of a joint purpose. If the audiences chose to believe in the mythical story, they would become a part of America's future greatness.[135] This required the communicated message to include historical events into the configuration of the future. There is no vision of the future that is separated from the past and present, but the future must be narratively created (with an almost solid existence instead of being merely one possibility) by tying together a continuous teleological timeline that connects the past to the present and the choices that must be made to follow "on the right path" into the "right" future.

> I'm convinced that in 1980 America faced one of those historic choices that come to a nation only a few times a century. We could continue our decline, perhaps comforting ourselves by calling it inevitable, or we could realize that there is no such thing as inevitable, and choose instead to make a new beginning. The American people chose the way of courage, and on this January day 3 years ago, this administration and all of you began to make a new beginning.[136]

Zelinsky claims that America has never been on familiar and companionable terms with its history, and that the past and the present do not blend seamlessly.[137] Reagan created narrative binds between the past and present and used these storylines to bind the future as well. To achieve this, he created a story with America as the main character and drafted a plot for its course through time. History has to be emplotted and storied in order to be in any way communicable. It is only a huge mass of events, actions, and states, and to produce anything graspable for such a limited mind as a human's, the historian has to put in place beginnings, middles, and ends. If the historian refuses to make choices concerning where exactly he starts the telling, there can be nothing to tell. The flow of history has to be controlled by setting dams and breaking it into temporal units with beginnings and endings.[138] The seams Zelinsky mentioned disappear and fade as history gets storied. In the early times of American historiography, the historians had a sense of mission to explain how the country achieved its uniqueness, and the concept of national unity became the interpretative credo.[139] In other words, unity worked as the theme for the emplotment of the American history as they tried to weld together a common national heritage.

Polkinghorne argued that we tend to retrieve stories about our own and the community's past to provide us models to understand the how actions are linked to consequences. It is with the help of these models that we plan our own actions and interpret those of others.[140] These historical narratives, gone through the process of mythification, provide our contemporary times with points of reference and tools of interpretation. At the same time they shape our future as well, since these models of the past influence the strategic planning of our futures, while we might not advocate a return to the past itself. The reason to emphasize some of the mythical moments in American history, such as the founding or the time of the Puritans, and connecting them to present-day America lies in Bruce Lincoln's argument that individuals who feel attached to the same moment in the past can be brought together to feel attached to each other.[141] Thus narrativizing the past in a manner that people can associate with, creates a sense of unity in the present as well. This is why the foundational myths are of crucial importance even after over two centuries have passed from the days they took place in.

Hayden White tried in his "Metahistory" to make the point that historical narrative is best understood as the construction of a story about reality rather than as a direct representation of it. There is not, nor ever was, a way to actually know the past as it was, unless one lived in it, and even then the limits of human perception and memory create hindrances.[142] Any historical narrative differs from more paradigmatic discourses in producing a coherence of events ordered by story logic. Historical narrative is for Polkinghorne only one of three narrative discourses. Two others that produce meanings through plot structures are literature and myth. They are all results of cultural attempts to

> impose a satisfactory, graspable, humanizing shape on experience. The historical narrative [and myth] takes the types of plot developed by literature and subjects them to the test of endowing real events with meaning. . . . Historical narratives are a test of the capacity of a culture's fictions to endow real events with the kinds of meaning patterns that its stories have fashioned from imagined meanings.[143]

In other words, myths, literature, and narrative history are deeply connected. Myths are often refined in literature to more elaborate stories, and these stories are used in creating history. Reagan's process of creating narratively a mythical America is about using myths to emplot a version of a historical narrative. Mythical narratives provide us with an alternative means of knowing that resonates with community and identity. They also form a connection with religion as everyday experience providing certainty in a manner Aaltola describes as "politico-religious."[144] According to Frye, it is in the form of metahistory that most history reaches the general public. The historian proper confines his imitations of action to human events, always looks for a human cause, and avoids the miraculous or the providential. He works inductively, and tries to avoid any informing patterns, except those that can be seen in the facts themselves. The metahistorian works deductively by seeking to impose a certain pattern on his subject. He chooses a certain historical, legendary, or contemporary theme to use to give his story of history perspective.[145] While there certainly is something called historical reality, it gets sullied as soon as humans try to process, store, or communicate it. It no longer is a "fact" but only an interpretation, a narration about what took place. Frye sees similarities between a historian and a poet, but the difference is that the poet "makes no specific statements of fact, and hence is not judged by the truth or falsehood of what he says." The poet "imitates the universal, not the particular; he is concerned not with what happened but with what happens."[146] Thus, Reagan did not have to tell the truth of what actually happened but only describe what tends to occur in his mythical America. Of course he formulated his story so that he seemed to narrate the events with the objectivity of a historian but took poetic liberties in blending fact and fiction.

> We are kind of a miracle. I have always said—you may call it mysticism if you will—but there had to be some divine plan that placed these great continents here between the two great oceans to be found by that kind of people. And that, maybe, is our purpose in life.[147]

Edmund Morris writes about Reagan that "there never was a politician more interested in the past,"[148] but I strongly disagree with him. It was the actual events and people in recent history that Reagan took no interest in. On the contrary he was very keen on the past, but it was the mythified past of the stories.

> History's no easy subject. Even in my day it wasn't, and we had so much less of it to learn then. [Laughter] But one of the most valuable benefits of a study of the past is that it gives you a perspective on the present. I think it's probably true that every generation, every age, is prone to think itself beset by unusual and particularly threatening

difficulties and to look back on the past as a golden age when issues were not so complex and politics not so divisive and when problems didn't seem so intractable. Sometimes we're tempted to think of the birth of our country as one such golden age: a time characterized primarily by harmony and cooperation and reason.[149]

MacIntyre notes that in all those cultures where moral thinking and action is structured according to classical schemes, the chief means of moral education is the telling of stories. Every one of these cultures "possesses a stock of stories which derive from and tell about its own vanished *heroic age*."[150] This stock of stories for example about the Founding Fathers, provide the historical memory of the society, whether adequate or inadequate.

> If America is to remain the free and vibrant country that we want her to be, and if she's to be the great land of opportunity, we can't lose sight of those principles laid down by our Founding Fathers. And we must have the same courage and dedication as those brave souls who built America.[151]

In order to understand contemporary America, we need to understand a heroic society, whether it indeed actually ever has existed anywhere or in any age. "We're a country of heroes,"[152] claims Reagan. A person in a heroic society is what he does, and thus every individual has been a given role and status within a well-defined and determinate system. In fact, morality and social structure are the one and the same in a heroic society, and a person becomes one only through his role. For Mead identity is rooted in the sense of solidarity with the ideas and ideals of a historical community, and thus man is at the same time a creature as well as creator of his culture.[153] Identity of the self is a social creation, not an individual one.[154] As MacIntyre notes, we are what our past has turned us into, and

> we cannot eradicate from ourselves, even in America, those parts of ourselves which are formed by our relationship to each formative stage in our history. If this is so, then even a heroic society is still an inescapably a part of us all, and we are narrating a history that is peculiarly *our own* history when we recount its past in the formation of our moral culture.[155]

The heroic American society is a part of the contemporary society, because it exists in the past that has formed today. For Reagan America is still a heroic society and, following his political vision, will forever

remain so. "Our future can be as heroic and as exciting as we will it
to be. Each day brings new opportunities for great dreams and great
feats. Let's begin now—united, confident, and determined to get
the job done."[156] In a heroic society, storytelling is the main means
of educating people to the virtues of the society,[157] but as Niebuhr
argued, there is an "ironic tendency of virtues to turn into vices when
too complacently relied upon."[158] Thus, if the American way of life
and the dream are to remain healthy, every now and then an evaluation of their basics has to be performed and modifications made into
the national narrative to keep the heroic society vibrant. The purpose
of the political storyteller is to choose the most fitting cultural myths
to use in each occasion. The difficulty lies in the ability to retrieve
these stories so that the possible connotations are likely to advance
his political purposes. The story of George Washington on his knees
at Valley Forge[159] can be used to bring up connotations of a people
not too proud to believe in God and pray for his help or to back up
a vision of a country used to overcoming hardships. For the context
of Reagan era foreign policies and "peace through strength" another
story must be employed. Certain storylines of the cultural collection
fit certain occasions, and Reagan was gifted in choosing the most
fitting ones and embellishing them. History and fiction blended in
his narration.

> Those rebels may not have had fancy uniforms or even adequate
> resources, but they had a passion for liberty burning in their
> hearts....The morning of the surrender must have been very much
> like this one today. The first real chill of autumn was in the air. The
> trees were burning brilliant with the hues of red and gold and brown.
> The sky was bright and clear. Quiet had finally returned to the coun-
> tryside. How strange the silence must have seemed after the thunder-
> ing violence of war. And then the silence was broken by a muffled beat
> of British drums, covered with black handkerchiefs, as the Redcoats
> marched to surrender. The pageantry was spectacular. The French
> in their spotless uniforms lined one side of the road. The ragged
> Continentals were brown and dreary on the other side....On that day
> in 1781 a philosophy found a people and the world would never be the
> same....The beacon of freedom shines here for all who will see, inspir-
> ing free men and captives alike and no wall, no curtain, nor totalitar-
> ian state can shut it out.[160]

In this "recollection" of the British surrender Reagan positioned
himself as a spectator to the event and tried to transmit the way
things looked like. Just as in his early days as a sports caster, he used

words to paint pictures of events just as he himself had been there that day. This is a characteristic feature in his storytelling. By creating scenes to his audiences he simultaneously re-creates and mythifies history. In his words the "pageantry was spectacular," "the first real autumn chill was in the air," "the morning *must* have been like the one today." With references between the time of narration and the time of narrated, and by depicting the scene he cued the listeners to his speech to "see" the narrated events through his words. It does not matter what that day centuries ago was like, because it had been created anew in storytelling as a greater than life experience. The scene Reagan depicts is removed from the context of history and taken as a separate scene of a foundational myth to back up Reagan's narration of the world-changing importance of the event depicted. When historical events are narrated in this manner, they turn into the stuff of myth. Alterations of the past will reflect on what must be done in the future. Reagan gives a new shape to the history of America, but, as Riessman argues, "The 'truths' of narrative accounts is not in their faithful representations of a past world, but in the shifting connections they forge among past, present and future."[161] All narrators, including Reagan, interpret the past in their stories, rather than producing the past as it was. Genette notes that the most persistent function of recalls is "to modify the meaning of past occurrences after the event, even by making significant what was not so originally or by refuting a first interpretation and replacing it with a new one."[162] In Reagan's narrative this is evident, since history is twisted to fit into Reagan's world view and the importance or nonsignificance is determined in the course of the narration.

History always has a meaning in Reagan's narration. The meaning of the past may perhaps not be found in the events themselves without an explanation. This process of explanation or interpretation, according to Jerome Bruner, gives new meanings and points of emphasis.[163] By employing a certain perspectival interpretation of the American history, Reagan could pass on his promise of the future. Sticking to the values embedded in the American way of life, past events are interpreted so that the future can become the glorious epoch of Reagan's vision. He seemed to realize that his narration alone was not enough to alter the perception of the past sufficiently, and therefore he called for assistance to make the chosen value-embedded perception of the past the accepted norm of the America.

So, we've got to teach history based not on what's in fashion but what's important—why the Pilgrims came here, who Jimmy Doolittle was, and what those 30 seconds over Tokyo meant. You know, 4 years ago on the 40th anniversary of D—day, I read a letter from a young woman writing to her late father, who'd fought on Omaha Beach. Her name was Lisa Zanatta Henn, and she said, "We will always remember, we will never forget what the boys of Normandy did." Well, let's help her keep her word. If we forget what we did, we won't know who we are. I'm warning of an eradication of the American memory that could result, ultimately, in an erosion of the American spirit. Let's start with some basics: more attention to American history and a greater emphasis on civic ritual. And let me offer lesson number one about America: All great change in America begins at the dinner table. So, tomorrow night in the kitchen I hope the talking begins. And children, if your parents haven't been teaching you what it means to be an American, let 'em know and nail 'em on it. That would be a very American thing to do.[164]

Most of Reagan's farewell address to the nation is a call for rearticulation of America. He calls American's to reflect upon the true nature of America. He calls for "informed patriotism," but the content of the information to be taught is reaffirmation of his mythical America. Reagan's generation, he tells, got the meaning of being American from their families, schools, and communities, or if all else failed, from popular culture. The idea of teaching "an ambivalent appreciation of America" to children has lost popularity, and children themselves need to tell their parents that they have not done proper teaching. None of this reads like "informed patriotism." It is essentially about telling stories that cue their listeners to love their country, and what it is told to stand for unquestioningly. Reagan talks about teaching history based not "on fashion, but what's important." There is no room for objectivity. "What's important" are not essentially the "facts" of history, but things like reason behind the pilgrimage to America, or the meaning of 30 seconds over Tokyo, or Jimmy Doolittle. Certain things need to be taught, and those are the things that teach, coerce, and even force one into loving "my country, right or wrong." If the Reaganesque view of history does not get sedimented into the accepted version of history, Americans will "forget what we did" and will not know "who we are." Lest the patriotic teachings of history get institutionalized into the way people think, the "erosion of American spirit" is what ultimately could happen. Love of America, American way of life, and the American dream are the things he wishes he could leave imprinted in the collective memory of the American people.

Reagan viewed narrative as a legitimate mode of historical representation, because the communicative function of narrative is so central to all of his politics. If history is seen as communication, then it boils down to being a message about a referent, and its content is both information and explanation. The past takes the place of a referent, and the narrative account provides the explanations necessary. The correspondence of the story to the events it describes is at the level of the conceptual content of the message.[165] Reagan's view of narrative history differs from its social scientific counterpart by dramatizing events and novelizing historical processes, and thus aiming to produce meanings peculiar to American culture as opposed to "real" events.[166] History has to be emplotted, restructured, and narrated anew so that what is politically "important" gets to be told. By emplotment, separate events can be brought together by enforcing causality on them, and a unified and extraordinary meaning is established.

> I preach no manifest destiny, but I do say we Americans cannot turn our backs on what history has asked of us. Keeping alive the hope of human freedom is America's mission, and we cannot shrink from the task or falter in the call to duty.[167]

In the Reagan era American history was packaged, as Garry Wills calls it, the myth of "original sinlessness."[168] According to Reagan's interpretation America started anew on a clean slate and thus was not marred by the original sin, which according to a multitude of theologians has tainted all of humanity since the exile from Eden. With the founding of America, Eden was reentered and paradise regained. The use of original sinlessness is one of the factors that enabled Reagan to view his mythical America as a perfect society, since there was no flaw in the beginning and the foundational myths can be pure. The United States of America certainly has a history, which has been written down and researched thoroughly, but Reagan replaces the United States with his America through the manipulation of a storyverse. The story recipient is transported into the America where history is the stuff of myths and not of scholarly studies. Reagan's mythical America exists out of historical time flow. It is contained in its own bubble of *kairos* time. Barthes gives one plausible explanation why Reagan is able to use such fuzzy temporality in his narration. For him "mythical history [has] a time-scale different to that of political history."[169]

Myth fuzzes temporality and blends all time periods into one, mythical time instead of separate periods, some of which are still yet to occur. The millennium has not yet happened, but it just as well could have, since it is taken as a certainty. Lévi-Strauss goes further to argue that in our times and societies "history has replaced mythology and fulfils the same function."[170] He claims that in those societies, which emphasize the importance of myths, the future is faithful to the present and the past, but in our times "the future should always be different, and ever more different, from the present, some difference depending, of course on our political preferences."[171] This is why Reagan's concept of an ever better future cannot be denied. His political narration was based on a past and a future that, despite their differences, are similar in their myth-like qualities. The use of mythical time allowed Reagan to blend all time into one unified sphere of experience. Thus the Founding Fathers can be treated as if they still were giving advice to the nation, or that the American Revolution never ended but continues in a political form.

> The impossible dream of those patriots was about to be transformed into the reality of a bright new Nation. The King's troops came slowly down the road to the surrender field; legend has it that they struck up the tune "The World Turned Upside Down." And, indeed, the old order was to be turned upside down, for the creative powers of Democracy were about to be released on an unsuspecting world.[172]

The world is turned upside down, old history has ended, the slate has been wiped clean, and America makes a new beginning, starting history all over again. Ordinary time has been replaced with mythical time. While every myth refers to events that allegedly have taken place in the distant past, "what gives the myth operational value is that the specific pattern described is timeless; it *explains the present and the past as well as the future*."[173] Myths and narratives are commonly seen to concern themselves only about the past, but this is a gross misunderstanding. For Lévi-Strauss, "any myth represents a guest for the remembrance of things past."[174] Creating and telling myths work toward trying to remember things long forgotten, or even creating a past that has never existed, and remembering that past as if it had once taken place.

Simultaneously politics are eschatological and strive toward a Utopia, which is the collective dream of a society as it wishes itself to be some time in the future (or as it envisions itself to have been in the past.) Myths of national greatness of goodness enable the society to idolize itself. The transcendent world of heroes and ancestors (or the Founding Fathers) has to remain accessible by the means of ritual, which abolishes chronological time, and recovers the sacred time. According to Eliade, this revolt against the irreversibility of time allows the society to both construct reality and assure that the past can be abolished and life began anew with the re-creation of the world.[175] This does not demand an apocalyptic worldview but only the inbuilt timelessness and ahistoricity of the myth. Like any narrative, a myth can begin *in medias res*, since mythical time is unconnected to historical time. At any moment the slate can be wiped clean, and Reagan kept offering citizens the choices that can wipe the history away and turn the tide toward the future glory.

> History's verdict will depend on us—on our courage and our faith, on our wisdom and our love. It'll depend on what we do or fail to do for the cause of millions who carry just one dream in their hearts: to live lives like ours, in this special land between the seas, where each day a new adventure begins in a revolution of hope that never ends.[176]

Adventures require heroes, and as we have discussed, Reagan created a heroic role for himself. Indeed, Joseph Campbell's "hero with a thousand faces" is to some degree what any politician using narratives as his tools of leadership should aim for. Whether this mythical hero slays a dragon, or performs any act of heroism, he always attacks the status quo which binds today into the past.[177]

> My opponent and his allies live in the past. They are celebrating the old and failed policies of an era that has passed them by, as if history had skipped over those Carter-Mondale years. On the other hand, millions of Americans join us in boldly charting a new course for the future.[178]

The task of the hero is therefore to "release" the future or actually to make possible the switch from immobility into progress. What existed, according to the story logic before his administration took over was "that moment of misfortune and malaise, that 'Reign of Error'."[179] The present moment of narration is "America of pride and power: powerful at home, powerful in the councils of the world, powerful in our ability to maintain the peace."[180] Tomorrow, on the other hand, is such that "America's future can be determined by our dreams and by our visions. Together, we've opened new doors to discovery, opportunity, and progress."[181] While new doors are opened and future released, it is worthwhile to note that the hero may also take the place of the beast he has slain and become the tyrant of tomorrow.[182] Another political narrator may arise and portray the politics, no matter how much progress is being made, as stagnated and immobile in his storytelling.

Reagan was not a figure situated in the present, since the present is ambivalent. Each tick of the clock transforms future into the past. Present is just a time for choosing, when political decisions have to be made and each of these moments enable a different future to come into existence. The present is always a moment of instantaneous choices, and the eyes of Reagan looked only to the past and the future. "For one tick of the history's clock we gave the world a shining golden hope. Mankind looked to us. Now the door is closing on that hope and it could be your destiny to keep it open."[183] James Combs articulates fittingly the task facing Reagan. He had to "re-enchant the world, to imbue the profane present with the aura of sacral past in order to forestall or reverse the rapid decomposition of value orientations."[184] This is what Reagan did with his concept of mythical America that is sanctified by the past, yet looking toward the future.

> Our vision is not an impossible dream; it's a waking dream. As Americans, let us cultivate the art of seeing things invisible. . . . The dream of America is much more than who we are or what we do. It is, above all, what we will be. We must always be the New World—the world of discovery, the world that reveres the great truths of its past, but that looks forward with unending faith to the promise of the future. In my heart, I know we have that faith. The dream lives on. America will remain future's child, the golden hope for all mankind.[185]

When narration is what Uri Margolin calls "concurrent narration," events are narrated in present tense, as if happening simultaneously with the process of narration. The stages of narration are matched with the stages of the narrated, and the narration itself becomes the "gradual figuring out what the case is as it evolves."[186] One cannot in fact live a story and narrate it at the same time; the attempt to do so results rather in ongoing reporting. "My friends, we live in a world that's lit by lightning. So much is changing and will change, but so much endures and transcends time."[187] Reagan's idea of temporality is very clearly expressed here. The world is "lit by lighting" refers to the suddenness of change; the mere fact that we get glimpses of our world while for microseconds the darkness is chased away by a flash only to return again. And when the next flash takes place, everything looks different. There is nothing steady, the pace of life is hectic, and progress is continuous, and yet the old-fashioned, old-time wisdoms and values are omnipresent and remain unchanged between flashes of lightning. The "now" is just a fleeting moment, and the world may seem entirely different when the next flash comes by. "Well, everything we do is a fragment of history, a passing moment in time."[188]

Nevertheless the "now" has meaning in a political narration. The past needs to be a beautiful picture, and while today can be depicted as merely a bleak moment in time, Reagan's internal optimism, which was part of his fascination for Americans, did not consider even the present as hopeless.

> There are generations that preside over transition periods like this, when there are great changes in the world. And we've been one of those. And no generation in history, no people have ever fought harder, paid a higher price for freedom, or done more to advance the dignity of man than our generation. And I'm not going to apologize to anyone for what we've done with our lives so far.[189]

Garry Wills put the point fittingly when he argued that Reagan saw America clearly poised "between the Good Old Days and the Brave New World. We pass from one perfection to another, through an interspace it were best not to advert to."[190] But some of the glory of the future is at least occasionally reflected on the here and now.

> Memory is far from infallible and when it comes to the "good old days" it leaves out a lot of the not so good. . . . Now, don't get me wrong my memories are pretty happy and I enjoy closing my eyes now and then for a re-run or two. But I also find life exciting and good today, *in truth better in most respects.*[191]

There are great risks involved if a politician focuses too much on the present moment. The narrated world is continuously in the process of becoming. It takes shape as it is narrated. It is not a bounded world but only turning into one, and no pattern, plot, or narrative theme can be used to describe such an evolving story.[192] Just because of this, concurrent narration should be avoided in political narratives. Since the present can only be described or reported and not storied in such a manner that a coherent plot could be progressively built, the narrator has no control upon how the story will evolve. This helps us understand why the weakest moment of Reagan's entire storytelling was the period when he had to narrate the Iran-Contra scandal, while the entire process was still ongoing. This also explains Reagan's extensive isolation from the press during the process when hearings of Oliver North and Admiral John Pointdexter were still continuing. Reagan was not in control of the way the plot emerged from one moment to another. Only when the Tower Board had published its report, did Reagan again participate, and contribute to the story. By then it had become possible to set all events within a narrative macrostructure and turn them into a coherent whole, or in other words, retrospectively emplot the events that had or had not taken place. During such perilous moments when failures were discussed, Reagan attempted to get his story recipients to move their focus away from the "now." This is also evident during his campaign for the second term of presidency.

> We shouldn't be dwelling on the past, or even the present. The meaning of this election is the future.[193]

By projecting the meaning of the election, of any choice to be made, out of its contemporary context and into the future, Reagan was able to at least attempt to escape the failures of his politics that were manifest in the time of the campaign. It is in religious terms an attempt at expiation from the sins. The Reagan administration had continuously promised a "brighter tomorrow," and when it had not actualized, the electorate should according to his storytelling turn its interest into the future to come. There has been practically a promise of deliverance by the administration but no actual delivery due to the vagueness of promises. After all, how can one define whether Reagan's America really "turned the tide of history away from totalitarian darkness and into the warm sunlight of human freedom"[194] or if America has been moved "into a great promised land of freedom, dignity, and happiness?"[195] If there had been more tangible promises, would failure or success have been verifiable objectively. Since there were failures, such as increasing taxation and growing national debts, there was a need for redemption. The unifying factors of the failures of economic policies, for example, were individual policy decisions and not a part of the grand vision Reagan had of mythical America. He could quite effectively narrate himself around these failures, but had they been part of the all-encompassing myth, the failures would have collapsed the entire story logic and taken the plausibility of the storyverse of the American dream with it. Now the failures could be depicted as minor and not deadly sins as such.

> As we work to make the American dream real for all, we must adhere to traditional values, keep our faith in God, and put our trust in people, rather than in the Government, to solve the problems before us. . . .

> Through a recommitment to our fundamental values, we can achieve a collective vision for a rising America—now, and for the future.[196]

A myth need not be only a eulogy of past greatness but also a political tool to bring about that greatness again. While *kronos-time* irreversibly turns the present into the past, the mythical narrative in it is able to work in nonlinear and reversible time and blur the distinctions between what has happened, what is happening, and what will happen. Storytelling allows the narrator to present things in the future as if they had already happened, and the timelessness allows a skillful narrator to explain the past with the same ease as the future. This is the benefit of entering the mythical *kairos-time*, where every moment has special significance while yet every moment is fundamentally one and the same. Things will happen as narrated, since in mythical time they are so connected with the past, that there is no way for them not to.

In the words of Livia Polanyi, narratives "tell about a series of events which took place at specific unique moments in a unique past time world."[197] All of the American experience is unique to Reagan. But when discussing the features of the present or describing the glorious future of America, the tenses in Polanyi's citation need to be replaced with present and future tenses. There is nothing that would prevent this logically, only the focalization of the narrative turns toward the unique things to come and anticipating them. While myths are used for the perfection of the beginnings, they are at the same time projected into the timeless future. The past mythical America of the Founding Fathers that was the origin of the American dream echoes into the future as well. As Eliade writes, "The 'origin' is no longer found only in the mythical past but also in a fabulous future.... It is in conceptions of eschatology understood as a cosmogony of the future that we find the sources of all beliefs that proclaim the Age of Gold to be not merely (or no longer) in the past but also (or only) in the future."[198] The mythical America lies still ahead in all Her glory. The past is crucial in any mythical political narrative, but it has to be a past distant enough to be mythified and turned into something with a profound meaning and purpose. The very recent past is marred and impure. Only the mythified past can be used as the soil where the political narrator plants the seeds of his story and cultivates it to grow a future more glorious than ever before. As Reagan put it, "The heritage of our past will bring forth the harvest of our future."[199]

Edmund Morris claims that even Reagan's tendency to reminisce about his days as the Governor of California or the Hollywood days, was not looking back but rather "an eager application of history to today and tomorrow."[200] According to Cannon, Reagan used his optimistic imagination to transform his childhood and rest of his past into an idyll, and later managed to create an America that never was, founded on an imagined version of the past. This vision had meaning to others because of its sheer power and Reagan's personal belief in it.[201] And this vision is projected into the future without advocating a return to the past at all. Even when Reagan seemed to dwell in the past golden age of America, he was already dreaming of the glorious tomorrow. Wills articulates this by claiming that for Reagan, "we were suspended between two glowing myths: the religious past and the technological future."[202] Or, in the words of Reagan himself,

> The dream of America is much more than who we are or what we do; the dream is what we will be. We must always be the New World, the world of discovery, the world that reveres the great truths of its past but that pushes on with unending faith toward the promise of the future. In my heart, I know we have that faith. The dream lives on. America will remain future's child, the golden hope of all mankind.[203]

Storytelling is not only retrospective activity intended to delineate the meanings of past actions but self-making and world-making activity where identity and context of the past, present, and future are delineated and a unified conception of reality is projected into the world.[204] Reagan's first secretary of state Alexander M. Haig saw Reagan's political views to include the notion that "to make foreign policy for a powerful state is, to a degree, to make the future."[205] Politics that concern today, must not limit themselves to making today better, but essentially to create, primarily narratively, but also in a more concrete manner, the future.

> We all believe in America's mission. We believe that in a world wracked by hatred and crisis, America remains mankind's best hope. The eyes of history are upon us, counting on us to protect the peace, promote a new prosperity, and provide for a better tomorrow.[206]

To release the future and to enter the better future it is necessary that history can be eradicated anytime. During Reagan's 20-minute walkabout around the city of Moscow during the 1988 summit with Gorbachev, a reporter was able to confront Reagan with a question about whether he still though he was in an evil empire, and Reagan denied. When asked why he replied "I was talking about another time in another era."[207] Times and eras seem to fluctuate very rapidly since the "evil empire" speech had been just five years earlier. Twenty years earlier Reagan had been even harsher by arguing that in another decade, the world will be headed either in the direction of freedom or slavery. Peaceful coexistence on Russia's terms is a satanic, diabolical device of the enemy to blunt our sword while he moves into position for the kill. Freedom is never more than one generation away from extinction. We must save it now or spend our sunset years telling our children and our children's children what it was like when men were free.[208]

Some criticized Reagan of being guilty of "vaporization" in the terms of George Orwell. This meant that "Big Brother" wants to change a historical or present fact and contradictory evidence is made to disappear. This is a prominent part of Reagan's leadership, and as Reeves notes "that skill, that gift was at the heart of Reagan's formidable politics. He imagined a past. He imagined a world. And he made people believe in the past he imagined, and a future, too."[209] Past is like a vast array of stories, a bag the politician can dip in on choice and bring up features that support his storytelling and more importantly the storyverse where American dream has fused with the way of life—the future.

> Knowledge of the past is one of our most treasured possessions, for only with an accurate picture of where we have been can we see where we must go....We must ensure that the gains of the past are not lost in the future and in so doing we can look to tomorrow with confidence.[210]

The past can also be treated as is a mirror for the politician to hold in front of the society but for the purposes of politics the mirror has to be like of the carnival funhouse mirrors. It has to distort the past to make it look better, so that the society could see a reflection of itself that is closer to the Durkheimian ideals than the reality. This metaphorical mirror distorts the present and the future as well. The negative aspects of the present, such as the homeless, do not show in the mirror, and when it comes to the future, it is reflected in all the glory it is possible to narrate to possess. But always, the future can be seen only as a reflective image of the past. It is not similar to the past, but by decoding the past, the future can be deduced.

Crable and Vibbert referred to Reagan's strategy of instilling calm, not heightening anxieties, and focusing of references to the future as "political faith healing."[211] But the problem with faith healing as a metaphor is that its success is dependent on the actual healing process taking place. What Reagan did, was not predicting what the future would hold, but rather providing the story recipients with a rough outline of the future. He envisioned a future, depicted it promisingly, and led the people toward this vision. The essential characteristics of this vision are well articulated by Boer, who writes that each and every political system "operates in terms of an ideal or utopian projection of what it might be. The key to realizing that ideal is overcoming some obstruction or other."[212] But the obstruction is important since such a limit makes the system work. "Should the ideal be realized, the system would collapse."[213] In a sense every vote, every decision, every election, and every moment is an obstacle, and it is important to keep new obstructions appearing constantly so that new choices have to be made in striving toward the ultimate utopia. As Bruce Lincoln argues, "extremely important" myths are not set in the past but in the future, "a mythic future that—like the mythic past—enters discourse in the present always and only for the reasons of the present."[214]

The ultimate utopia is narrated as attainable but in practice there is no way to determine whether it has been or even could be reached. Thus the promise of the future utopia beckons the people forward but itself moves further all the time. While the ultimate state of bliss is the objective or destination, progress can be depicted as practically an eternal force, and balancing the certainty of the future utopia against the uncertainty concerning how much more needs to be done before it would actualize, creates a politically favorable environment where the citizens strive forward without cessation. Narrative is always controlled by time and the recognition that temporality is the primary dimension of human existence.[215] We are creatures of time, and thus the stories we tell cannot completely escape temporality although temporality can and often is manipulated for some purposes within the narrative. "Never has there been a more exciting time to be alive, a time of rousing wonder and heroic achievement. As they said in the film 'Back to the Future,' 'Where we're going, we don't need roads.'"[216] While it is an invigorating thought for the citizenry to hang on to, Reagan's America with its mission was a frightening concept internationally, since his policies were founded on the fact that

we'll never stop. America will never stop. We never give up. We'll never give up on our special mission. There are new worlds on the horizon, and we're not going to stop until we all get there together. America's best days are yet to come. You ain't seen nothin' yet.[217]

Coda

Philosophy ages; poetry rejuvenates.

Mohammad Allama Iqbal[1]

In 1994 Reagan addressed the American public for the very last time in a letter that revealed he was suffering from Alzheimer's disease. This letter was short, frank, and candid, but it clearly revealed that the Great Communicator still existed. At the end of the handwritten letter are the following words:

> When the Lord calls me home, whenever that may be, I will leave with the greatest love for this country of ours and eternal optimism for its future. I now begin the journey that will lead me into the sunset of my life. I know that for America there will always be a bright dawn ahead.[2]

Even when Alzheimer's disease had begun to affect his life, this optimism was an ineradicable part of Reagan's nature even to such a degree that, according to Michael Deaver, he survived politically only by having people around him protecting him from himself.[3] While optimism was on the one hand a liability in politics, it was certainly the most important factor that enabled Reagan to communicate his message of an ever more glorious future to come for America. While Reagan lived long ridden with the Alzheimer's disease, his public appearances practically faded away. There were a few speaking occasions, which proved to be somewhat humiliating, since Reagan was no longer fully compos mentis due to the disease. Thus he practically disappeared from the public to be taken care of by his loving Nancy. We can say that the farewell letter was the coda of Reagan's long life story, or at least the version that he narrated for his beloved America. It is fitting that in his farewell letter he for the last time affirmed his faith in America's future. Reagan remained true to his narration to the end.

Now it is time to start drawing this story to its closure, and write a coda. I have used repetitive tellings and even tautology to point out the obvious. Those religious beliefs, myths we tell ourselves about ourselves, ideologies we support and politics we follow, culture that encompasses us, are all interconnected in numerous ways. But I cannot stress enough the importance of noticing the obvious in this context. Stories and their use bind all these things together. Each of the individual topics is best communicated—and perhaps only communicable—through narrative form. The use of narratives allows all these aspects of our beliefs and values to bind together into a Gordian knot, which is difficult to untangle. But we must untangle it to escape the belief that our politics are carried out based on cool calculation and rational decisions of pure intellect. Belief, whatever is its objective, is still a huge factor in the way we perceive ourselves as individuals and as societies. We must analyze our political actions by questioning the foundational basis of our thinking. We must be able to dissect the web of myths and beliefs to understand how they influence the ideologies and policies we choose when we accept certain parts of our existence as "common sense" and act under the illusion of rationality.

> We must preserve the noble promise of the American dream for every man, woman, and child in this land. And, make no mistake, we can preserve it, and we will. That promise was not created by America. It was given to America as a gift from a loving God—a gift proudly recognized by the language of liberty in the world's greatest charters of freedom, our Declaration of Independence, the Constitution, and the Bill of Rights.[4]

I have attempted to prove that myths, political and ideological stories, and religious beliefs in the shape of narratives are tightly interconnected into a web where each supports the other; myths originally based on religious beliefs, cultural stories supported by ideologies, which are in turn founded on myths et cetera. The combinations are stupefying and need to be put under further scrutiny in future studies in order to understand the forces in play in driving our contemporary politics. We live in an age of increased rationalization inflicting every sphere of our lives, and it is important to understand that our beliefs and the "common sense" of mythical thinking affect the policymaking. We should not restrict ourselves to using mere game theory or other ultrarational approaches in the study of politics.

After having spent years immersed in the storyverse of Reagan, the man behind the stories still remains a mystery to me. His character is an enigma, a puzzle almost impossible to solve. A researcher cannot decipher what the true personality of the man behind the image of the "all-American" president with his amicable smile is. We can easily home in on his enacted and narrated persona or the public image, but as soon as we try to close in on the "real" Reagan, the stories block our path. Reagan spun a carapace of stories around him, and that is difficult to penetrate. Anything Reagan wrote about himself cannot be accepted at face value, since he embellished facts to create more compelling stories. We can still research the political life of Reagan with relative ease, but even then the narrative framework partially obscures much of the information we would wish to gain. Too many serious scholars have made the mistake of treating what Reagan said about his life as factual, and that has caused us to think we know the real Reagan. The ones who take into account the mythical stories Reagan told about his life seem to agree that only his wife Nancy Reagan was able to penetrate the protective shell Reagan had created. And even she has hinted that there were places she could not enter.

What arises from the stories told by Reagan, however, is Reagan himself. Not the real Reagan, but the narrated version. When he recounted his life experiences, he was also creating a self. To tell about experience is to make oneself known to the story recipients, and thus a new addition is made to the identity of the teller whenever he tells about his life.[5] Ronald Reagan's life story blends into one with the sacred story of the American dream and so does his love for America and the American way of life. He loved America not only for having been taught to but also because of everything America offered him. His life story is the story of the fulfillment of the American dream. He was a poor son of an alcoholic Irishman from rural Midwest, who nevertheless seemed to have success in every walk of life.[6] His success was living proof that the American dream had a true foundation as a cultural myth. Even Reagan did not think that the dream was perfect, but everybody had an equal chance. He knew that life was full of injustice and hard to live, but at the same time he saw the American system as ripe with promise. The mere fact of Reagan's personal "rags-to-riches" story could act as a proof that his great vision of American way of life and dream could be fulfilled, and by being an example of this, his story metamorphoses into a part of the American belief system he tried to create. While his life story becomes a micronarrative within the entire mythical superstructure, he is transformed from a minister of the faith in American dream into an object of faith almost in the same manner a saint in Christianity is.

Reagan was a part of his story of a mythical America and its dreams in a complex manner. On one hand he was a hero, since his life story "proves" the truth of the myth, and he acted as a character in that mythical story. On the other hand his role as a manifestation of the American dream made him an ingredient in the storyworld as well. He became a part of the circumstances, part of the storyline, and such an essential part of the foundation of the storyworld that he is hard to separate from the myth he narrated, while leaving its plausibility intact. This made the creation of a storyworld about the American way of life and dream easier for Reagan, since his character, the story cum flesh, appeared in front of the people and made it hard to question the possibility of the American dream's fulfillment. To use a Biblical comparison, the actual moment of seeing Reagan speaking and preaching his political sermon was like hearing the voice and seeing the burning bush.

"My candidacy is based on my record and for that matter my entire life."[7] All his life Reagan was involved in a continuous process of self-creation by narrative means. A son of a drifter found a home for a while in Dixon, Illinois but again re-created himself while moving from regional celebrity in Des Moines to stardom in Hollywood. After his career faded there, he created himself anew as a political player first in his GE speeches, then as the Governor of California and then on a nationwide scale first as a political speaker on the radio and ultimately the president. Yet surprisingly the American public found in Reagan "unchanging American values and beliefs. He seemed to provide a solid foundation of ancient verities for people disturbed by their society's rootlessness."[8] The fact that a man without roots could appear in a rootless and unstable world as a figure of permanence was in itself a tribute to Reagan's skills as a storyteller and creator of narrative identities both for himself and Americans.

The only truly stable things about Reagan were the values he represented and communicated. They were old and practically set in stone. As he said, some sprung from his interpretation of the Constitution; others had been carved in stone during his personal political awakening during his Hollywood years and ultimately got their final form in the crucible of his GE years. They were the values behind his politics and as time would show, modern and even futuristic policies were able to enchant Reagan, as long as they would work on behalf of his old values and ideals. The Laffer curve behind Reaganomics just as well as the dream of SDI could be employed in support of Reagan's politics just because he saw these modernistic concepts to strengthen the age-old values. In a sense it is frightening that the president of a superpower did not seem to make the slightest alteration to his values for the last 30 years of his life.

Diana L. Eck's research shows how America during the immigration boost in the last three decades has, in terms of religious diversity, exponentially grown to be perhaps the world's most religiously diverse nation. In addition to the multitude of Christian denominations, there were in the beginning of the twenty-first century more Muslims than Episcopalians or Presbyterians in the United States, that is, about 6 million, which is the number of Jews living in America.[9] While religious diversity has exploded, the religious voices most commonly heard within the public sphere have their origins in evangelical and occasionally fundamentalist Christianity, as exemplified in the Moral Majority or the Christian Coalition. These organizations have been very eager to attempt to dominate the religious dialogue with their interpretation of "Christian America," and indeed, to an outsider it often sounds like America is more devoutly Christian than ever. I am not arguing that there are not today many liberal voices resounding and gaining influence among the public or even that during Reagan's administration other religious voices would have been silent. It is rather a case of only the ones screaming at the top of their lungs being heard and recognized out of the commotion. Nevertheless, the more reasonable and toned-down voices from the diverse field of religions have to be included within the American story to gain a more comprehensive understanding.

Since the motto of the republic is E Pluribus Unum or, "from many, one," there is a need to get these other world religions to participate in the re-creation of the nation. Religion is never a finished product, which could be transferred from one generation to another in sacred texts, doctrines, and rituals, which in turn would remain unchanged. All religious traditions are dynamic, and even American civil religion cannot try to remain unchanged throughout changing times.[10] The era of Reagan portrayed one type or version of civil religion, which could not be used to unify all faiths of contemporary America. But certain aspects of Reagan's religious politics can be used to re create, or perhaps merely retell in a new manner, the story of the American dream, which lies at the eye of the storm of the tumultuous concept of civil religion. Perhaps a narrative-based civil religion can be created, but this requires another "awakening." Maybe this time it would be awakening from the American dream, as it has been for a long time conceived, and a rearticulation of that dream.

In a somewhat paradoxical sense the religious pluralism in America, which implies a huge diversity of religious beliefs, can be beneficial. As Mead wrote, "Pluralism means that two people may bring quite different conceptual orders to an event both experience. In this sense they live in different worlds, and they simply do not, and cannot "see" the same thing in it."[11] He continues that "two persons may use the same words and phrases and each may think the other is talking about the same thing he is, when actually their minds are not meeting at all."[12] This difference of thought can be used by the politician attempting to reformulate a version of American civil religion with the means of storytelling, since it allows his calculated words to be nonsectarian enough that each and every religious or atheistic person can interpret them in a manner, which builds a storyworld he can accept and not see that he is living "in different worlds" than others.

A storyverse could prove to be a useful tool for politicians to use as a superstructure that would join these different worlds into a unified whole. Our world has become so complex and multifaceted that it is next to impossible to achieve a completely unified view within even a single nation on any imaginable topic. Thus the only thing we can aim for is an illusion of unity to rally the people behind. This illusion can only be provided with a storyverse, where each citizen constructs his own storyworld due to the vagueness embedded in political narration, and its important concepts will fail to realize its actual individuality. Only by an illusion of a unified belief system and vague values such as "freedom," can people be brought together to rally behind these intangible and impalpable causes.

As I have proved, Reagan's storyverse was an elaborate construction that managed to ensnare a huge amount of the population, but the ones who could not be persuaded to enter are the ones who could not abide Reagan. They did not see the "magical, intoxicating power of America" Reagan narrated. They did not accept his vision of mythical America, but saw a septuagenarian telling tales instead of leading the country as the head of state. They are the people who called Reagan an "amicable dunce" or even worse. But whatever Reagan was, he was not an idiot. He was an exceptionally gifted storyteller and a visionary. His visions were based on the mythical past that never existed but were no less powerful because of that. A lot has been written about the manipulation of polls by Reagan aides Richard Wirthlin and Mike Deaver, and Wynton C. Hall even argues that the Reagan presidency gave birth to something called "quantifiably safe rhetoric," a method of using pretested and approved content in the speeches.[13] In a way this was true, but the "pre-testing" had rather been carried out earlier in the process of electing Reagan as the president. He was an old man whose ideas and ideology were set in stone long before he became president, in some cases even before he was a governor. The basic ideology remained unaltered through the decades, and so did the narration. Rowland and Jones wrote that Reagan did not let ideology to stop him from supporting fundamental changes in Soviet Society, and calling this moral clarity tempered with pragmatism, thus giving the impression that Reagan was flexible in his ideology.[14] I both agree and disagree with them. Reagan had certain fundamental beliefs that he would not give up in any condition, such as cooperation with Communism. Reagan worked with Gorbachev to inflict changes in the communist system. It was just another attack toward the atheistic Communism he abhorred. Reagan was extremely pragmatic, allowing the pragmatism to temper his policies in almost anything as long as the benefits were worthy of the compromise. Yet there remained the core values he would not have sacrificed for any purpose; these values had been formulated in the 1950s and 1960s in his public speeches. As another example, Reagan would have done practically everything to rid the world of nuclear weapons—except compromise the American military strength. As President Reagan was an old man, with old values.

Yet Reagan had a childlike belief in progress, both in terms of humanity and technology. As he had argued, his generation went from horse buggy to space shuttles, and Reagan had a child's fascination on what else science could do for the mankind. This love of technology and his eternal optimism kept him from ever being stalled in his search for the "morning in America" and certainly does not allow for us to label him as a conservative. Reagan wanted to conserve an America for future generations, and that America would have all the mythic qualities he narrated the past to be endowed with, but the America he wanted to leave behind was in process. America would always, always progress and strive for the ultimate best as long as the people could dream of new things and better times.

All along these pages I have discussed Reagan's optimism numerous times. His worldview was romantic to the extreme, and he created a fantasy version of his mythical America around him and lived in that bubble of dream world. Should I be asked to define Reagan with only one adjective, my choice would for these reasons be "quixotic." Thus the words of Cervantes from the epitaph of famous knight are suitable to describe the meaning and influence Reagan had on the politics of his time and our contemporary moment. Ronald Reagan indeed "had the fortune in his age to live a fool and die a sage."[15] With this description I mean no disrespect but merely wish to again point out that his life story has undergone a substantial change in the retellings. Reagan created himself anew in his stories of the mythical America he was a part of, and while his opposition saw him as merely a fool, historians have accredited him with much more value.

The political scientist Larry Berman states that Reagan had a greater impact on the American political system than no other president since Franklin D. Roosevelt. Berman argues Reagan was able to demonstrate that the demands of the presidency were not after all unmanageable, and that they need not engulf the president. When Reagan left office his overall approval rate was 68 percent, which is just another statistic that goes to show that Reagan was psychologically suited for the presidency.[16] Stuckey makes a piercing observation when she claimed that presidential rhetoric of the future would be strongly affected by the Reagan years. She argues that "no one has analyzed candidates' public speech in terms of *values* rather than policy, or *vision* instead of programs."[17] To a certain degree all the candidates say the same things, and that these can be safely ignored, since everyone talks of patriotism, national unity, and the American way of life, but all of them present these symbols in different ways. To understand US politics, one must work to understand the presentation and especially the reception of the stories.[18] The lasting part of the Reagan legacy is that in the future politicians will have to convey difficult problems in emotionally satisfying and simple terms, and this task is to become both difficult and emotionally dishonest, since the world has gotten and will get even more complex.[19] Not everybody is as competent and comfortable in using stories as the tools of leadership. Traditional rhetoric remains a powerful means of political persuasion, but narratives can transgress the boundaries of rhetoric and provide political narrators with a new toolkit to employ.

Writing in 1982 Walter Fisher argued that Reagan could become a presidential hero only if he could capture the American imagination. To do so, he would need to overcome the perception that his policies served only some, rather than all of the Americans. For Fisher presidential heroes were always "liberal" in outlook and future-oriented.[20] In this age Reagan has become the hero for both modern Democrats and Republicans; we must rethink the ultraconservative label on Reagan, and in future studies reevaluate his impact on America and especially the American dream. Calvin Coolidge was a hero for Reagan, and in a similar manner both presidents initiated a fundamental rethinking of American conservatism.[21] All this having been said, all these pages written (and hopefully even read), I wish to conclude with a quotation from Reagan himself, which I hope illustrates my point that research in the field of the American dream is by no means exhausted.

> And if I could leave you with one last thought from my heart, it's that the American dream is a living thing—it's always growing, always presenting new challenges, new vistas, and new dreams.[22]

Notes

Preface

1. Speech, "California Council for Adult Education, International Hotel 12 March 1966," p. 99, Folder: 1966 Campaign: RR speeches and statements, Book I (3), Box C30, Research Unit, Ronald Reagan Governor's papers, Ronald Reagan Library.
2. Reagan (January 19, 1989) Remarks at the Presentation Ceremony for the Presidential Medal of Freedom http://www.reagan.utexas.edu/archives/speeches/1989/011989b.htm.
3. Lewis (1987).
4. Phelan (1996) p. 4.
5. Lewis (1987) p. 281.
6. In this book I will use the term "United States of America" to refer only to the official state apparatus. Most of the time I will be using the expression "America" to refer to the nation as an imagined community, which consists of a collectivity of people who firstly are US citizens and more importantly view themselves as "Americans." The populations of Canada, Mexico, and South America are thus excluded from my concept of "America." Very often "America" is also used to describe the mythical version of the imagined community Reagan wanted to narrate into existence as a storyworld. But I trust that the reader will be able to follow which one of the usages is under discussion.
7. Bakhtin (1986) p. 7.
8. Ibid., p. 126.
9. Ibid. Bakhtin emphasizes that there is no "third" party in the arithmetical sense of the word because in every dialogue there potentially can be an unlimited number of participants.
10. Rabinowitz and Sullivan. Cited in Riessman (1993) p. 14.
11. Ibid., p. 22.
12. Rabinowitz (1987) pp. 19–20.
13. Ibid., p. 48.
14. See Riessman (1993) p. 15.
15. Labov and Waletzky (2006) p. 1.
16. Bakhtin (1986) pp. 71, 76.
17. Ibid., pp. 108–109.
18. Ricoeur (1995) p. 38.

19. Address, "Republican State Convention, August 6, 1966," p. 10, Speech, "Elk Grove, May 14, 1966," p. 257 Folder: 1966 Campaign: RR speeches and statements, Book II (2), Box C30, Research Unit, Ronald Reagan Governor's papers, Ronald Reagan Library.
20. Lyotard (1993) p. 87.
21. Edelman (1977) p. 113.
22. Smith (1997) pp. 813–814.
23. Ford. Cited in Cannon (2003) p. 398.
24. Unfortunately the further we move back in time the less documented material is there from Reagan's speeches. This is partially due to the fact that in his GE speeches he began with a short introduction and then answered questions from the audience. As his speeches started evolving Reagan would bring in more and more political material but in these GE speeches as well as in many of his gubernatorial addresses before Reagan had full-time speechwriters he used "cue cards." These were 4x6 inch cards he carried in his pocket where his speech was in an abbreviated and compressed form. One single speech took easily a dozen cards since more often than not one topic he spoke of during the speech occupied one card. Acting upon the reactions of the audience Reagan altered the order of the cards and replaced some cards with others, suspecting that they would influence the audience better or just added new cards depending on the composition of the audience he would address. The Ronald Reagan Presidential Library has boxes full of these cue cards and while analyzing them can tell a researcher what Reagan liked to talk about, the fact that he kept intermingling them makes it an impossible task to fully reconstruct a speech given on any particular occasion.
25. Both Reagan autobiographies were more than partially ghostwritten. Paradoxically the man who communicated everything in the form of stories was not able to formulate his own story alone.
26. Chatman (1978) p. 172.
27. Denzin (1989). Cited in Holstein and Gubrium (2000) p. 106.
28. Bakhtin (1986) pp. 114–115, 125.
29. Czarniawska (2004) p. 88.
30. Riessman (1993) p. 1.
31. Niebuhr (1986) p. 26.
32. Reagan (May 31, 1988) Remarks at a Luncheon Hosted by Artists and Cultural Leaders in Moscow http://www.reagan.utexas.edu/archives/speeches/1988/053188a.htm.
33. Wills (2000) p. 349.
34. Weatherford and McDonnell (1990) p. 123.
35. Ibid.
36. Most of the study of political narratives seems to concentrate on "giving voice to the silenced" and not discussing the stories used to silence them in the first place. While researchers such as Molly Andrews (2007) have made important contributions to the study of political narratives, it

speakes volumes about the level of research put into political narratives in general that the Routledge Encyclopedia of Narrative Theory (2007) does not even contribute a mention to "political narratives" while such genres as "pornographic narratives" have their own entries. When it comes to the narratives of political leadership, there is even less work that has been done.

37. See Barthes (1990).
38. Frye (1969) p. 119. Italics in the original.
39. See for example Genette (1993) pp. 54–84.
40. Lincoln (1999) introduction.

1   The Narrative Approach to Reagan's Policymaking

1. Barthes (1977) p. 79.
2. Czarniawska (2004) pp. 40–41.
3. MacIntyre (1984) p. 216.
4. Herman (1999) p. 2.
5. Ibid., pp. 2–3.
6. Reagan (October 3, 1983) Remarks at a Dinner Marking the 10th Anniversary of the Heritage Foundation http://www.reagan.utexas.edu/archives/speeches/1983/100383h.htm.
7. Fisher (1982) p. 304.
8. Prince (1987) p. 4.
9. Prince (1973) p. 31.
10. Bal (1997) p. 182. Italics mine.
11. Herman (2002) p. 83.
12. Ibid., p. 84.
13. Labov and Waletzky (2006) p. 37.
14. Ibid.
15. Ibid., p. 28.
16. Genette (1993) p. 27.
17. Ricoeur (1981). Cited in Ochs and Capps (2001) p. 207.
18. Polkinghorne (1988) p. 160.
19. Polkinghorne (1987). Cited in Czarniawska (2004) p. 125.
20. Barthes (1974) p. 5. Italics in the original.
21. Holstein and Gubrium (2000) p. 132.
22. Labov and Waletzky (2006) p. 33.
23. Todorov (1981) p. 51.
24. Czarniawska (2004) p. 19.
25. Reagan (May 7, 1985) Remarks to Community Leaders in Madrid, Spain http://www.reagan.utexas.edu/archives/speeches/1985/50785b.htm.
26. Rimmon-Kenan (1983) p. 27.
27. Speech draft, no date. Box 43 Subseries E, Reagan, Ronald: Pre-presidential papers, Series I Speeches and writings, Ronald Reagan Library.

28. Polkinghorne (1988) p. 168.
29. Reagan (September 14, 1988) Remarks at a Republican Party Rally in Cape Girardeau, Missouri http://www.reagan.utexas.edu/archives/speeches/1988/091488e.htm.
30. Aristotle (1940) pp. 17–18, 46.
31. Ibid., pp. 17–18.
32. Andrews (2007) pp. 108–109.
33. Barthes (1977) p. 129.
34. Andrews (2007) p. 187.
35. White. Cited in Polkinghorne (1988) p. 68.
36. Mink. Cited in ibid.
37. Andrews (2007) p. 189.
38. Derrida (1988) pp. 21–22.
39. Reagan (January 11, 1989) Farewell Address to the Nation http://www.reagan.utexas.edu/archives/speeches/1989/011189i.htm.
40. Rabinowitz (1987) pp. 160–161.
41. Polkinghorne (1988) p. 18.
42. Ibid., p. 69.
43. Reagan (June 14, 1985) Remarks at a Flag Day Ceremony in Baltimore, Maryland http://www.reagan.utexas.edu/archives/speeches/1985/61485f.htm.
44. Chatman (1978) p. 45.
45. Labov and Waletzky (2006) p. 35.
46. Reagan (December 1, 1988) Remarks at a Dinner Honoring Representative Jack F. Kemp of New York http://www.reagan.utexas.edu/archives/speeches/1988/120188c.htm.
47. Reagan (August 1, 1983) Remarks at the Annual Meeting of the American Bar Association in Atlanta, Georgia http://www.reagan.utexas.edu/archives/speeches/1983/80183a.htm.
48. Greimas (1983) pp. 146–147, 151.
49. Ibid., p. 178.
50. Chatman (1978) p. 44. Italics in the original.
51. Ibid.
52. This statement is a generalization, since for example Roland Barthes shifted his thinking into a more psychological view of character and was by no means the only one. Barthes's S/Z is a good example of this shift. But essentially in structuralism the characters are "slaves" to the structure and serve its needs rather than have deep meanings *an sich*.
53. Chatman (1978) p. 111. Italics in the original.
54. Propp (1968) p. 20.
55. Speech draft, no date. Box 43 Subseries E, Reagan, Ronald: Pre-presidential papers, Series I Speeches and writings, Ronald Reagan Library
56. Chatman (1978) p. 119.
57. MacIntyre (1984) p. 27.
58. Wills (2000) p. 197.

59. Combs (1993) p. 7.
60. Reagan (May 25, 1984) Remarks at a Ceremony Honoring an Unknown Serviceman of the Vietnam Conflict http://www.reagan.utexas.edu/archives/speeches/1984/52584c.htm.
61. Barthes (1991) p. 121.
62. Ibid., p. 123.
63. Warner (1962) p. 13. See also Smith (1997) p. 816.
64. Speech draft, no date. Box 43 Subseries E, Reagan, Ronald: Pre-presidential papers, Series I Speeches and writings, Ronald Reagan Library.
65. George Gipp was a character that Reagan got to play in one of his most memorable movies, "Knute Rockne—All-American." Reagan even borrowed his nickname "the Gipper" from this character, a rebellious young man (but naturally smoothed over in the Hollywood presentation) who played football for Notre Dame and died young of pneumonia. A more thorough discussion on this character can be found in White (1998) pp. 1–6.
66. Barthes (1991) p. 122.
67. Reagan (July 19, 1982) Remarks at a Rally Supporting the Proposed Constitutional Amendment for a Balanced Federal Budget. s. 939.
68. Reagan (April 27, 1983) Remarks to Daily News Crime Fighter Award Winners in New York City http://www.reagan.utexas.edu/archives/speeches/1983/42783a.htm.
69. On the concept of ordinary people as heroes see Lewis (1987) pp. 284–285.
70. Shogan (2006) p. 219.
71. Reagan (January 26, 1982) Address before a Joint Session of the Congress Reporting on the State of the Union. ss. 78–79 http://www.reagan.utexas.edu/archives/speeches/1982/12682c.htm Accessed September 7. 2009.
72. Radio address, Folder Speeches and Writings—Radio Broadcast, Taping date—March 6, 1979, "The 100 Club," Typescript 3/4, Box 32, Reagan, Ronald: Pre-presidential papers, Series I Speeches and writings, Ronald Reagan Library.
73. Reagan (June 29, 1983) Remarks and a Question-and-Answer Session with Participants in the National Conference of the National Association of Student Councils in Shawnee Mission, Kansas http://www.reagan.utexas.edu/archives/speeches/1983/62983b.htm.
74. Czarniawska (2004) p. 6.
75. For this see also White (1998) p. 178.
76. Shogan (2006) p. 220.
77. See White (1998) pp. 70, 76–77.
78. Reagan (February 2, 1981) Message on the Observance of National Afro-American (Black) History Month. s. 68.
79. Forster (1953) pp. 122–124.
80. Reagan (May 25, 1984) Remarks at a Ceremony Honoring an Unknown Serviceman of the Vietnam Conflict http://www.reagan.utexas.edu/archives/speeches/1984/52584c.htm.

81. Reagan (January 26, 1982) Address Before a Joint Session of the Congress Reporting on the State of the Union. s. 78.
82. Phelan (1996) p. 29.
83. Ibid.
84. Forster (1953) p. 62. Italics mine.
85. See Morris (1999) pp. 181, 394.
86. Ibid., p. 333.
87. D'Souza (1997) p. 45.
88. On very rare occasions can we see Reagan without his "mask." In the photos where Reagan watches the news coverage after the Challenger space shuttle explosion we can get a glimpse of a tired old man and not the smiling aged "all-American boy."
89. Anonymous campaign associate. Cited in Linden (1981) pp. 122–123.
90. See Lewis (1987) pp. 285–286.
91. Reagan (April 30, 1984) Remarks and a Question-and-Answer Session with Students at Fudan University in Shanghai, China http://www.reagan.utexas.edu/archives/speeches/1984/43084d.htm.
92. Reagan. Cited in Hayward (2001) p. 660. Interestingly enough this quote also points out that in Reagan's mind acting or show business in general is different from telling stories, because in show business and politics Reagan lays the importance on openings and closings while in his storytelling the focus was always in moving the story smoothly along.
93. Answer, "Questions and Answers, Orange County, March 30, 1986," p. 187, Folder: 1966 Campaign: RR speeches and statements, Book I (5), Box C30, Research Unit, Ronald Reagan Governor's papers, Ronald Reagan Library.
94. Ritter (1968) p. 56.
95. D'Souza (1997) p. 44.
96. Smith (1997) p. 821.
97. On this see the excellent Jewett and Lawrence (1977) and their discussion on the "American Monomyth," which they define as a myth of innocent, Edenic society, which is under a threat but is saved by a mysterious hero who appears from nowhere and vanishes again after performing his deed.
98. Smith (1997) p. 822.
99. Ritter (1968) p. 56. Reagan himself had attended college in Eureka and had no educational background from Notre Dame. Likewise the Notre Dame football team is named "Fightin' Irish," but prior to his presidential visit to Ireland Reagan did not emphasize his ancestral roots.
100. Reagan (June 5, 1985) Remarks at a Fundraising Luncheon for Senator Don Nickles in Oklahoma City, Oklahoma http://www.reagan.utexas.edu/archives/speeches/1985/60585b.htm. The song was called *Mamas, don't let your babies grow up to be cowboys* sung by Waylon Jennings and later by numerous other big stars of country music.

101. Zelinsky (1988) p. 44.
102. Jewett and Lawrence (1977) pp. 44–45.
103. See Rantapelkonen (2006) p. 27.
104. On Reagan, the ranch, and the cowboy image in general see Fisher (1982).
105. Reagan (December 13, 1988) Remarks to Administration Officials on Domestic Policy http://www.reagan.utexas.edu/archives/speeches/1988/121388a.htm.
106. Ivie (1984) p. 45.
107. Knelman (1985) p. 224.
108. Knelman (1985) p. 239.
109. Culler (1975) pp. 234–237.
110. Palmer (2004) p. 38.
111. Speakes and Pack (1988) p. 136.
112. Nathan (1990) p. 195.
113. de Tocqueville (2000) p. 127.
114. Barthes (1990) p. 40.
115. Arendt (1963) p. 94.
116. Radio address, Folder Speeches and Writings—Radio Broadcast, Taping date—August, 1975, "Images," Holograph, Box 1, Reagan, Ronald: Pre-presidential papers, Series I Speeches and writings, Ronald Reagan Library.
117. Berman (1990) p. 7. The same idea can be read between the lines in Speakes and Pack (1988).
118. Berman (1990) p. 8.
119. Statement, "San Bernadino County Elementary School Admin. Assn. Luncheon. Casa Loma Hall—Redlands University, February 15, 1966," p. 18, Folder: 1966 Campaign: RR speeches and statements, Book I (1), Box C30, Research Unit, Ronald Reagan Governor's papers, Ronald Reagan Library.
120. Speech, "A Plan for Action: Announcement of Candidacy, January 4, 1966," Folder: 1966 Campaign: RR speeches and statements, Book I, Box C30, Research Unit, Ronald Reagan Governor's papers, Ronald Reagan Library.
121. Boorstin (1962) pp. 194–195.
122. Ricoeur. Cited in Polkinghorne (1988) p. 65.
123. Reagan (September 26, 1984) Remarks and a Question-and-Answer Session at Bowling Green State University in Bowling Green, Ohio http://www.reagan.utexas.edu/archives/speeches/1984/92684b.htm.
124. Peterson (1997) p. 76.
125. Reagan essentially began the writing process himself but for once in his life got stuck, and the publisher brought in Richard C. Hubler to help him finish the story (Reagan and Hubler 1965). Hubler was a Hollywood writer who had written everything from screenplays to "as-told-to" books like this autobiography. The first-person voice in the book sounds authentically Reagan, but Hubler's influence on the final

198 Notes

form of the book remains unclear (Cannon 2003, pp. 10–11). In the process of editing Hubler cut out a lot of the political message Reagan had inserted into his memoir and tried to keep it closer to the form of biography than a political manifesto. It is actually surprising that a man of such a talent with written words was unable to independently produce an autobiography. His second autobiography *An American Life* (Reagan 1990) was a ghostwritten book at the behest of his wife, Nancy. See Morris (1999) p. 92.

126. Reagan (July 19, 1982) Remarks at a Rally Supporting the Proposed Constitutional Amendment for a Balanced Federal Budget. s. 939.
127. Jewett and Lawrence (1977) pp. 171–172.
128. Speech, Men of All Saints Episcopal Church Dinner, Los Angeles, March 21, 1969, Box 44 Subseries E, Reagan, Ronald: Pre-presidential papers, Series I Speeches and writings, Ronald Reagan Library.
129. Frye (1957) p. 151.
130. Combs (1993) p. 9.
131. Ochs and Capps (2001) p. 201.
132. Reagan (November 1, 1984) Remarks at a Reagan-Bush Rally in Boston, Massachusetts http://www.reagan.utexas.edu/archives/speeches/1984/110184d.htm.
133. Speech, ("Losing freedom by installment") Rotary Club of Long Beach, June 6, 1962, Box 43 Subseries E, Reagan, Ronald: Pre-presidential papers, Series I Speeches and writings, Ronald Reagan Library.
134. Barthes (1977) p. 111.
135. Ibid., pp. 111–112.
136. Reagan (May 14, 1982) Remarks and a Question-and-Answer Session at a Fundraising Reception for Senator John Heinz in Philadelphia, Pennsylvania. s. 641.
137. This tendency is referred to in most of the books written about him. See for ex. Morris (1999), Cannon (1991), Noonan (2002), or even his diary notes Reagan (2007).
138. Ginsburg, Rimmon, and Kenan (1999) p. 75.
139. Reagan (March 1, 1985) Remarks at the Annual Dinner of the Conservative Political Action Conference http://www.reagan.utexas.edu/archives/speeches/1985/30185f.htm.
140. Todorov (1981) p. 40.
141. Ibid.,) pp. 38–39.
142. Prince (1987) p. 42.
143. Palmer (2004) p. 17.
144. Ryan (1991) pp. 138–150, Czarniawska (2004) p. 23.
145. Incredibly the abbreviation for the name of the radio station comes from "World of Chiropracy." Along with Reagan's first wife Jane Wyman, another character that leaves a gap in Reagan's storyworlds is B. J. Palmer, the man who owned the radio station. Garry Wills argues that he is omitted because for Reagan he was "an unpleasant part of his life he would rather dismiss." Wills (2000) p. 123. Reagan is *very* adept in leaving excluding unpleasant things from his lifestory.

146. One version of this often occurring anecdote can be found in Reagan (1981) pp. 78–79.
147. Wills (2000) p. 142.
148. Cannon (2003) p. 105.
149. Ryan (1991) p. 141.
150. Pemberton (1997) p. 15.
151. Cannon (2003) pp. 38–39.
152. According to a GE slogan at that time progress was their main product. And surely the gospel of progress and scientific invention became part of the message in Reagan's storytelling even during the presidency.
153. Kengor (2004) p. 102.
154. Reagan (1981) pp. 293–294.
155. Erickson (1985) p. 19.
156. In the aftermath of the Iran-Contra affair this aspect of Reagan's narration diminished. While the entire affair was not only embarrassing, but politically significant, the Reagan administration did not enable the members of the press to ask many questions from the president.
157. Morris (1999).
158. Noonan (2002) p. 83.
159. Reagan (1981) p. 303.
160. The articles used in the research, original draft, Reagan's editing, and the final product can be found at the Reagan Library Folder Hannaford/CA HQ—R. Reagan Speeches—1/1977, New Business Speech (Gavin) (1/2) and (2/2), Box 21, Ronald Reagan 1980 Campaign Papers, Series I, Ronald Reagan Library. In the same box can be found other examples as well and they attest to the fact that the editing Reagan performed on the speeches drafted for him was extensive, practically a rewrite.
161. For additional examples, see ibid. What Garry Wills said about Alexander Campbell, the founder of Reagan's denomination fits Reagan just as well. "The Disciples not only preached well, they proofread carefully." Wills (2000) p. 26.
162. Speakes and Pack (1988) p. 117.
163. Erickson (1985) p. 8.
164. Wallison (2003) p. 30.
165. Here she refers to the book *Stories in His Own Hand* edited by Skinner, Anderson, and Anderson. (Reagan 2001).
166. Noonan (2002) p. 39.
167. Robinson, Peter. Cited in D'Souza (1997) p. 250.
168. Reagan (2007) p. 152. Diary entry for May 3, 1983.
169. Ibid., p. 354. Diary entry for September 18, 1985.
170. Ibid., p. 565. Diary entry for January 5, 1989.
171. Barthes (1993) pp. 111–112. It is interesting to note however that Barthes links the death of the author to only those texts that do not attempt to influence the reality directly but a conscious choice has been made to tell the story symbolically and without functionality. Ibid., p. 111. This is not as exclusive toward political narratives as one might

surmise on the basis of one reading; since political narratives *do* try to influence the reality, *but* try to do it in a symbolic manner.

172. Barthes (1993) pp. 114–117.
173. Barthes (1977) this should NOT read "ibid" but "Barthes (1977)" p. 146.
174. Peter Rabinowitz chose to use the term "assumptions" from the part of the author considering the scope of knowledge of his audience. He claims that the success of stories partially rely on the assumptions upon the readers, whether they are "actual," "hypothetical," or "authorial" audiences the author has to aim his text for. An author has to consider *who* is reading. Rabinowitz (1987) pp. 20–22.
175. Reagan (March 8, 1983) Remarks at the Annual Convention of the National Association of Evangelicals in Orlando, Florida http://www.reagan.utexas.edu/archives/speeches/1983/30883b.htm.
176. Reeves (2005) pp. 110, 140, 503. The drafts can be found at the Ronald Reagan Presidential Library.
177. Chambers (1952) p. 8.
178. D'Souza (1997) p. 251.
179. Ibid., p. 135. Famous presidential historian Henry Steele Commager was quoted saying, "It was the worst presidential speech in American history. I've read them all. No other presidential speech has ever so flagrantly allied the government with religion." Cited in Reeves (2005) p. 141.
180. Kengor (2004) pp. 246–247. The copy of the speech where the editing by Reagan is visible can be found the Ronald Reagan Presidential Library.
181. Morris (1999) p. 472.
182. It is worth noting that in this quotation Reagan simultaneously offers proof of his beliefs in favor of creationism against Darwin's theory of evolution. It is common in creationist circles to claim that the world was created 6,000 years ago.
183. Reagan (June 16, 1981) The President's News Conference http://www.reagan.utexas.edu/archives/speeches/1981/61681b.htm.
184. Goodnight (1986) pp. 400–401.
185. Noonan (2002) p. 87. One early version of this speech with the identical title but slightly different content can be found in Speech ("A Time For Choosing") 71st Annual Convention of the United States Savings and Loan League, San Francisco, California, July 11, 1963, Box 44 Subseries E, Reagan, Ronald: Pre-presidential papers, Series I Speeches and writings, Ronald Reagan Library. The name in brackets for some reason was on the original version but is not used in the archives. The most famous version, the Goldwater address, is archived under Speech, A Time for Choosing, 1964, Box 44 Subseries E, Reagan, Ronald: Pre-presidential papers, Series I Speeches and writings, Ronald Reagan Library. Even researches have used the same expression, see for example Wills (2000).

186. A good history of the early versions of "The Speech" and its contents can be found in Ritter (1968).
187. Deaver (2003) p. 60.
188. Holstein and Gubrium (2000) p. 117.
189. Radio address, Folder Speeches and Writings—Radio Broadcast, Taping date—July 15, 1978, "Stanley Yankus," Typescript 3/4, Box 24, Reagan, Ronald: Pre-presidential papers, Series I Speeches and writings, Ronald Reagan Library.
190. On actual speechwriting see Reagan (2007) pp. 33, 50, 67, 176, 181, 191, 212, 216, 218. Diary entries for July 25, 1981; November 18, 1981; February 6, 1982; September 5, 1983; September 21, 1983; November 27, 1983; January 16, 1984; January 28, 1984; September 22, 1984. Some of these occasions are for important speeches like after the invasion of Grenada, an address to the UN, State of the Union address, or on the tragedy of KAL-007, but some are on more mundane matters and for more mundane audiences. On the editing of his speeches see Reagan (2007) pp. 139, 570, 685, 686. Only the first two of these belong to the first term and the last two are connected with dealing with Peggy Noonan who, sent a draft Reagan did not like and upon hearing it, got upset.
191. I have been using the first version of Reagan's diaries edited by Douglas Brinkley, and thus I cannot assert that there would not have been more mentions, since Brinkley edited the content somewhat.
192. Reagan (January 11, 1989) Farewell Address to the Nation http://www.reagan.utexas.edu/archives/speeches/1989/011189i.htm.
193. Reagan (January 22, 1983) Radio Address to the Nation on Domestic Social Issues http://www.reagan.utexas.edu/archives/speeches/1983/12283a.htm.
194. Reagan (1993) in Noonan (2002) p. 317.
195. Frye (1957) p. 96.
196. Pope (1903) p. 12.
197. Darman (1984). Cited in Erickson (1985) p. 100.
198. Rimmon-Kenan (1983) p. 100.
199. Ibid.
200. Reagan (March 4, 1987) Address to the Nation on the Iran Arms and Contra Aid Controversy http://www.reagan.utexas.edu/archives/speeches/1987/030487h.htm.
201. Indeed there are numerous references in Reagan's personal diaries that point out to the fact that Reagan knew a lot more about the affair than he publicly admitted to. As an example might suffice, "We sit quietly by & never reveal how we got them [hostages] back." Reagan (2007) p. 381. Diary entry for January 7, 1986. In hearings concerning the matter Reagan's memory as related to the incident was vague to the extreme while he could easily have consulted his diary for confirmations of dates and actions taken. So, perhaps Reagan was not that reliable as a narrator as the American public presumed. Reagan claims to

have consulted his diaries from 1985 prior to a meeting with the Tower commission and claims that "it sure is helping my memory." Reagan (2007). Diary entry for January 22, 1987. Thus it is intriguing that he still remained almost useless in giving testimony.

202. See also Lewis (1987) p. 290.
203. Erickson (1985) p. 9.
204. Hayward (2001) p. 399.
205. Ibid.
206. Horace (1940), ll. 99–100.
207. Deaver (2003) pp. 53–54.
208. Ibid., p. 56.
209. Lewis (1987) p. 284.
210. Rabinowitz (1987) p. 23.
211. Ibid., pp. 22–25. He also notes that the assumed contract between the writer and the reader does often not lead to readers interpreting texts in the way writer wants them to even if the readers wish to do so. (Ibid., pp. 43, 53, 56) Intentionality is ever present in political narratives, but this does not guarantee the intentions of the politician as narrator and those of the citizen as narratee coincide in any manner. Texts and their interpretations are unpredictable.
212. Riessman (1993) p. 11.
213. Reagan (November 11, 1983) Address Before the Japanese Diet in Tokyo http://www.reagan.utexas.edu/archives/speeches/1983/111183a.htm.
214. Bellow. Cited in Martin (1987) p. 158.
215. Reagan (May 31, 1983) Interview with American and Foreign Journalists at the Williamsburg Economic Summit Conference in Virginia http://www.reagan.utexas.edu/archives/speeches/1983/53183a.htm.
216. Reagan (1984) Remarks on the Caribbean Basin Initiative to the Permanent Council of the Organization of American States, February 24, 1982. s. 210.
217. Reagan (December 14, 1983) Remarks and a Question-and-Answer Session with Editors of Gannett Newspapers on Domestic and Foreign Policy Issues http://www.reagan.utexas.edu/archives/speeches/1983/121483e.htm.
218. Stuckey (1990) pp. 32–33.
219. Draft, Folder Hannaford/CA HQ—R. Reagan Speeches—May 21, 1979, Speech Draft, Box 25, Ronald Reagan 1980 Campaign Papers, Series I, Ronald Reagan Library. The underline is in the original.
220. See Rantapelkonen (2006) p. 252.
221. Barthes (1990) p. 16.
222. Barthes (1974) p. 151. Italics in the original.
223. Bakhtin (1986) p. 68.
224. Jameson (2002).
225. Reagan (December 6, 1983) Interview with Garry Clifford and Patricia Ryan of People Magazine http://www.reagan.utexas.edu/archives/speeches/1983/120683c.htm.

226. Aristotle (1940) p. 33.
227. Todorov. Cited in Culler (1975) p. 109.
228. Forster (1953) p. 41.
229. Reagan (2007) p. 571. Diary entry for January 25, 1988 "The 7th & best of the St. of the U. [State of the Union] I've never had such reception with even the Dem's clapping. I was interrupted 37 times by applause. The speech ran 43 min's because of it." For other examples see among others pp. 50, 99, 128, 164, 185, 216.
230. Reagan (1981) p. 334.

2 RE-CREATING THE MYTHICAL AMERICA AS A STORYVERSE

1. Reagan (September 17, 1982) Remarks at the Swearing-In Ceremony for United States Citizens in White House Station, New Jersey. s. 1179.
2. White (1987) p. ix.
3. Ibid.
4. Bruner (1986) p. 122.
5. Greimas (1983) p. 135.
6. Chatman (1978) p. 30. Italics mine.
7. Ryan (2004a) p. 3.
8. Genette (1980) p. 236.
9. Ryan (2004a) pp. 8–9 and Ryan (2004b) p. 337. While for Ryan language is indeed the native tongue of narrative, she sees it in cognitive terms not as a linguistic object but rather as a mental image and a cognitive construct.
10. Dolezel (1998). Cited in Palmer (2004) p. 33.
11. Dolezel. Cited in Palmer (2004) pp. 12, 198–199.
12. Ricoeur (1995) p. 43. Italics mine.
13. Ibid.
14. Dolezel (1999) pp. 253–254.
15. Ibid., p. 256.
16. Ibid.
17. See Kuhn (1970). These were the best attempts to describe the world in the time before scientific paradigms. Likewise the past alchemists were doing their best with paradigms that were scientific, but later as knowledge increased, the paradigms became more defined and described the actuality better.
18. Bruner (1986) pp. 42–43.
19. Ricoeur (1995) p. 43.
20. Lyotard (1997) p. 91.
21. Chatman (1978) pp. 21–22.
22. Ibid., p. 49.
23. Ibid., p. 176. Italics mine.
24. D'Souza (1997) p. 38.
25. This realm is "the textual actual world" in Ryan's terminology.

26. Ryan (1999) p. 118.
27. Ibid.
28. Speech, "Pacifica Junior Chamber of Commerce Annual Meeting, April 2, 1966," p. 216 Folder: 1966 Campaign: RR speeches and statements, Book I (5), Box C30, Research Unit, Ronald Reagan Governor's papers, Ronald Reagan Library.
29. Palmer (2004) p. 33.
30. Morris (1999) p. 398. To clarify, "Dutch" was the nickname Reagan carried in his boyhood years. As he explained it, his father had commented on the look of him as a baby that "he looks like a fat Dutchman."
31. As an example we can use the story of witnessing firsthand the horror of Nazi concentration camps that Reagan told to several prominent Jewish leaders. In real life during the war Reagan never travelled to Germany and was able to witness the horror only on film, but the documentary made such a strong impression on him that later in life he told the story as if he had been one of the soldiers liberating the victims.
32. Herman (2002) pp. 9–10.
33. Ibid.
34. Ibid., pp. 14–15.
35. Rabinowitz (1987) pp. 100–101.
36. Herman (2002) p. 15.
37. Culler (1975) pp. 138–139.
38. Chatman (1978) p. 49.
39. Herman (2002) p. 50.
40. Ibid.
41. Ibid.
42. Ibid., p. 55.
43. Ibid., p. 16.
44. Dolezel (1998). Cited in Palmer (2004) p. 34.
45. Ibid., p. 35. This same idea is expressed in more detail in Rabinowitz (1987) pp. 104–105.
46. Reagan (March 8, 1983) Remarks at the Annual Convention of the National Association of Evangelicals in Orlando, Florida http://www.reagan.utexas.edu/archives/speeches/1983/30883b.htm.
47. Wills (2000) p. 459.
48. Reagan (July 19, 1982) Remarks at a Rally Supporting the Proposed Constitutional Amendment for a Balanced Federal Budget. s. 939.
49. Reagan (March 14, 1985) Remarks and a Question-and-Answer Session During a White House Briefing for Members of the Magazine Publishers Association http://www.reagan.utexas.edu/archives/speeches/1985/31485a.htm.
50. Reagan. Cited in Noonan (2003) p. 147.
51. Reagan (2003) in a letter p. 5.
52. Pemberton (1997) pp. 5–6.
53. Wills (2000) p. 111.
54. Dolezel. Cited Herman (2004) p. 67.

55. Chatman (1978) p. 120.
56. Iser. Cited in Rimmon-Kenan (1983) p. 127.
57. Ibid., p. 129.
58. Kafalenos (1999) p. 34.
59. Ibid., p. 35.
60. Rabinowitz (1987) p. 148.
61. Ryan. Cited Herman (2004) p. 68.
62. Stuckey (1989) p. 60.
63. Kristeva. Cited in Culler (1975) p. 139.
64. Barthes (1974) p. 21.
65. Palmer (2004) p. 147.
66. Rimmon-Kenan (1983) p. 121.
67. Ryan (1991) p. 156.
68. Ibid.
69. Frye (1957) p. 125.
70. Palmer (2004) p. 188.
71. Ryan (1991), p. 156.
72. Margolin (1999) p. 149.
73. Young (1999) pp. 198–199.
74. Ryan (1999) p. 131.
75. Bruner (1986) p. 24.
76. Reagan (November 16, 1987) Remarks at the Annual Meeting of the American Council of Life Insurance http://www.reagan.utexas.edu/archives/speeches/1987/111687a.htm.
77. Barthes (1974) p. 52.
78. Ibid.

3 American Religion

1. Reagan (May 6, 1982) Remarks at a White House Ceremony in Observance of National Day of Prayer. s.
2. Wilson (1979) pp. 95–96. Italics mine.
3. Reagan (August 1, 1983) Address to the American Bar Association. s. 160.
4. Frye (1957) p. 127.
5. Tillich. Cited in Mead (1977) p. 62.
6. Wilson (1979) pp. 24–25.
7. Reagan (July 26, 1984) Remarks at the St. Ann's Festival in Hoboken, New Jersey http://www.reagan.utexas.edu/archives/speeches/1984/72684c.htm.
8. Iqbal (1992) pp. 84–85.
9. Durkheim (1995) p. 421. Italics mine.
10. James (1981) p. 12.
11. Durkheim (1995) p. 9.
12. Weber (1959) p. 355. Italics in the original.
13. Kelly (1984) p. 28.

14. Reagan (April 16, 1985) Remarks at a Conference on Religious Liberty http://www.reagan.utexas.edu/archives/speeches/1985/41685d.htm.
15. de Tocqueville (2000) pp. 43–44.
16. Reagan (July 4, 1984) Remarks at a Spirit of America Festival in Decatur, Alabama http://www.reagan.utexas.edu/archives/speeches/1984/70484e.htm.
17. Durkheim (1995) p. 34.
18. Ibid., p. 185.
19. Smith (1982) p. 55.
20. Durkheim (1995) p. 33.
21. Ibid., p. 44.
22. Mead (1975). Even named his book after this notion of Chesterton.
23. Ibid., p. 51.
24. Reagan (July 19, 1982) Remarks at a Rally Supporting the Proposed Constitutional Amendment for a Balanced Federal Budget. p. 942.
25. Reagan (June 3, 1988) Remarks Upon Returning From the Soviet-United States Summit Meeting in Moscow http://www.reagan.utexas.edu/archives/speeches/1988/060388c.htm.
26. Deneen (1964) p. xvi.
27. James (1981) pp. 48–49.
28. Durkheim (1995) pp. 36–37.
29. Ibid., p. 322.
30. Ibid., p. 323.
31. Aaltola (2007) pp. 71–72.
32. Kelly (1984) p. 249.
33. Aaltola (2007) p. 15. It has to be noted that in the endnotes referring to Mika Aaltola's "Sowing the Seeds of Sacred" the page numbers may not correspond to the book, since I have been using a manuscript I received from the author.
34. de Tocqueville (2000) pp. 280–281.
35. Kelly (1984) pp. 18–19.
36. Ibid.
37. Schmitt (2005) p. 36.
38. Blumenberg. Cited in Campbell (1998) p. 46.
39. Ibid., p. 47.
40. Reagan (November 13, 1987) Remarks at the Presentation Ceremony for the Young American Medals for Bravery and Service http://www.reagan.utexas.edu/archives/speeches/1987/111387b.htm.
41. James (1981) pp. 27–28. Naturally this argument is dependent upon whether one wants to consider religion as personal or as institutionalized. The church as an organization is naturally religious, but in the personal, private life of people, religion or religiosity is only a part of a greater whole.
42. Durkheim (1995) p. 227.
43. Ibid.

44. de Tocqueville (2000) p. 275. Italics in the original.
45. Weber (1987). Reagan seems to agree since he once argued that "capitalism works best and creates the greatest wealth and human progress for all when it follows the teachings of scripture: Give and you will be given unto . . . search and you will find . . . cast your bread upon the waters and it will return to you manyfold. In the Parable of the Talents, the man who invests and multiplies his money is praised." Reagan (May 14, 1983) Radio Address to the Nation on Small Business http://www.reagan.utexas.edu/archives/speeches/1983/51483a.htm.
46. Edelman (1977) p. 25.
47. Ibid., p. 152.
48. Reagan (March 28, 1985) Remarks to the Students and Faculty at St. John's University in New York, New York http://www.reagan.utexas.edu/archives/speeches/1985/32885b.htm.
49. Niebuhr (1986).
50. Hughes (2003) p. 54. This gave birth to the myth of Nature's Nation. Ibid., p. 56
51. As an example one can use Jerry Falwell who in 1980 wrote "Any diligent student of American history find that our great nation was founded by godly men upon godly principles to be a Christian nation." Cited in Meacham (2006) p. 219.
52. Declaration of Independence.
53. Eisenhower. Cited in Herberg (1960) p. 84.
54. Mead (1975) p. 8.
55. Phillips (2006) p. 100.
56. Reagan (October 4, 1988) Remarks at the Republican Governors Club Dinner http://www.reagan.utexas.edu/archives/speeches/1988/100488e.htm.
57. Speech, Welcoming the Reverend Billy Graham, September 28, 1969, Box 44 Subseries E, Reagan, Ronald: Pre-presidential papers, Series I Speeches and writings, Ronald Reagan Library.
58. McLoughlin (1978). Cited in Gutterman (2005) p. 8.
59. Schurmann (1995) p. 52.
60. McLoughlin (1978).
61. Feldman (2005) pp. 13–14.
62. Ibid., p. 190.
63. Reagan (December 16, 1988) Remarks and a Question-and-Answer Session at the University of Virginia in Charlottesville http://www.reagan.utexas.edu/archives/speeches/1988/121688b.htm.
64. Reagan (October 7, 1985) Remarks at a White House Meeting With Reagan-Bush Campaign Leadership Groups http://www.reagan.utexas.edu/archives/speeches/1985/100785b.htm.
65. Reagan (January 19, 1989) Remarks at the Presentation Ceremony for the Presidential Medal of Freedom http://www.reagan.utexas.edu/archives/speeches/1989/011989b.htm.

66. Reagan (February 7, 1984) Remarks at the Annual Convention of the National Association of Secondary School Principals in Las Vegas, Nevada http://www.reagan.utexas.edu/archives/speeches/1984/20784a.htm.
67. Reagan (March 15, 1982) Address before a Joint Session of the Alabama State Legislature in Montgomery. s. 296.
68. Reagan (January 20, 1982) Remarks to the Reagan Administration Executive Forum. s. 45.
69. Reagan (September 25, 1982) Remarks at a Candle-Lighting Ceremony for Prayer in Schools. s. 1219.
70. Reagan (1984). Ecumenical Prayer Breakfast (August 23, 1984) p. 111.
71. Boorstin (1953) p. 159.
72. Reagan (1984). Ecumenical Prayer Breakfast (August 23, 1984) p. 111.
73. Reagan (November 3, 1984) Written Responses to Questions Submitted by France Soir Magazine http://www.reagan.utexas.edu/archives/speeches/1984/110384a.htm.
74. For a good discussion about the religiosity of Carter and Reagan see Boase (1989) pp. 1–7.
75. Kosmin and Lachman (1993) p. 182.
76. Phillips (2006) p. 187.
77. Safire. Cited in Kosmin and Lachman (1993) p. 158.
78. White (1998) p. ix.
79. Lakoff (1996).
80. Clinton (1991). Cited in Kosmin and Lachman (1993) p. 160.
81. Herberg (1960) p. 265.
82. This is what Billy Graham called Reagan in National Prayer Breakfast of 1986. See Reagan (2007) p. 389. Diary entry for February 6, 1986.
83. Cited in Noonan (2002) p. 98. A cynic might argue that this had something to do with Reagan's almost pathological fear of flying, which he decided to overcome during the governorship that included a lot of travel. All his trips during the General Electric years he did by train or car.
84. Chernus (2006) p. 70.
85. Harding. Cited in Chernus (2006) p. 70.
86. Bruner (2006) pp. 101–102.
87. Reagan (2007) p. 12. Diary entry for March 30, 1981. The actual date of the entry and its validity as an autobiographical piece of evidence can be put to question, since the date specified was the date of shooting, and after that there is a thirteen-day gap in entries, which continue only after Reagan has been sent to convalesce at the White House.
88. Deaver (2003) p. 3.
89. Box 1–44, Reagan, Ronald: Pre-presidential papers, Series I Speeches and writings, Ronald Reagan Library.
90. Stuckey (1989) p. 17.
91. This is evident from the typescripts and handwritten originals of his gubernatorial papers and radio addresses held at the Ronald Reagan

Presidential Library. The small number of evocations of God's name is striking when compared to the presidential papers.

92. Linden (1981) pp. 26–27. Italics in the original.
93. Reagan (January 2, 1967) Inaugural Invocation and Prayer Breakfast Invocation Delivered by the Rev. Donald L. Moomaw http://www.reagan.utexas.edu/archives/speeches/govspeech/01021967b.htm.
94. Reagan. Cited in Linden (1981) p. 86.
95. Kelly (1984) p. 144.
96. Conkin (1997) p. 1. Indeed, it was in 1830 that the Disciples of Christ and Christians broke from each other. See Ibid., pp. 25–26.
97. Ibid., pp. 13–16.
98. Kelly (1984) p. 146.
99. Hughes (2003) p. 122.
100. Ibid., p. 123.
101. Conkin (1997) pp. 26–27.
102. Reagan (August 25, 1983) Remarks at the Hispanic Economic Outlook Preview Luncheon in Los Angeles, California http://www.reagan.utexas.edu/archives/speeches/1983/82583b.htm.
103. Reagan (March 23, 1982) Remarks in New York City on Receiving the Charles Evans Hughes Gold Medal of the National Conference of Christians and Jews. s. 361.
104. Kelly (1984) p. 151.
105. Ibid., p. 191.
106. (RR) "Viewpoint," Disc 75–04, Taping date—February 23, 1975, Box 39, Subseries C, Reagan, Ronald: Pre-presidential papers, Series I Speeches and writings, Ronald Reagan Library.
107. Herberg (1960) p. 122.
108. Kengor (2004) p. 34.
109. Herberg (1960) p. 104.
110. Kengor (2004) p. 34. This is essentially the same idea of "light to shine before men" as in Matthew 5:16.
111. See for example "the beacon of hope for all mankind" in Reagan (February 24, 1982) Remarks on the Caribbean Basin Initiative to the Permanent Council of the Organization of American States. s. 215.
112. Conkin (1997) p. 37.
113. Cannon (2003) p. 14. Originally the source is Wills (2000) p. 21. Wills made a very thorough research into Reagan's past and surely is one of the best sources of issues related to Reagan's early life.
114. Reagan (October 7, 1984) Debate between the President and Former Vice President Walter F. Mondale in Louisville, Kentucky http://www.reagan.utexas.edu/archives/speeches/1984/100784a.htm.
115. Wright (1903). The hero of the book is Dick Walker, who after his mother's death flees his violent drunkard of a father. He becomes a tramp, wandering around until he walks into a church that becomes something of an anchor in his life and a man named Udell hires him as an apprentice

printer. Dick Walker grows up, becoming a Christian but not attaching himself to any denomination and being a "practical" Christian. In his adulthood he comes up with a plan to save Boyd City, the city he lives in, from moral decadence. He sees himself as inspired by God to do the work of Christ and embarks on a mission of social welfare that distinguished between the deserving and undeserving. His attempts take place on a local level of grassroots initiatives and ultimately, as is fitting for such an "educational" book, bars are closed down and whores acquire new careers while church attendance is soaring. Even Walker himself decides to join a church, and, a practicing and good Christian that he is, he naturally joins the Disciples of Christ, marries a good girl from the church, and ultimately is sent to do his good deeds in Washington D.C. as a representative elected from Boyd City. There are a lot of interesting comparisons with Reagan's own life, if one chooses to read the book looking for them. On this see Kengor(2004) pp. 18–26 who practically casts Reagan into the role of Walker.

116. Reagan (1990) p. 32. The quotation is from Reagan (1984), a letter in Kinner, Anderson, and Anderson (2003) p. 6. It has to be said that his favorite book keeps on changing, but always it is something he had read in his youth. Another example is a book called *Northern Trails*, which, according to Reagan, gave him his love of the outdoors. On this see Reagan (November 3, 1984) Written Responses to Questions Submitted by France Soir Magazine http://www.reagan.utexas.edu/archives/speeches/1984/110384a.htm.

117. Reagan (1990) p. 32.

118. Reagan (2003) in a letter. p. 256.

119. We are talking about a president publicly making the claim of being born-again. Carter was certainly not afraid of expressing his beliefs. He was the first US president, as so far the only one, who has officially reported a UFO sighting.

120. Phillips (2006) p. 106.

121. Reagan (2003) in a letter p. 5.

122. Ibid., in a letter pp. 278–279.

123. Ibid.

124. Wills (2000) p. 134. It was indeed Cleaver who broke the engagement.

125. Reagan's mother joined the same church after he and Jack moved to California in 1937. See Wills (2000) p. 29.

126. Kengor (2004) p. 49.

127. Reeves (2005) p. 74. As Kengor notes, Reagan joined the Bel Air Presbyterian after his marriage to Nancy. Kengor (2004) p. 117.

128. D'Souza (1997) pp. 213–214.

129. Reagan way by no means the only associate Graham had in the world of politics, while naturally his presidency made him the most important. Graham had friends in the Reagan administration as well, for example Alexander Haig. See Haig (1984) p. 69.

130. As an example, Reagan (2007) p. 31. Diary entry July 17, 1981.
131. Kengor (2004) pp. 119–120 discusses Moomaw's meaning to Reagan.
132. Linden (1981) p. 90.
133. Reagan (February 4, 1982) Remarks at the Annual National Prayer Breakfast. s. 109. For more info of the relationship between Reagan and Cooke see Deaver (2003) pp. 145–147.
134. Reagan (1990) pp. 49, 57, 70, 123.
135. Reagan (January 20, 1982) Interview with Reporters From the Los Angeles Times. s. 62.
136. Reagan (2001) p. 85.
137. Reagan. Cited in Linden (1981) pp. 90–91.
138. Porter (1990) p. 33.
139. Campbell (1988) p. 79.
140. Ibid.
141. Ibid.
142. Reagan (February 3, 1983) Remarks at the Annual National Prayer Breakfast. s. 122–123.
143. Reagan spoke of his creationistic beliefs during the 1980 campaign for presidency on the 22nd of August to an audience in Dallas participating in a "Roundtable National Affairs Briefing." Reagan argued that the theory of evolution "is a scientific theory only. And in recent years it has been challenged in the world of science and is not believed in the scientific community to be as infallible as it once was. I think that recent discoveries down through the years have pointed up great flaws in it." Los Angeles Times, August 23, 1980, A1–A2. The descriptive name of the article by Richard Bergholtz was *Reagan Tries to Cement His Ties with TV Evangelicals.* While the composition of the audience undoubtedly was a reason why Reagan expressed this belief that he had kept out of his narration throughout the eight-year presidency, it cannot be discounted as merely telling his audience what it wanted to hear. The implications of admitting to such a belief were potentially extremely harmful to a presidential candidate, and the PR people of the Reagan campaign encouraged the future president to avoid such controversial opinions.
144. Isaiah 40:8.
145. Reagan (January 31, 1983) Remarks at the Annual Convention of the National Religious Broadcasters http://www.reagan.utexas.edu/archives/speeches/1983/13183b.htm.
146. Reagan (1984). Ecumenical Prayer Breakfast (August 23, 1984) p. 109.
147. Kengor (2004) p. 106. The text of John 3:16 reads, "For God so loved the world, that he gave his only begotten Son, that whosoever believeth in him should not perish, but have everlasting life."
148. See for example Kengor (2004) p. 158.
149. Reagan (2003) p. 654.

150. Reagan (May 6, 1982) Remarks at a White House Ceremony in Observance of National Day of Prayer. s. 575.

151. Chronicles 7:11–16.

152. Clarck. Cited in Kengor (2004) p. 279.

153. Reagan (July 17, 1980) http://www.reaganlibrary.com/reagan/speeches/speech.asp?spid=18.

154. Aaltola (2007) p. 7.

155. Reagan (January 25, 1984) Address before a Joint Session of the Congress on the State of the Union http://www.reagan.utexas.edu/archives/speeches/1984/12584e.htm. please remove the page numbers.

156. Gutterman (2005) p. 9. He also notes that revivals can differ widely in their descriptions of the crises facing the society and in the development of concomitant paths to the resolutions for them.

157. Speech, "Dinner Speech, Hollywood Palladium, April 20, 1966," p. 242 Folder: 1966 Campaign: RR speeches and statements, Book II (1), Box C30, Research Unit, Ronald Reagan Governor's papers, Ronald Reagan Library.

158. See Hanska (2007) pp. 103–119. For Reagan "the Russians" are good and decent people like the Americans, but they are misled by the "Soviet" system, which crushes initiative, efficiency, and spiritual values. The source of evil is the totalitarian communist system that removes the freedom of the citizen with tight control. With a deeper analysis of Reagan's speeches we can note that he even refers in negative terms to only a few communist leaders, Qaddafi and Castro in the forefront, with their names and usually chooses to talk of "Soviet leaders." These leaders, just as the system itself, are stripped of human characteristics. In the case of the Ayatollah, "Now, I think he's as big a Satan as he thinks I am." Reagan (December 3, 1987) Interview With Television Network Broadcasters http://www.reagan.utexas.edu/archives/speeches/1987/120387d.htm. What Reagan did with the Soviet Union is directly comparable to what Christianity did to the notion of evil itself; it invented Satan. In a similar manner Reagan "invented" Soviet Union as the "focus of evil." To combat fear of evil Christianity personified evil and condensed it into one force, Satan. Whether Satan (or Soviet Union) is an independent force or a tool of God, his (its) mere existence generates a driving force for action. In a way, it is this powerful antagonist that makes one strong. However powerful evil is depicted to be, once it has been personified, it can be confronted. See Hall (2006) pp. 187–188.

159. Reagan (October 13, 1983) Remarks and a Question-and-Answer Session with Women Leaders of Christian Religious Organizations http://www.reagan.utexas.edu/archives/speeches/1983/101383d.htm.

160. Reagan (2001) p. 23. From a letter to Sister Mary Ignatius.

161. Reagan (September 18, 1982) Radio Address to the Nation on Prayer http://www.reagan.utexas.edu/archives/speeches/1982/91882b.htm.
162. Reagan (February 3, 1983) Remarks at the Annual National Prayer Breakfast http://www.reagan.utexas.edu/archives/speeches/1983/20383a.htm.
163. Reagan (December 24, 1983) Radio Address to the Nation on Christmas http://www.reagan.utexas.edu/archives/speeches/1983/122483a.htm.
164. Reagan (2007) p. 369. Diary entry for November 18, 1985.
165. Ochs and Capps (2001) pp. 231–239.
166. Reagan (January 25, 1984) Address Before a Joint Session of the Congress on the State of the Union http://www.reagan.utexas.edu/archives/speeches/1984/12584e.htm
167. Lincoln. Cited in Meacham (2006) p. 24. Italics in the original.
168. Wilson (1979) p. 12.
169. Reagan (October 27, 1983) Address to the Nation on Events in Lebanon and Grenada http://www.reagan.utexas.edu/archives/speeches/1983/102783b.htm.
170. Porter (1990) p. 33.
171. Reagan (2001) p. 17. Radio address for January 9, 1978. Original to be found in Radio address, Folder Speeches and Writings—Radio Broadcast, Taping date—January 16, 1978, "Christmas," Holograph 1/4, Box 17, Reagan, Ronald: Pre-presidential papers, Series I Speeches and writings, Ronald Reagan Library.
172. Meacham (2006) pp. 20–23.
173. Reagan (2007) p. 36. Diary entry September 6, 1981.
174. Ibid., p. 41. Diary entry October 4, 1981.
175. Radio address, Folder Speeches and Writings—Radio Broadcast, Taping date— April 13, 1977, "Redwoods," Edited Typescript 2/4, Box 8, Reagan, Ronald: Pre-presidential papers, Series I Speeches and writings, Ronald Reagan Library.
176. Reagan. Cited in Noonan (2002) p. 105.
177. Regan (1989).
178. Reagan (May 17, 1988) Remarks and a Question-and-Answer Session with Reporters. http://www.reagan.utexas.edu/archives/speeches/1988/051788b.htm.
179. Ibid. Regan (1989) asserts that all the schedules of the president had to pass the judgment of an astrologist to determine if they were suitable and especially safe. According to him this practice came into effect after the 1981 assassination attempt on Reagan by John Hinckley. Regan claims that this practice was initiated and continued due to demands from the First Lady.
180. Reeves (2005) pp. 455–456.
181. Berman (1990) p. 5.

182. Boyarsky (1981) p. 16.
183. Morris (1999) p. 345. Mrs. Dixon actually predicted that Reagan would be a president one day. Since this happened in 1966, and she predicted on the same occasion on television that the Chinese would invade Russia, the United States and the USSR would ally together against them, and that the Soviets would land the first man on the moon, there seem to be slight inaccuracies in her mystical powers. See Kengor (2004) p. 189.
184. Wills (2000) p. 355.
185. Kengor (2004) pp. 184–196 argues that Reagan disavowed astrology because of his belief in the guidance of the Christian God, and the fact that he never brought up the subject and yet he freely discussed flying saucers, ghosts, aliens, and Antichrist for example. He was not a man to hide his beliefs.
186. Reagan (2007) p. 604. Diary entry for May 3, 1988.
187. Ibid., p. 385. Diary entry for January 22, 1986. "I think the ghost of Abe Lincoln is stirring upstairs where we live."
188. Reagan (September 21, 1987) Address to the 42nd Session of the United Nations General Assembly in New York, New York http://www.reagan.utexas.edu/archives/speeches/1987/092187b.htm
189. Fisher (1982) p. 306.
190. Durkheim (1995) p. 429.
191. de Tocqueville (2000) p. 89.
192. Herberg (1960) p. 39.
193. In his diaries Reagan describes a meeting with a "cabinet room full of religious leaders covering *every denomination*—Protestant, Catholic & Hebrew." It is easy to see that Reagan clearly thought along the same lines as Herberg about the faiths that are America. Reagan (2007) p. 450. Diary entry for November 14, 1986. Italics mine.
194. Herberg (1960) p. 38.
195. Ibid., p. 263.
196. Ibid. Italics mine.
197. Ibid.
198. Durkheim (1995) pp. 350–351. Italics mine.
199. Mead (1977) p. 2.
200. Wilson (1979) pp. 172–174.
201. White (1987) p. x.
202. Ibid.
203. Ibid.
204. Draft, Folder Hannaford/CA HQ—R. Reagan Speeches—January 7, 1980, Acceptance Speech (Research)—Convention (2/2) Box 25, Ronald Reagan 1980 Campaign Papers, Series I, Ronald Reagan Library. Underlining in the original, perhaps to place emphasis on the blessing itself.
205. Chernus (2009).

206. Reagan (July 19, 1985) Proclamation 5357—Captive Nations Week, 1985 http://www.reagan.utexas.edu/archives/speeches/1985/71985d. htm.
207. Reagan (July 3, 1986) Remarks on the Lighting of the Torch of the Statue of Liberty in New York, New York http://www.reagan.utexas. edu/archives/speeches/1986/70386e.htm.
208. Reagan (February 6, 1985) Address before a Joint Session of the Congress on the State of the Union http://www.reagan.utexas.edu/ archives/speeches/1985/20685e.htm.
209. Reagan (September 18, 1986) Remarks at a Senate Campaign Rally for Representative W. Henson Moore in Metairie, Louisiana http://www. reagan.utexas.edu/archives/speeches/1986/091886a.htm.
210. Smith (1982) p. xi.
211. Chernus (2009).
212. Ibid.
213. Aaltola (2007) p. 35.
214. Eck (2001) p. 31.
215. Madsen (1991) pp. 451–456.
216. Reagan (April 5, 1982) Remarks at the National Legislative Conference of the Building and Construction Trades Department, AFL-CIO. p. 432.
217. Herberg (1960) p. 75.
218. Niebuhr and Heimert (1963) p. 63.
219. Herberg (1960) p. 75.
220. Ibid.
221. Bellah (1967) p. 12.
222. Anderson (1991).
223. Reagan (July 13, 1982) Remarks at the Annual Convention of the National Association of Counties in Baltimore, Maryland. s. 918. The expression "Big Brother government" had been a part of "The Speech" ever since the 1950s. See Ritter (1968) p. 52.
224. Reagan (June 5, 1985) Remarks at a Fundraising Luncheon for Senator Don Nickles in Oklahoma City, Oklahoma http://www.reagan.utexas. edu/archives/speeches/1985/60585b.htm.
225. Reagan (June 4, 1984) Address before a Joint Session of the Irish National Parliament http://www.reagan.utexas.edu/archives/ speeches/1984/60484a.htm.
226. Reagan (May 15, 1982) Radio Address to the Nation on Armed Forces Day. s. 645.
227. Reagan (February 9, 1982) Address before a Joint Session of the Indiana State Legislature in Indianapolis. s. 154.
228. Luoma-aho (2009).
229. Speech, Young Republicans' Convention, Omaha June 23, 1963, Box 44 Subseries E, Reagan, Ronald: Pre-presidential papers, Series I Speeches and writings, Ronald Reagan Library.

230. Reagan (September 9, 1984) Remarks at a Polish Festival in Doylestown, Pennsylvania http://www.reagan.utexas.edu/archives/speeches/1984/90984a.htm.

231. Reagan (September 25, 1984) Remarks at the Annual Meeting of the Boards of Governors of the International Monetary Fund and World Bank Group http://www.reagan.utexas.edu/archives/speeches/1984/92584a.htm.

232. Reagan (January 25, 1984) Address Before a Joint Session of the Congress on the State of the Union http://www.reagan.utexas.edu/archives/speeches/1984/12584e.htm.

233. Schmitt (2005) p. 49.

234. de Tocqueville (2000) p. 55.

235. Reagan (January 10, 1989) Remarks at the Franklin D. Roosevelt Library 50th Anniversary Luncheon http://www.reagan.utexas.edu/archives/speeches/1989/011089c.htm.

236. Reagan (April 21, 1987) Proclamation 5634—Law Day, U.S.A., 1987 http://www.reagan.utexas.edu/archives/speeches/1987/042187t.htm.

237. Reagan (February 12, 1982) Proclamation 4897—National Day of Prayer. s. 171.

238. Reagan (February 13, 1981) Message on the Observance of National Brotherhood Week. s. 100.

239. Reagan (November 6, 1981) Remarks in New York, New York, at the 84th Annual Dinner of the Irish American Historical Society. s. 1024. The concept of "melting pot" to describe America was first concocted, at least in a manner that attracted attention, by the Jewish writer Israel Zangwill in his 1908 play thus named. He saw America as "God's crucible" where the "feuds and vendettas" of Europe's religious strife would be burnt away, and the races of Europe melted and reformed. Theodore Roosevelt saw the play on its opening night and agreed that "we Americans are the children of the crucible." Ever since the idea of a melting pot has been central to the way the popular image of creating unum out of pluribus has been expressed. Eck (2001) p. 55.

240. Reagan (August 15, 1988) Remarks at the Republican National Convention in New Orleans, Louisiana http://www.reagan.utexas.edu/archives/speeches/1988/081588b.htm.

241. Rowland and Jones (2006) pp. 21–22. Mostly this attitude of seeing beyond the conservative rhetoric has been manifested in articles, but books have begun to emerge as well. See for example Wilentz (2008).

242. Reagan (April 5, 1982) Remarks at the National Legislative Conference of the Building and Construction Trades Department, AFL-CIO. s. 433.

243. Niebuhr (1986) p. 84.

244. Reagan (August 2, 1982) Remarks at the Annual Convention of the National Corn Growers Association in Des Moines, Iowa. s. 999. Italics mine.

245. Herberg (1960) p. 264.

246. Ibid.

247. Bellah (1967) p. 18.
248. Naturally there are numerous and occasionally even almost contradictory definitions of what "democracy" means, but I ask the reader
not to be offended by my use of it here, which follows the common
usage in American political discourse with additional elements from
Republican, Conservative, and even Reaganesque interpretations.
249. Bellah (1967) p. 18.
250. Reagan (June 29, 1987) Remarks at a White House Briefing for
Administration Supporters http://www.reagan.utexas.edu/archives/
speeches/1987/062987a.htm.
251. Reagan (November 9, 1987) Remarks to Representatives of the
Organization of American States http://www.reagan.utexas.edu/
archives/speeches/1987/110987c.htm.
252. Reagan (January 30, 1984) Remarks at the Annual Convention of
the National Religious Broadcasters http://www.reagan.utexas.edu/
archives/speeches/1984/13084b.htm.
253. Hughes (2003) p. 193.
254. Reagan (July 4, 1984) Remarks at a Spirit of America Festival
in Decatur, Alabama http://www.reagan.utexas.edu/archives/
speeches/1984/70484e.htm
255. Prestowitz (2003) pp. 36–37.
256. Reagan (2007) p. 44. Diary entry for October 16, 1981.
257. Reagan (January 1, 1982) Remarks to the People of Foreign Nations
on New Year's Day. s. 2.
258. See Reagan (January 19, 1989) Remarks at the Presentation Ceremony
for the Presidential Medal of Freedom http://www.reagan.utexas.edu/
archives/speeches/1989/011989b.htm.
259. de Tocqueville (2000) p. 155.
260. Reagan (January 1, 1982) Remarks to the People of Foreign Nations
on New Year's Day. s. 2.
261. Reagan (October 1, 1984) Remarks at Naturalization Ceremonies for
New United States Citizens in Detroit, Michigan http://www.reagan.
utexas.edu/archives/speeches/1984/100184a.htm.
262. Reagan (April 30, 1984) Remarks at Fudan University in Shanghai,
China.
263. Reagan (1952). Cited in Kengor (2004) p. 94.
264. Lyrics by Springsteen, Bruce. Available at www.brucespringsteen.net.
Rather surprisingly during the 1984 campaign Reagan and his associates wanted to get the rock singer Bruce Springsteen to support the
campaign, but Springsteen politely declined (White, 1998, pp. 131–
134). One could claim that Springsteen in his songs rather portrayed
the dark side of the American dream. If it was not the nightmare, it
certainly was a moment of insomnia. In 1980 after Reagan's electoral
win, Springsteen had said to his audience that what happened last night
was "pretty terrifying." Ibid., p. 134.
265. X (1964).
266. Schurmann (1995) pp. 32–33.

267. Speech, "A Plan for Action: Announcement of Candidacy, January 4, 1966," Folder: 1966 Campaign: RR speeches and statements, Book I, Box C30, Research Unit, Ronald Reagan Governor's papers, Ronald Reagan Library. Indeed, Reagan goes further to argue that "we can demonstrate to our sister states—to the entire nation—that government should be of and by as well as for the people. That this way of ours is still the greatest adventure, the newest experiment in man's relation to man."
268. Stuckey (1989) p. 46.
269. Reagan(January20,1984)RemarkstotheReaganAdministrationExecutive Forum   http://www.reagan.utexas.edu/archives/speeches/1984/12084a.htm.
270. Frye (1957) p. 106.
271. Ibid., pp. 83, 107.
272. Ibid., pp. 118–119.
273. White (1998) p. 33.
274. Muir (1995) p. 262.
275. Reagan (July 19, 1982) Remarks at a Rally Supporting the Proposed Constitutional Amendment for a Balanced Federal Budget http://www.reagan.utexas.edu/archives/speeches/1982/71982d.htm.
276. Schurmann (1995) p. 146. The irony inbuilt into Reagan's vision of the continuous American Revolution through the ages has to be noted, since before his presidency he commented on the "perpetual revolution" that Mao Tse-tung kept China in for 27 years, and how this may sweep the revolutionaries away and cause hindrance to getting a stable leadership established. Communist revolution just is not as good as the American Revolution, while both are in a sense just as perpetual. For this see Radio address, Folder Speeches and Writings—Radio Broadcast, Taping date—1976, September "Mao's China," Edited typescript, Box 2, Reagan, Ronald: Pre-presidential papers, Series I Speeches and writings, Ronald Reagan Library.
277. Speech, Men of All Saints Episcopal Church Dinner, Los Angeles, March 21, 1969, Box 44 Subseries E, Reagan, Ronald: Pre-presidential papers, Series I Speeches and writings, Ronald Reagan Library.
278. Speech, Marlborough College Preparatory School for Girls Commencement Exercises June 6, 1974, Box 44 Subseries E, Reagan, Ronald: Pre-presidential papers, Series I Speeches and writings, Ronald Reagan Library.
279. Schurmann (1995) p. 216.
280. Reagan (July 3, 1986) Remarks at the Opening Ceremonies of the Statue of Liberty Centennial Celebration in New York, New York http://www.reagan.utexas.edu/archives/speeches/1986/70386d.htm.
281. Erickson (1985) p. 3. Italics mine.
282. Reagan (April 28, 1981) Address before a Joint Session of the Congress on the Program for Economic Recovery. http://www.reagan.utexas.edu/archives/speeches/1981/42881c.htm.

283. Lewis (1987) p. 284.
284. Reagan (September 5, 1984) Remarks and a Question-and-Answer Session at the "Choosing a Future" Conference in Chicago, Illinois http://www.reagan.utexas.edu/archives/speeches/1984/90584a.htm.
285. Durkheim (1995) p. 425.
286. Boorstin (1962) p. 239.
287. Ibid., p. 240.
288. Reagan (February 22, 1982) Remarks at a Mount Vernon, Virginia, Ceremony Commemorating the 250th Anniversary of the Birth on George Washington. s. 200.
289. Nixon (1968) Acceptance speech for the Republican Presidential Candidate Nomination. Cited in White (1998) p. 26.
290. Wallace (1997) p. 8. Italics in the original.
291. Speakes and Pack (1988) p. 70.
292. At the same time he often told a story of his friend Franklin Burghardt who played in the same football team, and the racist encounter with a player from the other team who finally confessed that Burgie was the "whitest man he ever knew." During the presidency the story had been changed so that Burghardt was "the greatest human being," but otherwise the anecdote was the same. Reagan (January 15, 1986) Remarks to the Students and Faculty at Martin Luther King, Jr. Elementary School http://www.reagan.utexas.edu/archives/speeches/1986/11586b. htm. Another story concerning Burghardt was that once when the team could not get a hotel because of him and two other blacks on the team, Reagan took them overnight to his parents' house. Burghardt himself confirmed this latter anecdote to be true. Thus, it is just another example of Reagan perfecting his America that he chose not to take these two incidents as proof of the racism in his youth.
293. Reagan (May 19, 1981) Remarks at the White House Luncheon Honoring the Astronauts of the Space Shuttle Columbia. s. 441.
294. Deaver (2003) p. 5.
295. Warner (1962) pp. 128–130.
296. Zelinsky (1988) p. 57.
297. Lyotard (1993b) p. 29. Italics in the original.
298. Reagan (June 3, 1984) Toasts of the President and Prime Minister Garret FitzGerald of Ireland at a Dinner Honoring the President in Dublin http://www.reagan.utexas.edu/archives/speeches/1984/60384b. htm.
299. Lyotard (1993b) p. 41.
300. Reagan (January 25, 1984) Address before a Joint Session of the Congress on the State of the Union http://www.reagan.utexas. edu/archives/speeches/1984/12584e.htm. please remove the page number...
301. Rushing (1986) p. 421.
302. Reagan (May 1, 1982) Remarks at Dedication Ceremonies for the U.S. Pavilon at the Knoxville International Energy Exposition (World's Fait) in Tennessee. s. 549.

303. Niebuhr (1954) p. 72.
304. Reagan (August 15, 1988) Remarks at the Republican National Convention in New Orleans, Louisiana http://www.reagan.utexas.edu/archives/speeches/1988/081588b.htm
305. Fisher (1982) p. 301.
306. White (1998) pp. 34–35.
307. Fisher (1982) p. 301.
308. Reagan (July 22, 1982) Remarks at the Mathews-Dickey Boys' Club in St. Louis, Missouri. s. 963.
309. Reagan (September 17, 1982) Remarks at the Swearing-In Ceremony for United States Citizens in White House Station, New Jersey. s. 1178.

4   BLENDING THE MYTHICAL AND RELIGIOUS INTO POLITICAL

1. Reagan (1984). Fudan University, Shanghai (April 30, 1984) p. 44.
2. Smith (1982) p. xii.
3. Ibid., p. xiii.
4. Grottanelli (1999) p. 88.
5. Ibid., p. 161.
6. Ibid.
7. Genette (1993) p. 24.
8. Ibid.
9. Reagan (February 4, 1985) Remarks at the Annual Convention of the National Religious Broadcasters http://www.reagan.utexas.edu/archives/speeches/1985/20485d.htm.
10. Propp (1968) p. 106. Italics mine.
11. Ibid., p. 87.
12. Ibid., p. 90.
13. Lyotard (1993) p. 19.
14. Marty (1984) p. 12.
15. Campbell (1988) p. 36.
16. Ricoeur (1995) p. 1.
17. Aaltola (2007) p. 17.
18. Ricoeur (1995) p. 46.
19. Durkheim (1995) p. 384. Italics mine.
20. Ibid., p. 386.
21. Ricoeur (1995) p. 68.
22. The choice to use this term may be caused by the fact that Ricoeur was in his own words "frightened by this word 'sacred'." Ibid., p. 72.
23. Ibid., p. 69.
24. Smith (1982) p. 44.
25. Ricoeur (1995) pp. 69–70.
26. Ibid., p. 70.
27. Ibid.
28. Durkheim (1995) p. 79.

29. Frye (1957) p. 64.
30. Shapiro (2006) pp. 168–169.
31. de Tocqueville (2000) p. 407.
32. Eliade (1963) p. 19.
33. Lévi-Strauss (1969) p. 219.
34. Cited in Eliade (1963) p. 165.
35. Origen, *De principiis 4, 2, 9.* Cited in Eliade (1963) p. 166. Origen was an original thinker in other aspects as well as the story about his self-castration to avoid the sin of lust exemplifies.
36. Eliade (1963) p. 166.
37. Ibid., p. 163.
38. Ibid., p. 1.
39. Lincoln (1989) p. 24.
40. Eliade (1963) p. 2.
41. Ibid., pp. 8–11.
42. Ibid., p. 19.
43. Frye (1957) p. 51.
44. Levin (1969) p. 107.
45. Boer (2009) p. 22.
46. Ibid.
47. Ibid.
48. Ibid., p. 31.
49. Barthes (1991) p. 110.
50. Ibid., pp. 110–111.
51. Ibid., p. 120.
52. Propp (1968) pp. 76–86.
53. Ibid., p. 113.
54. Barthes (1977) p. 169. Italics in the original.
55. Lincoln (1999) p. 150.
56. McLoughlin (1978) p. 103.
57. Reagan (January 20, 1984) Remarks to the Reagan Administration Executive Forum http://www.reagan.utexas.edu/archives/speeches/1984/12084a.htm. This biblical quotation is from the *Book of Joel*, another prophet Reagan often cites.
58. Reagan (April 22, 1986) Remarks at the Heritage Foundation Anniversary Dinner http://www.reagan.utexas.edu/archives/speeches/1986/42286f.htm.
59. Sorel. Cited in Levin (1969) p. 109.
60. Barthes (1991) p. 130.
61. Boer (2009) p. 15.
62. Barthes (1991) p. 144.
63. Ibid., pp. 144–145.
64. Weber (2005) p. 6–7.
65. Bruner (1969) p. 281.
66. Ibid., pp. 282–283.
67. Lincoln (1989) p. 32.

68. Hughes (2003) p. 2.
69. Ibid., pp. 6–8.
70. Bellah (1975) p. 159.
71. Chernus (2009).
72. Frye (1957) p. 349. Italics mine.
73. Ibid.
74. Reagan (September 3, 1984) Remarks at a Reagan-Bush Rally in Cupertino, California http://www.reagan.utexas.edu/archives/speeches/1984/90384c.htm.
75. Campbell (1969) p. 19.
76. Jameson (2002) p. 46.
77. Ibid., pp. 45–46.
78. Culler (1975) p. 50.
79. Hall (2006) p. 179.
80. Lévi-Strauss (1978) p. 17. Italics in the original.
81. Eliade (1963) p. 141. Italics in the original.
82. Ivie (1984) p. 44.
83. Speech, "Excerpts from remarks by the Hon. Ronald Reagan at Friends of Kirby Holmes Luncheon, Monte Carlo Banquet Hall, Utica, Michigan, Friday, September 29, 1978," Folder Hannaford/CA HQ—R. Reagan Speeches—September 29, 1976, Friends of Kirby Holmes, Utica MI, Box 21, Ronald Reagan 1980 Campaign Papers, Series I, Ronald Reagan Library.
84. de Tocqueville (2000) p. 155.
85. Stuckey (1989) p. 15.
86. Reagan (January 31, 1984) Remarks at the Annual Convention of the Concrete and Aggregates Industries Associations in Chicago, Illinois http://www.reagan.utexas.edu/archives/speeches/1984/13184b.htm.
87. Shogan (2006) p. 216. Shogan presents a very good account of the rhetorical elements common to Reagan and Coolidge and how Coolidge was treated by Reagan in his speeches as a source for quotations.
88. Lyotard (1984) p. 37.
89. Jameson (1984) pp. xi-xii.
90. Reagan (September 9, 1982) Remarks at Kansas State University at the Alfred M. Landon Lecture Series on Public Issues http://www.reagan.utexas.edu/archives/speeches/1982/90982d.htm.
91. Harle (1998) pp. 100–101.
92. Lyotard (1997) pp. 81–82.
93. Chernus (2006) p. 3.
94. Reagan (October 24, .1985) Address to the 40th Session of the United Nations General Assembly in New York, New York http://www.reagan.utexas.edu/archives/speeches/1985/102485a.htm.
95. Stuckey (1989) p. 3.
96. Aaltola (2007) p. 44.
97. Jewett and Lawrence (1977) p. 7.
98. Exum (1996) p. 9.
99. Ricoeur (1995) p. 44.

100. Reagan (June 6, 1982) Address to the British Parliament. s. 197.
101. Reagan (October 3, 1983) Remarks at a Dinner Marking the 10th Anniversary of the Heritage Foundation http://www.reagan.utexas.edu/archives/speeches/1983/100383h.htm.
102. Gutterman (2005) p. 26.
103. Hughes (2003) p. 28.
104. See Ibid., p. 33.
105. Bercovich (1993) p. 40.
106. Ibid., p. 87.
107. Gutterman (2005) p. 6.
108. Phillips (2006) p. 129.
109. As an example might serve the stories the slaves and their African-American descendants have told where America is depicted as their Egypt.
110. Gutterman (2005) pp. 11–12.
111. See Stephanson (1996).
112. Gutterman (2005).
113. Kelly (1984) p. 40.
114. Boer (2009) p. 17. Italics in the original.
115. Reagan (August 13, 1983) Remarks at the Annual Convention of the American G.I. Forum in El Paso, Texas http://www.reagan.utexas.edu/archives/speeches/1983/81383b.htm.
116. Reagan (July 4, 1984) Remarks at a Spirit of America Festival in Decatur, Alabama http://www.reagan.utexas.edu/archives/speeches/1984/70484e.htm.
117. Polkinghorne (1988) p. 167.
118. Ibid.
119. Matthew 5:14–16.
120. Reagan (January 11, 1989) Farewell Address to the Nation http://www.reagan.utexas.edu/archives/speeches/1989/011189i.htm.
121. Reagan (June 3, 1988) Remarks Upon Returning From the Soviet-United States Summit Meeting in Moscow http://www.reagan.utexas.edu/archives/speeches/1988/060388c.htm.
122. Reagan (July 8, 1985) Remarks at the Annual Convention of the American Bar Association http://www.reagan.utexas.edu/archives/speeches/1985/70885a.htm.
123. Reagan (September 4, 1984) Remarks at the Annual Convention of the American Legion in Salt Lake City, Utah http://www.reagan.utexas.edu/archives/speeches/1984/90484a.htm.
124. Frye (1969) p. 125.
125. Campbell (1988) p. 63. Italics in the original.
126. Reagan (January 11, 1989) Farewell Address to the Nation http://www.reagan.utexas.edu/archives/speeches/1989/011189i.htm.
127. Gutterman (2005) p. 12.
128. Culler (1975) p. 43.
129. Draft, Folder Hannaford/CA HQ—R. Reagan Speeches—January 7, 1980, Acceptance Speech (Research)—Convention (2/2) Box 25,

Ronald Reagan 1980 Campaign Papers, Series I, Ronald Reagan Library.

130. Campbell (1968) pp. 387–388.
131. Lewis (1987) p. 283.
132. Martin (1987) p. 87.
133. Polkinghorne (1988) p. 150. Italics mine.
134. Lewis (1987) p. 282.
135. Ibid., p. 283.
136. Reagan (January 20, 1984) Remarks to the Reagan Administration Executive Forum http://www.reagan.utexas.edu/archives/speeches/1984/12084a.htm.
137. Zelinsky (1988) p. 93.
138. Martin (1987) p. 73.
139. Zelinsky (1988) p. 145.
140. Polkinghorne (1988) p. 135.
141. Lincoln (1989) p. 23.
142. White (1973).
143. Polkinghorne (1988) p. 63.
144. Aaltola (2007) p. 9–10.
145. It would be tempting to use the French word for a story, "*histoire*" here, to further illustrate my point, but I refrain from it for reasons of clarity.
146. Frye (1969) p. 119.
147. Reagan (June 24, 1987) Remarks to Participants in the People to People International Youth Exchange Program http://www.reagan.utexas.edu/archives/speeches/1987/062487b.htm.
148. Morris (1999) p. 394.
149. Reagan (September 10, 1987) Remarks to the Winners of the Bicentennial of the Constitution Essay Competition http://www.reagan.utexas.edu/archives/speeches/1987/091087a.htm.
150. MacIntyre (1984) p. 121. Italics mine.
151. Reagan (October 10, 1984) Remarks to the Heritage Council in Warren, Michigan http://www.reagan.utexas.edu/archives/speeches/1984/101084c.htm.
152. Reagan (June 29, 1983) Remarks and a Question-and-Answer Session with Participants in the National Conference of the National Association of Student Councils in Shawnee Mission, Kansas http://www.reagan.utexas.edu/archives/speeches/1983/62983b.htm.
153. Mead (1975) p. 4.
154. MacIntyre (1984) pp. 121–129. It must be noted that for MacIntyre the age of the heroic society has long since passed and for example in Europe most countries had made the transition away from it by the middle ages. Ibid., p. 165–167.
155. Ibid., p. 130. Italics in the original.
156. Reagan (January 25, 1986) Radio Address to the Nation on the State of the Union http://www.reagan.utexas.edu/archives/speeches/1986/12586a.htm.
157. MacIntyre (1984) p. 216.

158. Niebuhr (1954) p. 133.
159. For example Reagan (July 3, 1983) Message to the Nation on the Observance of Independence Day http://www.reagan.utexas.edu/archives/speeches/1983/70383a.htm.
160. Reagan (October 19, 1981) Remarks at the Bicentennial Observance of the Battle of Yorktown in Virginia. s. 968. Italics mine.
161. Riessman (2004) p. 35.
162. Genette (1980) p. 56.
163. Bruner (1986).
164. Reagan (January 11, 1989) Farewell Address to the Nation http://www.reagan.utexas.edu/archives/speeches/1989/011189i.htm.
165. White (1987) p. 40. White goes on to claim that "the narrative form is only the medium for the message and has no more truth value or informational content than any other formal structure." Ibid.. This no longer applies to Reagan's storytelling, since narrative form provides most of the content of the message as well by turning it into something myth-like. White admits that arguments may be embedded in narratives in the form of explanations but insists on seeing them as "commentary" instead of a part of the narrative. Ibid., p. 43.
166. Ibid., p. 44.
167. Reagan (September 4, 1984) Remarks at the Annual Convention of the American Legion in Salt Lake City, Utah http://www.reagan.utexas.edu/archives/speeches/1984/90484a.htm.
168. Wills (2000) pp. 454–455.
169. Barthes (1977) p. 166.
170. Lévi-Strauss (1978) p. 43.
171. Ibid.
172. Reagan (September 14, 1981) Proclamation 4857—Yorktown Bicentennial. s. 785.
173. Lévi-Strauss (1969) p. 209. Italics mine.
174. Ibid., p. 204.
175. Eliade (1963) p. 140.
176. Reagan (March 18, 1985) Toast at a Luncheon with Provincial and Community Leaders in Quebec City, Canada http://www.reagan.utexas.edu/archives/speeches/1985/31885b.htm.
177. Campbell (1968) p. 337.
178. Reagan (October 12, 1984) Remarks During a Whistlestop Tour of Ohio http://www.reagan.utexas.edu/archives/speeches/1984/101284d.htm.
179. Reagan (October 12, 1984) Remarks at a Reagan-Bush Rally in Dayton, Ohio http://www.reagan.utexas.edu/archives/speeches/1984/101284b.htm.
180. Reagan (October 21, 1984) Remarks at a Reagan-Bush Rally in Kansas City, Missouri http://www.reagan.utexas.edu/archives/speeches/1984/102184a.htm.
181. Reagan (October 22, 1984) Remarks to Employees at a Rockwell International Facility in Palmdale, California http://www.reagan.utexas.edu/archives/speeches/1984/102284b.htm.

182. Campbell (1968) p. 337, 353.
183. Speech, Alf Landon Lecture, Kansas State University, Manhattan, KS, October 26, 1963, Box 44 Subseries E, Reagan, Ronald: Pre-presidential papers, Series I Speeches and writings, Ronald Reagan Library.
184. Combs (1993) p. 27.
185. Reagan (August 30, 1984) Remarks During a Visit to the Goddard Space Flight Centre in Greenbelt, Maryland http://www.reagan.utexas.edu/archives/speeches/1984/83084a.htm.
186. Margolin (1999) p. 151.
187. Reagan (January 21, 1985) Inaugural Address http://www.reagan.utexas.edu/archives/speeches/1985/12185a.htm.
188. Reagan (June 5, 1985) Remarks at a Fundraising Luncheon for Senator Don Nickles in Oklahoma City, Oklahoma http://www.reagan.utexas.edu/archives/speeches/1985/60585b.htm.
189. Reagan (July 6, 1982) Remarks and a Question-and-Answer Session with Senior Citizens in Los Angeles, California. s. 907.
190. Wills (2000) p. xxiii.
191. Reagan (2001) p. 94. Italics mine. the words about the radio address are given just to provide context. can be deleted as well, should you prefer it so
192. Margolin (1999) p. 153.
193. Reagan (October 21, 1984) Debate between the President and Former Vice President Walter F. Mondale in Kansas City, Missouri http://www.reagan.utexas.edu/archives/speeches/1984/102184b.htm.
194. Reagan (January 21, 1985) Inaugural Address http://www.reagan.utexas.edu/archives/speeches/1985/12185a.htm.
195. Reagan (January 25, 1985) Remarks at the 1985 Reagan Administration Executive Forum http://www.reagan.utexas.edu/archives/speeches/1985/12585a.htm.
196. Reagan (February 6, 1986) Message to the Congress on America's Agenda for the Future http://www.reagan.utexas.edu/archives/speeches/1986/20686c.htm.
197. Polanyi. Cited in Ochs and Capps (2001) p. 161.
198. Eliade (1963) pp. 52–53.
199. Reagan (August 19, 1984) Remarks at the Missouri State Fair in Sedalia http://www.reagan.utexas.edu/archives/speeches/1984/81984b.htm.
200. Morris (1999) p. 9.
201. Cannon (2003) p. 81.
202. Wills (2000) p. xxiv.
203. Reagan (September 5, 1984) Remarks and a Question-and-Answer Session at the "Choosing a Future" Conference in Chicago, Illinois http://www.reagan.utexas.edu/archives/speeches/1984/90584a.htm.
204. Gutterman (2005) p. 22.
205. Haig (1984) p. 13.
206. Reagan (September 14, 1983) Remarks at the Fundraising Dinner of the Republican National Hispanic Assembly http://www.reagan.utexas.edu/archives/speeches/1983/91483d.htm.

207. Reeves (2005) p. 473.
208. Speech "Encroaching Control," no date, Box 43 Subseries E, Reagan, Ronald: Pre-presidential papers, Series I Speeches and writings, Ronald Reagan Library.
209. Reeves (2005) p. 473.
210. Reagan (February 2, 1981) Message on the Observance of National Afro-American (Black) History Month. s. 68.
211. Crable and Vibbert (1983) pp. 291–292.
212. Boer (2009) p. 115.
213. Ibid.
214. Lincoln (1989) p. 38.
215. Polkinghorne (1988) p. 20.
216. Reagan (February 4, 1986) Address Before a Joint Session of Congress on the State of the Union http://www.reagan.utexas.edu/archives/speeches/1986/20486a.htm.
217. Reagan (October 22, .1984) Remarks at a Reagan-Bush Rally in Medford, Oregon http://www.reagan.utexas.edu/archives/speeches/1984/102284d.htm.

5 Coda

1. Iqbal (1992) p. 92.
2. Reagan (November 5, 1994). In a farewell letter to the public, Skinner, Anderson, and Anderson (2004) pp. 832–833.
3. Pemberton (1997) p. 17.
4. Reagan (August 1, 1983) Remarks at the Annual Meeting of the American Bar Association in Atlanta, Georgia http://www.reagan.utexas.edu/archives/speeches/1983/80183a.htm.
5. Riessman (1993) p. 11.
6. Interestingly the only "evidence" of Jack Reagan's alcoholism or "sickness" comes from his son's first autobiography and subsequent speeches. Wills claims that Jack Reagan's drinking was never a public disgrace, and his hard drinking is debated. If so, why did Reagan want to share the embarrassing story of his father's alcoholism with millions of people? Maybe Reagan just was an unembarrassed moralist. See Wills (2000) pp. 41–43.
7. Speech Draft re, Bicentennial, July 6, 1976, Box 44 Subseries E, Reagan, Ronald: Pre-presidential papers, Series I Speeches and writings, Ronald Reagan Library.
8. Pemberton (1997) p. 17.
9. Eck (2001) pp. 2–3.
10. Ibid., pp. 9, 29.
11. Mead (1975) p. 33.
12. Ibid.
13. Hall (2002) p. 321. It has to be noted, however, that by all accounts Wirthlin was a masterly pollster, but much of the Reagan success rested on the fact that *he* was delivering the speeches. Reaganism just could not have worked without Reagan.

14. Rowland and Jones (2006) p. 42.
15. Cervantes (1957) p. 432.
16. Berman (1990) p. 1. Berman also notes the fact that Reagan indeed was psychologically suited for the job "raises some rather ironic issues with respect to the presidential job description."
17. Stuckey (1990) p. 95. Italics in the original.
18. Ibid., pp. 95–96.
19. Ibid., p. 97.
20. Fisher (1982) p. 310.
21. Shogan (2006) p. 217.
22. Reagan (September 20, 1984) Remarks at a Reagan-Bush Rally in Cedar Rapids, Iowa http://www.reagan.utexas.edu/archives/speeches/1984/92084b.htm.

BIBLIOGRAPHY

PRIMARY SOURCES

Public Papers of the Presidents of the United States. Ronald Reagan 1981. January 20–December 31, 1981. United States Government Printing Office, Washington 1982

Public Papers of the Presidents of the United States. Ronald Reagan 1982. January 1–July 2, 1982. United States Government Printing Office, Washington 1983

Public Papers of the Presidents of the United States. Ronald Reagan 1982. July 3–December 31, 1982. United States Government Printing Office, Washington 1983

Reagan (January 2, 1967) Inaugural Invocation and Prayer Breakfast Invocation Delivered by the Rev. Donald l. Moomaw http://www.reagan.utexas.edu/archives/speeches/govspeech/01021967b.htm Accessed September 7, 2009

Reagan (July 17, 1980) http://www.reaganlibrary.com/reagan/speeches/speech.asp?spid=18 Accessed September 7, 2009

Reagan (April 28, 1981) Address before a Joint Session of the Congress on the Program for Economic Recovery http://www.reagan.utexas.edu/archives/speeches/1981/42881c.htm Accessed September 7, 2009

Reagan (June 16, 1981) The President's News Conference http://www.reagan.utexas.edu/archives/speeches/1981/61681b.htm Accessed September 7, 2009

Reagan (July 19, 1982) Remarks at a Rally Supporting the Proposed Constitutional Amendment for a Balanced Federal Budget http://www.reagan.utexas.edu/archives/speeches/1982/71982d.htm Accessed September 7, 2009

Reagan (September 9, 1982) Remarks at Kansas State University at the Alfred m. Landon Lecture Series on Public Issues http://www.reagan.utexas.edu/archives/speeches/1982/90982d.htm Accessed September 7, 2009

Reagan (September 18, 1982) Radio Address to the Nation on Prayer http://www.reagan.utexas.edu/archives/speeches/1982/91882b.htm Accessed September 7, 2009

Reagan (January 22, 1983) Radio Address to the Nation on Domestic Social Issues http://www.reagan.utexas.edu/archives/speeches/1983/12283a.htm Accessed April 29, 2007

Reagan (January 31, 1983) Remarks at the Annual Convention of the National Religious Broadcasters http://www.reagan.utexas.edu/archives /speeches/1983/13183b.htm Accessed April 29, 2007

Reagan (February 3, 1983) Remarks at the Annual National Prayer Breakfast http://www.reagan.utexas.edu/archives/speeches/1983/20383a.htm Accessed April 29, 2007

Reagan (March 8, 1983) Remarks at the Annual Convention of the National Association of Evangelicals in Orlando, Florida http://www.reagan.utexas .edu/archives/speeches/1983/30883b.htm Accessed April 30, 2007

Reagan (April 27, 1983) Remarks to Daily News Crime Fighter Award Winners in New York City http://www.reagan.utexas.edu/archives /speeches/1983/42783a.htm Accessed April 30, 2007

Reagan (May 14, 1983) Radio Address to the Nation on Small Business http://www.reagan.utexas.edu/archives/speeches/1983/51483a.htm Accessed April 30, 2007

Reagan (May 31, 1983) Interview with American and Foreign Journalists at the Williamsburg Economic Summit Conference in Virginia http://www.reagan .utexas.edu/archives/speeches/1983/53183a.htm Accessed May 2, 2007

Reagan (June 29, 1983) Remarks and a Question-and-Answer Session With Participants in the National Conference of the National Association of Student Councils in Shawnee Mission, Kansas http://www.reagan.utexas. edu/archives/speeches/1983/62983b.htm Accessed May 3, 2007

Reagan (July 3, 1983) Message to the Nation on the Observance of Independence Day http://www.reagan.utexas.edu/archives/speeches /1983/70383a.htm Accessed May 3, 2007

Reagan (August 1, 1983) Remarks at the Annual Meeting of the American Bar Association in Atlanta, Georgia http://www.reagan.utexas.edu/archives /speeches/1983/80183a.htm Accessed May 3, 2007

Reagan (August 13, 1983) Remarks at the Annual Convention of the American G. I. Forum in El Paso, Texas http://www.reagan.utexas.edu /archives/speeches/1983/81383b.htm Accessed May 3, 2007

Reagan (August 25, 1983) Remarks at the Hispanic Economic Outlook Preview Luncheon in Los Angeles, California http://www.reagan.utexas .edu/archives/speeches/1983/82583b.htm Accessed May 3, 2007

Reagan (September 14, 1983) Remarks at the Fundraising Dinner of the Republican National Hispanic Assembly http://www.reagan.utexas.edu /archives/speeches/1983/91483d.htm Accessed May 3, 2007

Reagan (October 3, 1983) Remarks at a Dinner Marking the 10th Anniversary of the Heritage Foundation http://www.reagan.utexas.edu/archives /speeches/1983/100383h.htm Accessed May 6, 2007

Reagan (October 13, 1983) Remarks and a Question-and-Answer Session with Women Leaders of Christian Religious Organizations http://www .reagan.utexas.edu/archives/speeches/1983/101383d.htm   Accessed May 6, 2007

Reagan (October 27, 1983) Address to the Nation on Events in Lebanon and Grenada http://www.reagan.utexas.edu/archives /speeches/1983/102783b.htm Accessed May 6, 2007

Reagan (November 11, 1983) Address before the Japanese Diet in Tokyo http://www.reagan.utexas.edu/archives/speeches/1983/111183a.htm Accessed May 6, 2007

Reagan (December 6, 1983) Interview with Garry Clifford and Patricia Ryan of People Magazine http://www.reagan.utexas.edu/archives /speeches/1983/120683c.htm Accessed May 6, 2007

Reagan (December 14, 1983) Remarks and a Question-and-Answer Session with Editors of Gannett Newspapers on Domestic and Foreign Policy Issues http://www.reagan.utexas.edu/archives/speeches/1983/121483e.htm Accessed May 6, 2007

Reagan (December 24, 1983) Radio Address to the Nation on Christmas http://www.reagan.utexas.edu/archives/speeches/1983/122483a.htm Accessed May 6, 2007

Reagan (January 20, 1984) Remarks to the Reagan Administration Executive Forum http://www.reagan.utexas.edu/archives/speeches/1984/12084a .htm Accessed May 6, 2007

Reagan (January 25, 1984) Address before a Joint Session of the Congress on the State of the Union http://www.reagan.utexas.edu/archives/speeches /1984/12584e.htm Accessed May 6, 2007

Reagan (January 30, 1984) Remarks at the Annual Convention of the National Religious Broadcasters http://www.reagan.utexas.edu/archives /speeches/1984/13084b.htm Accessed May 6, 2007

Reagan (January 31, 1984) Remarks at the Annual Convention of the Concrete and Aggregates Industries Associations in Chicago, Illinois http://www.reagan.utexas.edu/archives/speeches/1984/13184b.htm Accessed May 7, 2007

Reagan (February 7, 1984) Remarks at the Annual Convention of the National Association of Secondary School Principals in Las Vegas, Nevada http://www.reagan.utexas.edu/archives/speeches/1984/20784a.htm Accessed May 7, 2007

Reagan (April 30, 1984) Remarks and a Question-and-Answer Session with Students at Fudan University in Shanghai, China http://www.reagan .utexas.edu/archives/speeches/1984/43084d.htm Accessed May 9, 2007

Reagan (May 25, 1984) Remarks at a Ceremony Honoring an Unknown Serviceman of the Vietnam Conflict http://www.reagan.utexas.edu /archives/speeches/1984/52584c.htm Accessed May 9, 2007

Reagan (June 3, 1984) Toasts of the President and Prime Minister Garret FitzGerald of Ireland at a Dinner Honoring the President in Dublin http://www.reagan.utexas.edu/archives/speeches/1984/60384b.htm Accessed May 9, 2007

Reagan (June 4, 1984) Address before a Joint Session of the Irish National Parliament http://www.reagan.utexas.edu/archives/speeches /1984/60484a.htm Accessed May 11, 2007

Reagan (July 4, 1984) Remarks at a Spirit of America Festival in Decatur, Alabama http://www.reagan.utexas.edu/archives/speeches/1984/70484e.htm Accessed May 9, 2007

Reagan (July 26, 1984) Remarks at the St. Ann's Festival in Hoboken, New Jersey http://www.reagan.utexas.edu/archives/speeches/1984/72684c .htm Accessed May 11, 2007

Reagan (August 19, 1984) Remarks at the Missouri State Fair in Sedalia http://www.reagan.utexas.edu/archives/speeches/1984/81984b.htm Accessed May 11, 2007

Reagan (August 30, 1984) Remarks During a Visit to the Goddard Space Flight Centre in Greenbelt, Maryland http://www.reagan.utexas.edu /archives/speeches/1984/83084a.htm Accessed May 11, 2007

Reagan (September 3, 1984) Remarks at a Reagan-Bush Rally in Cupertino, California http://www.reagan.utexas.edu/archives/speeches /1984/90384c.htm Accessed May 11, 2007

Reagan (September 4, 1984) Remarks at the Annual Convention of the American Legion in Salt Lake City, Utah http://www.reagan.utexas.edu /archives/speeches/1984/90484a.htm Accessed May 11, 2007

Reagan (September 5, 1984) Remarks and a Question-and-Answer Session at the "Choosing a Future" Conference in Chicago, Illinois http://www .reagan.utexas.edu/archives/speeches/1984/90584a.htm Accessed May 11, 2007

Reagan (September 9, 1984) Remarks at a Polish Festival in Doylestown, Pennsylvania http://www.reagan.utexas.edu/archives/speeches/1984 /90984a.htm Accessed May 11, 2007

Reagan (September 20, 1984) Remarks at a Reagan-Bush Rally in Cedar Rapids, Iowa http://www.reagan.utexas.edu/archives/speeches/1984/92084b .htm Accessed May 11, 2007

Reagan (September 25, 1984) Remarks at the Annual Meeting of the Boards of Governors of the International Monetary Fund and World Bank Group http://www.reagan.utexas.edu/archives/speeches/1984/92584a.htm Accessed May 14, 2007

Reagan (September 26, 1984) Remarks and a Question-and-Answer Session at Bowling Green State University in Bowling Green, Ohio http://www .reagan.utexas.edu/archives/speeches/1984/92684b.htm Accessed May 14, 2007

Reagan (October 1, 1984) Remarks at Naturalization Ceremonies for New United States Citizens in Detroit, Michigan http://www.reagan.utexas .edu/archives/speeches/1984/100184a.htm Accessed May 14, 2007

Reagan (October 7, 1984) Debate between the President and Former Vice President Walter F. Mondale in Louisville, Kentucky http://www.reagan. utexas.edu/archives/speeches/1984/100784a.htm Accessed May 14, 2007

Reagan (October 10, 1984) Remarks to the Heritage Council in Warren, Michigan http://www.reagan.utexas.edu/archives/speeches /1984/101084c.htm Accessed May 14, 2007

Reagan (October 12, 1984) Remarks During a Whistlestop Tour of Ohio http://www.reagan.utexas.edu/archives/speeches/1984/101284d.htm Accessed May 14, 2007

Reagan (October 12, 1984) Remarks at a Reagan-Bush Rally in Dayton, Ohio http://www.reagan.utexas.edu/archives/speeches/1984/101284b.htm Accessed May 14, 2007

Reagan (October 21, 1984) Debate between the President and Former Vice President Walter F. Mondale in Kansas City, Missouri http://www.reagan .utexas.edu/archives/speeches/1984/102184b.htm Accessed May 14, 2007

Reagan (October 22, 1984) Remarks at a Reagan-Bush Rally in Medford, Oregon http://www.reagan.utexas.edu/archives/speeches/1984/102284d.htm Accessed May 14, 2007

Reagan (October 22, 1984) Remarks to Employees at a Rockwell International Facility in Palmdale, California http://www.reagan.utexas.edu/archives /speeches/1984/102284b.htm Accessed May 14, 2007

Reagan (November 1, 1984) Remarks at a Reagan-Bush Rally in Boston, Massachusetts http://www.reagan.utexas.edu/archives/speeches/1984 /110184d.htm Accessed May 14, 2007

Reagan (November 3, 1984) Written Responses to Questions Submitted by France Soir Magazine http://www.reagan.utexas.edu/archives/speeches /1984/110384a.htm Accessed May 14, 2007

Reagan (January 21, 1985) Inaugural Address http://www.reagan.utexas. edu/archives/speeches/1985/12185a.htm Accessed May 14, 2007

Reagan (January 25, 1985) Remarks at the 1985 Reagan Administration Executive Forum http://www.reagan.utexas.edu/archives/speeches /1985/12585a.htm Accessed May 14, 2007

Reagan (February 4, 1985) Remarks at the Annual Convention of the National Religious Broadcasters http://www.reagan.utexas.edu/archives /speeches/1985/20485d.htm Accessed May 14, 2007

Reagan (February 6, 1985) Address before a Joint Session of the Congress on the State of the Union http://www.reagan.utexas.edu/archives/speeches /1985/20685e.htm Accessed May 15, 2007

Reagan (March 1, 1985) Remarks at the Annual Dinner of the Conservative Political Action Conference http://www.reagan.utexas.edu/archives /speeches/1985/30185f.htm Accessed May 15, 2007

Reagan (March 14, 1985) Remarks and a Question-and-Answer Session During a White House Briefing for Members of the Magazine Publishers Association http://www.reagan.utexas.edu/archives/speeches/1985/31485a.htm Accessed May 15, 2007

Reagan (March 18, 1985) Toast at a Luncheon with Provincial and Community Leaders in Quebec City, Canada http://www.reagan.utexas .edu/archives/speeches/1985/31885b.htm Accessed May 15, 2007

Reagan (March 28, 1985) Remarks to the Students and Faculty at St. John's University in New York, New York http://www.reagan.utexas.edu /archives/speeches/1985/32885b.htm Accessed May 15, 2007

Reagan (April 16, 1985) Remarks at a Conference on Religious Liberty http://www.reagan.utexas.edu/archives/speeches/1985/41685d.htm Accessed May 15, 2007

Reagan (May 7, 1985) Remarks to Community Leaders in Madrid, Spain http://www.reagan.utexas.edu/archives/speeches/1985/50785b.htm Accessed May 15, 2007

Reagan (June 5, 1985) Remarks at a Fundraising Luncheon for Senator Don Nickles in Oklahoma City, Oklahoma http://www.reagan.utexas.edu /archives/speeches/1985/60585b.htm Accessed June 16, 2007

Reagan (June 14, 1985) Remarks at a Flag Day Ceremony in Baltimore, Maryland http://www.reagan.utexas.edu/archives/speeches/1985/61485f.htm Accessed May 16, 2007

Reagan (July 8, 1985) Remarks at the Annual Convention of the American Bar Association http://www.reagan.utexas.edu/archives/speeches/1985 /70885a.htm Accessed May 16, 2007

Reagan (July 19, 1985) Proclamation 5357—Captive Nations Week, 1985 http://www.reagan.utexas.edu/archives/speeches/1985/71985d.htm Accessed May 16, 2007

Reagan (October 7, 1985) Remarks at a White House Meeting With Reagan-Bush Campaign Leadership Groups http://www.reagan.utexas.edu /archives/speeches/1985/100785b.htm Accessed May 17, 2007

Reagan (October 24, 1985) Address to the 40th Session of the United Nations General Assembly in New York, New York http://www.reagan .utexas.edu/archives/speeches/1985/102485a.htm Accessed May 17, 2007

Reagan (January 15, 1986) Remarks to the Students and Faculty at Martin Luther King, Jr. Elementary School http://www.reagan.utexas.edu /archives/speeches/1986/11586b.htm Accessed May 17, 2007

Reagan (January 25, 1986) Radio Address to the Nation on the State of the Union http://www.reagan.utexas.edu/archives/speeches/1986/12586a.htm Accessed May 17, 2007

Reagan (February 4, 1986) Address Before a Joint Session of Congress on the State of the Union http://www.reagan.utexas.edu/archives/speeches /1986/20486a.htm Accessed May 17, 2007

Reagan (February 6, 1986) Message to the Congress on America's Agenda for the Future http://www.reagan.utexas.edu/archives/speeches/1986 /20686c.htm Accessed May 18, 2007

Reagan (April 22, 1986) Remarks at the Heritage Foundation Anniversary Dinner http://www.reagan.utexas.edu/archives/speeches/1986/42286f.htm Accessed May 18, 2007

AccessedReagan (July 3, 1986) Remarks at the Opening Ceremonies of the Statue of Liberty Centennial Celebration in New York, New York http://

www.reagan.utexas.edu/archives/speeches/1986/70386d.htm Accessed
    May 20, 2007
Reagan (July 3, 1986) Remarks on the Lighting of the Torch of the Statue of
    Liberty in New York, New York http://www.reagan.utexas.edu/archives
    /speeches/1986/70386e.htm Accessed May 20, 2007
Reagan (September 18, 1986) Remarks at a Senate Campaign Rally for
    Representative W. Henson Moore in Metairie, Louisiana http://www
    .reagan.utexas.edu/archives/speeches/1986/091886a.htm   Accessed
    May 21, 2007
Reagan (March 4, 1987) Address to the Nation on the Iran Arms and Contra
    Aid Controversy http://www.reagan.utexas.edu/archives/speeches/1987
    /030487h.htm Accessed May 24, 2007
Reagan (April 21, 1987) Proclamation 5634—Law Day, U.S.A., 1987
    http://www.reagan.utexas.edu/archives/speeches/1987/042187t.htm
    Accessed May 25, 2007
Reagan (June 24, 1987) Remarks to Participants in the People to People
    International Youth Exchange Program http://www.reagan.utexas.edu
    /archives/speeches/1987/062487b.htm Accessed May 27, 2007
Reagan (June 29, 1987) Remarks at a White House Briefing for
    Administration   Supporters   http://www.reagan.utexas.edu/archives
    /speeches/1987/062987a.htm Accessed May 27, 2007
AccessedReagan (September 10, 1987) Remarks to the Winners of the
    Bicentennial of the Constitution Essay Competition http://www.reagan
    .utexas.edu/archives/speeches/1987/091087a.htm Accessed May 27,
    2007
Reagan (September 21, 1987) Address to the 42nd Session of the United
    Nations General Assembly in New York, New York http://www.reagan
    .utexas.edu/archives/speeches/1987/092187b.htm Accessed May 29,
    2007
Reagan (November 9, 1987) Remarks to Representatives of the Organization
    of American States http://www.reagan.utexas.edu/archives/speeches
    /1987/110987c.htm Accessed May 27, 2007
Reagan (November 13, 1987) Remarks at the Presentation Ceremony for
    the Young American Medals for Bravery and Service http://www.reagan
    .utexas.edu/archives/speeches/1987/111387b.htm Accessed May 29,
    2007
Reagan (November 16, 1987) Remarks at the Annual Meeting of the
    American Council of Life Insurance http://www.reagan.utexas.edu
    /archives/speeches/1987/111687a.htm Accessed May 29, 2007
Reagan (December 3, 1987) Interview with Television Network Broadcasters
    http://www.reagan.utexas.edu/archives/speeches/1987/120387d.htm
    Accessed May 29, 2007
Reagan (May 17, 1988) Remarks and a Question-and-Answer Session with
    Reporters.   http://www.reagan.utexas.edu/archives/speeches/1988
    /051788b.htm Accessed May 31, 2007

Reagan (May 31, 1988) Remarks at a Luncheon Hosted by Artists and Cultural Leaders in Moscow http://www.reagan.utexas.edu/archives/speeches/1988/053188a.htm Accessed May 31, 2007

Reagan (June 3, 1988) Remarks upon Returning From the Soviet-United States Summit Meeting in Moscow http://www.reagan.utexas.edu/archives/speeches/1988/060388c.htm Accessed May 31, 2007

Reagan (August 15, 1988) Remarks at the Republican National Convention in New Orleans, Louisiana http://www.reagan.utexas.edu/archives/speeches/1988/081588b.htm Accessed May 31, 2007

Reagan (September 14, 1988) Remarks at a Republican Party Rally in Cape Girardeau, Missouri http://www.reagan.utexas.edu/archives/speeches/1988/091488e.htm Accessed June 1, 2007

Reagan (October 4, 1988) Remarks at the Republican Governors Club Dinner http://www.reagan.utexas.edu/archives/speeches/1988/100488e.htm Accessed June 1, 2007

Reagan (December 1, 1988) Remarks at a Dinner Honoring Representative Jack F. Kemp of New York http://www.reagan.utexas.edu/archives/speeches/1988/120188c.htm Accessed June 2, 2007

Reagan (December 13, 1988) Remarks to Administration Officials on Domestic Policy http://www.reagan.utexas.edu/archives/speeches/1988/121388a.htm Accessed June 3, 2007

Reagan (December 16, 1988) Remarks and a Question-and-Answer Session at the University of Virginia in Charlottesville http://www.reagan.utexas.edu/archives/speeches/1988/121688b.htm Accessed June 3, 2007

Reagan (January 10, 1989) Remarks at the Franklin D. Roosevelt Library 50th Anniversary Luncheon http://www.reagan.utexas.edu/archives/speeches/1989/011089c.htm Accessed June 3, 2007

Reagan (January 11, 1989) Farewell Address to the Nation http://www.reagan.utexas.edu/archives/speeches/1989/011189i.htm Accessed June 3, 2007

Reagan (January 19, 1989) Remarks at the Presentation Ceremony for the Presidential Medal of Freedom http://www.reagan.utexas.edu/archives/speeches/1989/011989b.htm Accessed June 3, 2007

Archival Material From Ronald Reagan Presidential Library

Address, "Republican State Convention, August 6, 1966," p. 10, Speech, "Elk Grove, May 14, 1966," p. 257 Folder: 1966 Campaign: RR speeches and statements, Book II (2), Box C30, Research Unit, Ronald Reagan Governor's papers, Ronald Reagan Library

Answer, "Questions and Answers, Orange County, March 30, 1966," p. 187, Folder: 1966 Campaign: RR speeches and statements, Book I (5), Box C30, Research Unit, Ronald Reagan Governor's papers, Ronald Reagan Library

Draft, Folder Hannaford/CA HQ—R. Reagan Speeches—May 21, 1979, Speech Draft. Box 25, Ronald Reagan 1980 Campaign Papers, Series I, Ronald Reagan Library

Draft, Folder Hannaford/CA HQ—R. Reagan Speeches—July 1, 1980, Acceptance Speech (Research)—Convention (2/2) Box 25, Ronald Reagan 1980 Campaign Papers, Series I, Ronald Reagan Library

New Business Speech (Gavin) (1/2) and (2/2) Folder Hannaford/CA HQ—R. Reagan Speeches—1/1977, Box 21, Ronald Reagan 1980 Campaign Papers, Series I, Ronald Reagan Library

(RR) "Viewpoint," Disc 75–04, Taping date—February 23, 1975, Box 39, Subseries C, Reagan, Ronald: Pre-presidential papers, Series I Speeches and writings, Ronald Reagan Library

Radio address, Folder Speeches and Writings—Radio Broadcast, Taping date—August, 1975, "Images," Holograph, Box 1, Reagan, Ronald: Pre-presidential papers, Series I Speeches and writings, Ronald Reagan Library

Radio address, Folder Speeches and Writings—Radio Broadcast, Taping date—September, 1976, "Mao's China," Edited Typescript, Box 2, Reagan, Ronald: Pre-presidential papers, Series I Speeches and writings, Ronald Reagan Library

Radio address, Folder Speeches and Writings—Radio Broadcast, Taping date—April 13, 1977, "Redwoods," Edited Typescript 2/4, Box 8, Reagan, Ronald: Pre-presidential papers, Series I Speeches and writings, Ronald Reagan Library

Radio address, Folder Speeches and Writings—Radio Broadcast, Taping date—January 16, 1978, "Christmas," Holograph 1/4, Box 17, Reagan, Ronald: Pre-presidential papers, Series I Speeches and writings, Ronald Reagan Library

Radio address, Folder Speeches and Writings—Radio Broadcast, Taping date—July 15, 1978, "Stanley Yankus," Typescript 3/4, Box 24, Reagan, Ronald: Pre-presidential papers, Series I Speeches and writings, Ronald Reagan Library

Radio address, Folder Speeches and Writings—Radio Broadcast, Taping date—March 6, 1979, "The 100 Club," Typescript 3/4, Box 32, Reagan, Ronald: Pre-presidential papers, Series I Speeches and writings, Ronald Reagan Library

Speech, ("Losing freedom by installment") Rotary Club of Long Beach, June 6, 1962, Box 43 Subseries E, Reagan, Ronald: Pre-presidential papers, Series I Speeches and writings, Ronald Reagan Library

Speech, Young Republicans' Convention, Omaha, June 23, 1963, Box 44 Subseries E, Reagan, Ronald: Pre-presidential papers, Series I Speeches and writings, Ronald Reagan Library

Speech, Alf Landon Lecture, Kansas State University, Manhattan, Kansas, October 26, 1963, Box 44 Subseries E, Reagan, Ronald: Pre-presidential papers, Series I Speeches and writings, Ronald Reagan Library

Speech, ("A Time For Choosing") 71st Annual Convention of the United States Savings and Loan League, San Francisco, California, November 7, 1963, Box 44 Subseries E, Reagan, Ronald: Pre-presidential papers, Series I Speeches and writings, Ronald Reagan Library

Speech, A Time for Choosing, 1964, Box 44 Subseries E, Reagan, Ronald: Pre-presidential papers, Series I Speeches and writings, Ronald Reagan Library

Speech, "A Plan for Action: Announcement of Candidacy, January 4, 1966," Folder: 1966 Campaign: RR speeches and statements, Book I, Box C30, Research Unit, Ronald Reagan Governor's papers, Ronald Reagan Library

Speech, "California Council for Adult Education, International Hotel March 12, 1966," p. 99, Folder: 1966 Campaign: RR speeches and statements, Book I (3), Box C30, Research Unit, Ronald Reagan Governor's papers, Ronald Reagan Library

Speech, "Pacifica Junior Chamber of Commerce Annual Meeting, April 2, 1966," p. 216, Folder: 1966 Campaign: RR speeches and statements, Book I (5), Box C30, Research Unit, Ronald Reagan Governor's papers, Ronald Reagan Library

Speech, "Dinner Speech, Hollywood Palladium, April 20, 1966," p. 242, Folder: 1966 Campaign: RR speeches and statements, Book II (1), Box C30, Research Unit, Ronald Reagan Governor's papers, Ronald Reagan Library

Speech, "Elk Grove, May 14, 1966," p. 257, Folder: 1966 Campaign: RR speeches and statements, Book II (1), Box C30, Research Unit, Ronald Reagan Governor's papers, Ronald Reagan Library

Speech, Men of All Saints Episcopal Church Dinner, Los Angeles, March 21, 1969, Box 44 Subseries E, Reagan, Ronald: Pre-presidential papers, Series I Speeches and writings, Ronald Reagan Library

Speech, Welcoming the Reverend Billy Graham, September 28, 1969, Box 44 Subseries E, Reagan, Ronald: Pre-presidential papers, Series I Speeches and writings, Ronald Reagan Library

Speech, Marlborough College Preparatory School for Girls Commencement Exercises, June 6, 1974, Box 44 Subseries E, Reagan, Ronald: Pre-presidential papers, Series I Speeches and writings, Ronald Reagan Library

Speech, "Excerpts from remarks by the Hon. Ronald Reagan at Friends of Kirby Holmes Luncheon, Monte Carlo Banquet Hall, Utica, Michigan, Friday, September 29, 1978," Folder Hannaford/CA HQ—R. Reagan Speeches—September 29, 1976, Friends of Kirby Holmes, Utica MI, Box 21, Ronald Reagan 1980 Campaign Papers, Series I, Ronald Reagan Library

Speech, "Encroaching Control," no date, Box 43 Subseries E, Reagan, Ronald: Pre-presidential papers, Series I Speeches and writings, Ronald Reagan Library

Speech draft re: Bicentennial, July 6, 1976, Box 44 Subseries E, Reagan, Ronald: Pre-presidential papers, Series I Speeches and writings, Ronald Reagan Library

Speech draft, no date, Box 43 Subseries E, Reagan, Ronald: Pre-presidential papers, Series I Speeches and writings, Ronald Reagan Library
Statement, "San Bernadino County Elementary School Admin. Assn. Luncheon. Casa Loma Hall—Redlands University, February 15, 1966," p. 18, Folder: 1966 Campaign: RR speeches and statements, Book I (1), Box C30, Research Unit, Ronald Reagan Governor's papers, Ronald Reagan Library

Lɪᴛᴇʀᴀᴛᴜʀᴇ

Aaltola, Mika (2007), Sowing the Seeds of Sacred—Political Religion of Contemporary World Order and the American Era. Manuscript. Published (2008) Martinus Nijhoff Publishers, Leiden & Boston

Anderson, Benedict (1991), *Imagined Communities: Reflections on the Origin and Spread of Nationalism.* Verso, London

Andrews, Molly (2007), *Shaping History: Narratives of Political Change.* Cambridge University Press, Cambridge

Arendt, Hannah (1963), *On Revolution.* Viking, New York

Aristotle (1940), *Poetics.* Rev. T. A. Moxon, ed. J. M. Dent & Sons Limited, London

Bakhtin, Mikhail (1986), *Speech Genres and Other Late Essays.* University of Texas Press, Austin

Bal, Mieke (1997), *Narratology: Introduction to the Theory of Narrative.* University of Toronto Press, Toronto

Barthes, Roland (1974), *S/Z.* Trans. Richard Miller. Hill and Wang, New York

Barthes, Roland (1977), *Image Music Text.* Hill and Wang, New York

Barthes, Roland (1990), *The Pleasure of the Text.* Basil Blackwell, Oxford

Barthes, Roland (1991), *Mythologies.* Noonday Press, New York

Barthes, Roland (1993), *Tekijän kuolema, Tekstin syntymä.* Vastapaino, Tampere

Bellah, Robert N. (1967), Civil Religion in America. *American Academy of Arts and Sciences* 96(1). Daedalus. Pp. 1–21

Bellah, Robert N. (1975), *The Broken Covenant: American Civil Religion in a Time of Trial.* Seabury Press, New York

Bercovich, Sacvan (1993), *The Rites of Assent—Transformations in the Symbolic Construction of America.* Routledge, New York

Berman, Larry (1990), Looking Back on the Reagan Presidency. In Larry Berman, ed., *Looking Back on the Reagan Presidency.* Johns Hopkins University Press, Baltimore. Pp. 1–17

Boase, Paul H. (1989), Moving the Mercy Seat into the White House: An Exegesis of the Carter/Reagan Religious Rhetoric. *The Journal of Communication and Religion*, September. Pp. 1–9

Boer, Roland (2009), *Political Myth: On the Use and Abuse of Biblical Themes.* Duke University Press, Durham and London

Boorstin, Daniel J. (1953), *The Genius of American Politics.* University of Chicago Press, Chicago and London

Boorstin, Daniel J. (1962), *The Image or What Happened to the American Dream.* Atheneum, New York

Boyarsky, Bill (1981), *Ronald Reagan: His Life and Rise to the Presidency.* Random House, New York

Bruner, Jerome (1969), Myth and Identity. In Henry A. Murray, ed., *Myth and Mythmaking.* Beacon Press, Boston. Pp. 276–288

Bruner, Jerome (1986), *Actual Minds, Possible Worlds.* Harvard University Press, Cambridge

Bruner, Jerome (2006) [1987], Life as Narrative. In Paul Atkinson and Sara Delamont, eds., *Sage Benchmarks in Social Research Methods—Narrative Methods*, Volume 1, Narrative Perspectives. Sage Publications, London, Thousand Oaks, and New Delhi. Pp. 99–117

Campbell, Alexander (1988), *An Alexander Campbell Reader.* Lester G. McAllister, ed. CBP Press, St. Louis

Campbell, David (1998), *Rewriting Security: United States Foreign Policy and the Politics of Identity.* Revised Edition. University of Minnesota Press, Minneapolis

Campbell, Joseph (1968), *Hero with a thousand faces.* Princeton University Press, Princeton

Campbell, Joseph (1969), The Historical Development of Mythology. In Henry A. Murray, ed., *Myth and Mythmaking.* Beacon Press, Boston. Pp. 19–45

Cannon, Lou (1991), *President Reagan: The Role of a Lifetime.* Simon & Schuster, New York

Cannon, Lou (2003), *Governor Reagan: His Rise to Power.* Public Affairs, New York

Cervantes, Miguel de Saavedra (1957), *Don Quixote of La Mancha.* Trans. Walter Starkie. New American Library, New York

Chambers, Whittaker (1952), *Witness.* Random House, New York

Chatman, Seymour (1978), *Story and Discourse: Narrative Structure in Fiction and Film.* Cornell University Press, Ithaca and London

Chernus, Ira (2006), *Monsters to Destroy: The Neoconservative War on Terror and Sin.* Paradigm Publishers, Boulder and London

Chernus, Ira (2009), American Civil Religion. www-document. http://www.colorado.edu/ReligiousStudies/chernus/4820-Nationalism/Readings/AmericanCivilReligion.htm Accessed October 1, 2009

Combs, James (1993), *The Reagan Range: The Nostalgic Myth in American Politics.* Bowling Green State University Popular Press, Bowling Green

Conkin, Paul K. (1997), *American Originals: Homemade Varieties of Christianity.* University of North Carolina Press, Chapel Hill and London

Crable, Richard E. and Steven L. Vibbert (1983), Argumentative Stance and Political Faith Healing: "The Dream Will Come True". *Quarterly Journal of Speech* 69. Pp. 290–301

Culler, Jonathan (1975), *Structuralist Poetics: Structuralism, Linguistics, and the Study of Literature*. Cornell University Press, Ithaca and New York

Czarniawska, Barbara (2004), *Narratives in Social Science Research*. Sage Publications, London

Deaver, Michael K. (2003), *A Different Drummer: My Thirty Years with Ronald Reagan*. Perennail, New York

Deneen, Patrick J. (1964), *Democratic Faith*. Princeton University Press, Princeton

Derrida, Jacques (1988), *Positioita*. Gaudeamus, Helsinki

Dolezel, Lubomir (1999), Fictional and Historical Narrative: Meeting the Postmodernist Challenge. In David Herman, ed., *Narratologies: New Perspectives for Narrative Analysis*. Ohio State University Press, Columbus. Pp. 247–273

D'Souza, Dinesh (1997), *Ronald Reagan: How An Ordinary Man Became An Extraordinary Leader*. Touchstone, New York

Durkheim, Emile (1995) [1912], *Elementary Forms of Religious Life*. Translated and with an introduction by Karen E. Fields. The Free Press, New York

Eck, Diana L. (2001), *a New Religious America: How a "Christian Country" Has Now Become the World's Most Religiously Diverse Nation*. HarperSanFrancisco, San Francisco

Edelman, Murray (1977), *Political Language: Words That Succeed and Policies That Fail*. Academic Press, New York, San Francisco, and London

Eliade, Mircea (1963), *Myth and Reality*. Trans. Willard R. Trask. Harper & Row Publishers, New York, Hagerstown, San Francisco, and London

Erickson, Paul D. (1985), *Reagan Speaks: The Making of an American Myth*. New York University Press, New York

Exum, J. Cheryl (1996), *Tragedy and Biblical Narrative*. Cambridge University Press, Cambridge

Feldman, Noah (2005), *Divided by God: America's Church-State Problem and What We Should Do About It?* Farrar, Straus and Giroux, New York

Fisher, Walter R. (1982), Romantic Democracy, Ronald Reagan, and Presidential Heroes. *The Western Journal of Speech Communication* 46 (Summer). Pp. 299–310

Forster, E. M. (1953), *Aspects of the Novel*. Edward Arnold & Co., London

Frye, Northrop (1957), *Anatomy of Criticism*. Four Essays. Princeton University Press, Princeton

Frye, Northrop (1969), New Directions from Old. In Henry A. Murray, ed., *Myth and Mythmaking*. Beacon Press, Boston. Pp. 115–131

Genette, Gerard (1980), *Narrative Discourse*. Translated from French by Jane E. Levin. Basil Blackwell, Oxford

Genette, Gerard (1993), *Fiction and Diction*. Translated from French by Catherine Porter. Cornell University Press, Ithaca

Ginsburg, Ruth and Shlomith Rimmon-Kenan (1999), Is There a Life after Death? Theorizing Authors and Reading Jazz. In David Herman, ed., *Narratologies: New Perspectives for Narrative Analysis*. Ohio State University Press, Columbus. Pp. 66–87

Goodnight, G. Thomas (1986), Ronald Reagan's Re-formulation of the Rhetoric of War: Analysis of the "Zero Option," "Evil Empire," and "Star wars" Addresses. *Quarterly Journal of Speech* 72. Pp. 390–414

Greimas, Algirdas-Julien (1983), *Structural Semantics: An Attempt at a Method*. University of Nebraska Press, Lincoln and London

Grottanelli, Cristiano (1999), *Kings & Prophets: Monarchic Power, Inspired Leadership, & Sacred Text in Biblical Narrative*. Oxford University Press, New York and Oxford

Gutterman, David S. (2005), *Prophetic Politics. Christian Social Movements and American Democracy*. Cornell University Press, Ithaca and London

Haig, Alexander M. Jr. (1984), *Caveat: Realism, Reagan, and Foreign Policy*. Macmillan Publishing Company, New York

Hall, Martin (2006), The Fantasy of Realism, or Mythology as Methodology. In Daniel H. Nexon and Iver B. Neumann, eds., *Harry Potter and International Relations*. Rowman & Littlefield Publishers, Inc., Oxford. Pp. 177–196

Hall, Wynton C. (2002), The Invention of "Quantifiably Safe Rhetoric": Richard Wrthlin and Ronald Reagan's Instrumental Use of Public Opinion Research in Presidential Discourse. *Western Journal of Communication* 66(3) (Summer). Pp. 319–346

Hanska, Jan (2007), They Are the Focus of Evil in the Modern World: Ronald Reaganin narratiivit Yhdysvaltojen identiteetin, viholliskuvan ja politiikan muokkaajina. Masters Thesis. Dept. Of Political Science and International Relations, University of Tampere, Tampere http://tutkielmat.uta.fi/pdf/gradu01572.pdf

Harle, Vilho (1998), *Ideas of Social Order in the Ancient World*. Greenwood Press, Westport

Hayward, Stephen (2001), *The Age of Reagan: The Fall of the Old Liberal Order*. Prima Publishing, Roseville

Herberg, Will (1960) [1955], *Protestant-Catholic-Jew: An Essay in American Religious Sociology*. A New Edition, Completely Revised. Doubleday & Company Inc., Garden City

Herman, David (1999), Introduction. In David Herman, ed., *Narratologies: New Perspectives for Narrative Analysis*. Ohio State University Press, Columbus. Pp. 1–30

Herman, David (2002), *Story Logic: Problems and Possibilities of Narrative*. University of Nebraska Press, Lincoln and London

Herman, David (2004), Toward a Transmedial Narratology. In Marie-Laure Ryan, ed., *Narrative Across Media: The Languages of Storytelling*. University of Nebraska Press, Lincoln. Pp. 47–76

Herman, David, Manfred Jahn, and Marie-Laure Ryan, eds. (2007). *Routledge Encyclopedia of Narrative Theory*. Routledge, London

Holstein, James A. and Jaber F. Gubrium (2000), *The Self We Live By: Narrative Identity in a Postmodern World*. Oxford University Press, New York and Oxford

Horace (1940), *The Art of Poetry*. Rev. T. A. Moxon, ed. J. M. Dent & Sons Limited, London

Hughes, Richard T. (2003), *Myths America Lives By*. University of Chicago Press, Urbana and Chicago

Iqbal, Muhammad Allama (1992), *Thoughts and Reflections*. Syed Abdul Wahid, ed. Sh. Muhammad Ashraf Publishers, Lahore

Ivie, Robert L. (1984), Speaking "Common Sense" About the Soviet Threat: Reagan's Rhetorical Stance. *The Western Journal of Speech Communication* 48 (Winter). Pp. 39–50

James, William (1981), *Uskonnollinen kokemus*. (Orig. The Varieties of Religious Experience.) Trans. Elvi Saari. Arvi A. Karisto Oy, Hämeenlinna

Jameson, Fredric (1984), Foreword. In Jean-Francois Lyotard, *The Postmodern Condition: A Report on Knowledge*. Trans. Geoff Bennington and Brian Massumi. Manchester University Press, Manchester

Jameson, Fredric (2002) [1981], *The Political Unconscious; Narrative as a socially symbolic act*. Routledge, London and New York

Jewett, Robert and John Shelton Lawrence (1977), *The American Monomyth*. Anchor Press/Doubleday, Garden City

Kafalenos, Emma (1999), Not (Yet) Knowing: Epistemological Effects of Deferred and Suppressed Information in Narrative. In David Herman, ed., *Narratologies: New Perspectives for Narrative Analysis*. Ohio State University Press, Columbus. Pp. 33–65

Kelly, George Armstrong (1984), *Politics and Religious Consciousness in America*. Transaction Books, New Brunswick and London

Kengor, Paul (2004), *God and Ronald Reagan: A spiritual life*. HarperCollins Publishers, New York

Knelman, F. H. (1985), *Reagan, God, and the Bomb: From Myth to Policy in the Nuclear Arms Race*. Prometheus Books, Buffalo

Kosmin, Barry A. and Seymour P. Lachman (1993), *One Nation Under God: Religion in Contemporary American Society*. Harmony Books, New York

Kuhn, Thomas S. (1970), *The Structure of Scientific Revolutions*. Second Edition, Enlarged. University of Chicago Press, Chicago

Labov, William and Joshua Waletzky (2006) [1967], Narrative Analysis: Oral Versions of Personal Experience. In Paul Atkinson and Sara Delamont, eds., Sage Benchmarks in Social Research Methods—Narrative Methods, Volume 1, Narrative Perspectives. Sage Publications, London, Thousand Oaks, and New Delhi. Pp. 1–41

Lakoff, George (1996), *Moral Politics: What Conservatives Know That Liberals Don't*. University of Chicago Press, Chicago

Levin, Harry (1969), Some Meanings of Myth. In Henry A. Murray, ed., *Myth and Mythmaking*. Beacon Press, Boston. Pp. 103–114

Lévi-Strauss, Claude (1969), *Structural Anthropology*. Translated from the French by Claire Jacobson and Brooke Grundfest Schoepf. Allen Lane the Penguin Press, London

Lévi-Strauss, Claude (1978), *Myth and Meaning*. Routledge & Kegan Paul, London and Henley

Lewis, William F. (1987), Telling America's Story: Narrative Form and the Reagan Presidency. *Quarterly Journal of Speech* 73. Pp. 280–302

Lincoln, Bruce (1989), *Discourse and the Construction of Society: Comparative Studies of Myth, Ritual, and Classification*. Oxford University press, New York and Oxford

Lincoln, Bruce (1999), *Theorizing Myth: Narrative, Ideology and Scholarship*. University of Chicago Press, Chicago and London

Linden, Frank van der (1981), *The Real Reagan: What He Believes. What He Has Accomplished. What Can We Expect from Him*. William Morrow and Company, Inc., New York

Luoma-aho, Mika (2009), Political Theology, Anthropomorphism and Person-hood of the State: The Religion of IR. *International Political Sociology* 3(3) (September). Pp. 293–309

Lyotard, Jean-Francois (1984), *The Postmodern Condition: A Report on Knowledge*. Trans. Geoff Bennington and Brian Massumi. Manchester University Press, Manchester

Lyotard, Jean-Francois (1993), *Toward the Postmodern*. Robert Harvey and Mark S. Roberts, eds. Humanities Press, New Jersey and London

Lyotard, Jean-Francois (1997), *Postmodern Fables*. Trans. Georges Van Den Abbeele. University of Minnesota Press, Minneapolis and London

MacIntyre, Alasdair (1984), *After Virtue: A Study in Moral Theory*. University of Notre Dame Press, Notre Dame

Madsen, Richard (1991), Contentless Consensus—The Political Discourse of a Segmented Society. In Alan Wolfe, ed., *America at Century's End*. University of California Press, Berkeley. Pp. 440–460

Margolin, Uri (1999), Of What Is Past, Is Passing, or to Come: Temporality, Aspectuality, Modality, and the Nature of Literary Narrative. In David Herman, ed., *Narratologies: New Perspectives for Narrative Analysis*. Ohio State University Press, Columbus. Pp. 142–166

Martin, Wallace (1987), *Recent Theories of Narrative*. Cornell University Press, Ithaca and London

Marty, Martin E. (1984), *Pilgrims in their Own Land, 500 years of religion in America*. Little, Brown and Company, Boston and Toronto

McLoughlin, William G. (1978), *Revivals, Awakenings, and Reform. An Essay on Religion and Social Change in America, 1607–1977*. University of Chicago Press, Chicago and London

Meacham, Jon (2006), *American Gospel: God, the Founding Fathers, and the Making of a Nation*. Random House, New York

Mead, Sidney E. (1975), *The Nation With the Soul of a Church*. Harper & Row Publishers, New York

Mead, Sidney E. (1977), *The Old Religion in the Brave New World—Reflections on the Relation between Christendom and the Republic*. University of California Press, Berkeley

Morris, Edmund (1999), *Dutch: A Memoir of Ronald Reagan*. Random House, New York

Muir, William K. Jr. (1995), Ronald Reagan: The Primacy of Rhetoric. In Fred I. Greenstein, ed., *Leadership in the Modern Presidency*. Harvard University Press, Cambridge. Pp. 260–295

Nathan, Richard P. (1990), The Presidency after Reagan: Don't Change It—Make It Work. In Larry Berman, ed., *Looking Back on the Reagan Presidency*. Johns Hopkins University Press, Baltimore. Pp. 195–206

Niebuhr, Reinhold (1954), *The Irony of American History*. Charles Scribner's Sons, New York

Niebuhr, Reinhold (1986), *The Essential Reinhold Niebuhr: Selected Essays and Addresses*. (Edited and introduced by Robert McAffee Brown). Yale University Press,. New Haven and London

Niebuhr, Reinhold and Alan Heimert (1963), *a Nation So Conceived— Reflections on the History of America from Its Early Visions to Its Present Power*. Charles Scribner's Sons, New York

Noonan, Peggy (2002), *When Character Was King: A Story of Ronald Reagan*. Penguin Books, New York

Noonan, Peggy (2003) [1990], *What I Saw at the Revolution: A Political Life in the Reagan Era*. Random House Trade Paperbacks, New York

Ochs, Elinor and Lisa Capps (2001), *Living Narrative; Creating Lives in Everyday Storytelling*. Harvard University Press, Cambridge

Palmer, Alan (2004), *Fictional Minds*. University of Nebraska Press, Lincoln and London

Pemberton, William E. (1997), *Exit with Honor: The Life and Presidency of Ronald Reagan*. M.E. Sharpe, London

Peterson, Paul (1997), Ronald Reagan and the Reformation of American Conservatism. In Eric J. Schmertz, Natalie Datlof, and Alexej Ugrinsky, eds., *Ronald Reagan's America. Contributions in Political Science*, Number 377. Greenwood Press, Westport and London. Pp. 67–79

Phelan, James (1996), *Narrative as Rhetoric: Technique, Audiences, Ethics, Ideology*. Ohio State University Press, Columbus

Phillips, Kevin (2006), *American Theocracy: The Peril and Politics of Radical Religion, Oil and Borrowed Money in the 21st Century*. Viking Penguin, London

Polkinghorne, Donald E. (1988), *Narrative Knowing and the Human Sciences*. State University of New York Press, Albany

Pope, Alexander (1903), *Essay on Criticism*. J. M. Dent & Co., London

Porter, Laurinda W. (1990), Religion and Politics: Protestant Beliefs in the Presidential Campaign of 1980. *The Journal of Communication and Religion* (September). Pp. 24–39

Prestowitz, Clyde (2003), *Rogue Nation: American Unilateralism and the Failure of Good Intentions*. Basic Books, New York

Prince, Gerald (1973), *A Grammar of Stories*. Mouton, Hague

Prince, Gerald (1987), *A Dictionary of Narratology*. Scolar, London

Propp, Vladimir (1968), *Morphology of the Folktale*. Trans. Laurence Scott. University of Texas Press, Austin

Rabinowitz, Peter (1987), *Before Reading; Narrative Conventions and the Politics of Interpretation*. Cornell University Press, Ithaca and London

Rantapelkonen, Jari (2006), The Narrative Leadership of War—Presidential Phrases in the War on Terror and Their Relation to Information Technology. Publication Series 1, Research no. 34, National Defence University, Department of Leadership and Management Studies, Helsinki

Reagan, Ronald (1984), *The Triumph of the American Spirit*. Emil Arca and Gregory P. Damel, eds. National Reproductions Corp, Detroit

Reagan, Ronald (1990), *An American Life*. Simon & Schuster, New York.

Reagan, Ronald (2001), *Stories in His Own Hand—The Everyday Wisdom of Ronald Reagan*. Kiron K. Skinner, Annelise Anderson, and Martin Anderson, eds. The Free Press, New York

Reagan, Ronald (2003), *A Life in Letters*. Kiron K. Skinner, Annelise Anderson, and Martin Anderson, eds. The Free Press, New York

Reagan, Ronald (2007), *The Reagan Diaries*. Douglas Brinkley, ed. HarperCollins Publishers, New York

Reagan, Ronald and Richard C. Hubler (1965) [1981], *Where's the Rest of Me?* Dell,. New York

Reeves, Richard (2005), *President Reagan: The Triumph of Imagination*. Simon & Schuster, New York

Regan, Donald T. (1989), *For the Record: From Wall Street to Washington*. New York, St. Martin's Press

Ricoeur, Paul (1995), *Figuring the Sacred: Religion, Narrative and Imagination*. Fortress Press, Minneapolis

Riessman, Catherine Kohler (1993), *Narrative Analysis. Qualitative Research Methods Series 30*. Sage Publications, London

Riessman, Catherine Kohler (2004), Accidental Cases: Extending the Concept of Positioning in Narrative Studies. In Bamberg Michael and Molly Andrews, eds., *Considering Counter-Narratives; Narrating, Resisting, Making Sense*. Studies in Narrative, Volume 4. John Benjamin Publishing Company, Amsterdam and Philadelphia. Pp. 33–38

Rimmon-Kenan, Shlomith (1983), *Narrative Fiction: Contemporary Poetics*. Methuen, London and New York

Ritter, Kurt W. (1968), Ronald Reagan and "The Speech": The Rhetoric of Public Relations Politics. *Western Speech* (Winter). Pp. 50–58

Rowland, Robert C. and John M. Jones (2006), Reagan at the Brandenburg Gate: Moral Clarity Tempered by Pragmatism. *Rhetoric & Public Affairs* 9(1). Pp. 21–50

Rushing, Janice Hocker (1986), Ronald Reagan's "Star Wars" Address: Mythical Containment of Technical Reasoning. *Quarterly Journal of Speech* 72. Pp. 415–433

Ryan, Marie-Laure (1991), *Possible Worlds, Artificial Intelligence, and Narrative Theory*. Indiana University Press, Bloomington

Ryan, Marie-Laure (1999), Cyberage Narratology: Computers, Metaphor, and Narrative. In David Herman, ed., *Narratologies: New Perspectives for Narrative Analysis*. Ohio State University Press, Columbus. Pp. 113–141

Ryan, Marie-Laure, ed. (2004a), *Introduction in Narrative Across Media: The Languages of Storytelling*. University of Nebraska Press, Lincoln. Pp. 1–47

Ryan, Marie-Laure, ed. (2004b), *Will New Media Produce New Narratives in Narrative Across Media: The Languages of Storytelling*. University of Nebraska Press, Lincoln. Pp. 337–361

Schmitt, Carl (2005), *Political Theology: Four Chapters on the Concept of Sovereignty*. Second Edition. Trans. George Schwab. University of Chicago Press, Chicago and London

Schurmann, Franz (1995), *American Soul*. Mercury House, San Francisco

Shapiro, Michael J. (2006), *Deforming American Political Thought: Ethnicity, Facticity, and Gender*. University Press of Kentucky, Lexington

Shogan, Colleen J. (2006), Coolidge and Reagan: The Rhetorical Influence of Silent Cal on the Great Communicator. *Rhetoric & Pubilc Affairs* 9(2). Pp. 215–234

Smith, John Kares (1997), "Why Shouldn't We Believe That? We Are Americans.": Rhetorical Myths and Fantasies in the Reagan Inaugurals. In Eric J. Schmertz, Natalie Datlof, and Alexej Ugrinsky, eds., *Ronald Reagan's America. Contributions in Political Science,* Number 377. Greenwood Press, Westport and London. Pp. 813–825

Smith, Jonathan Z. (1982), *Imagining Religion: From Babylon to Jonestown*. University of Chicago Press, Chicago and London

Speakes, Larry and Robert Pack (1988), *Speaking Out: The Reagan Presidency from Inside the White House*. Charles Scribner's Sons, New York

Stephanson, Anders (1996), *Manifest Destiny: American Expansionism and the Empire of Right*. Hill and Wang, New York

Stuckey, Mary E. (1989), *Getting into the Game: The Pre-Presidential Rhetoric of Ronald Reagan*. Praeger, New York

Stuckey, Mary E. (1990), *Playing the Game: The Presidential Rhetoric of Ronald Reagan*. Praeger, New York

de Tocqueville, Alexis (2000), *Democracy in America*. Translated, edited, and with an introduction by Harvey C. Mansfield and Delba Withrop. University of Chicago Press, Chicago and London

Todorov, Tzvetan (1981), *Introduction to Poetics*. University of Minnesota Press, Minneapolis

Wallace, Mike (1997), The Reagan Years: A Reporter's Notebook. In Eric J. Schmertz, Natalie Datlof, and Alexej Ugrinsky, eds., *Ronald Reagan's America. Contributions in Political Science,* Number 377. Greenwood Press, Westport and London. Pp. 5–10

Wallison, Peter J. (2003), *Ronald Reagan: The Power of Conviction and the Success of His Presidency*. Westview Press, Boulder

Warner, W. Lloyd (1962), *American Life: Dream and Reality*. University of Chicago Press, Chicago and London

Weatherford, Stephen M. and Lorraine M. McDonnell (1990), Ideology and Economic Policy. In Larry Berman, ed., *Looking Back on the Reagan Presidency*. Johns Hopkins University Press, Baltimore. Pp. 122–155

Weber, Cynthia (2005), *International Relations Theory: A Critical Introduction*. Second Edition. Routledge, London

Weber, Max (1959), The Profession and Vocation of Politics. In Peter Lassman and Ronald Speirs, eds., *Political Writings*. Cambridge University Press, Cambridge. Pp. 309–369

Weber, Max (1987), *The Protestant Ethic and the Spirit of Capitalism*. Trans. Talcott Parsons. Unwin, London

White, Hayden (1973), *Metahistory: The Historical Imagination in Nineteenth-Century Europe*. Johns Hopkins Press, Baltimore

White, Hayden (1987), *The Content of the Form: Narrative Discourse and Historical Representation*. Johns Hopkins University Press, Baltimore

White, John Kenneth (1998), *The New Politics of Old Values*. University Press of America, Lanham

Wilentz, Sean (2008), *The Age of Reagan: A History 1974–2008*. Harper, New York

Wills, Garry (2000), *Reagan's America—Innocents at Home*. Penguin Books, New York

Wilson, John F. (1979), *Public Religion in American Culture*. Temple University Press, Philadelphia

Wright, Harold Bell (1903), *That Printer of Udell's: A Story of the Middle West*. A.L. Burt Company Publishers, New York

X, Malcolm (1964), The Ballot or the Bullet. Speech. www-document http://www.famousquotes.me.uk/speeches/Malcolm_x/1.htm Accessed September 20, 2009

Young, Katharine (1999), Narratives of Indeterminacy: Breaking the Medical Body into its Discourses; Breaking the Discursive Body out of Postmodernism. In David Herman, ed., *Narratologies: New Perspectives for Narrative Analysis*. Ohio State University Press, Columbus. Pp. 197–217

Zelinsky, Wilbur (1988), *Nation into State—The Shifting Symbolic Foundations of American Nationalism*. University of North Carolina Press, Chapel Hill and London

INDEX